# Dublin 1916

The French Connection

# POBLACHT NA H EIREANN.

## THE PROVISIONAL GOVERNMENT

### OF THE

# IRISH REPUBLIC

## TO THE PEOPLE OF IRELAND.

IRISHMEN AND IRISHWOMEN In the name of God and of the dead generations from which she receives her old tradition of nationhood, Ireland, through us, summons her children to her flag and strikes for her freedom.

Having organised and trained her manhood through her secret revolutionary organisation, the Irish Republican Brotherhood, and through her open military organisations, the Irish Volunteers and the Irish Citizen Army, having patiently perfected her discipline, having resolutely waited for the right moment to reveal itself, she now seizes that moment, and, supported by her exiled children in America and by gallant allies in Europe, but relying in the first on her own strength, she strikes in full confidence of victory.

We declare the right of the people of Ireland to the ownership of Ireland, and to the unfettered control of Irish destinies, to be sovereign and indefeasible. The long usurpation of that right by a foreign people and government has not extinguished the right, nor can it ever be extinguished except by the destruction of the Irish people. In every generation the Irish people have asserted their right to national freedom and sovereignty, six times during the past three hundred years they have asserted it in arms. Standing on that fundamental right and again asserting it in arms in the face of the world, we hereby proclaim the Irish Republic as a Sovereign Independent State, and we pledge our lives and the lives of our comrades-in-arms to the cause of its freedom, of its welfare, and of its exaltation among the nations.

The Irish Republic is entitled to, and hereby claims, the allegiance of every Irishman and Irishwoman. The Republic guarantees religious and civil liberty, equal rights and equal opportunities to all its citizens, abd declares its resolve to pursue the happiness and prosperity of the whole nation and of all its parts, cherishing all the children of the nation equally, and oblivious of the differences carefully fostered by an alien government, which have divided a minority from the majority in the past.

Until our arms have brought the opportune moment for the establishment of a permanent National Government, representative of the whole people of Ireland and elected by the suffrages of all her men and women, the Provisional Government, hereby constituted, will administer the civil and military affairs of the Republic in trust for the people.

We place the cause of the Irish Republic under the protection of the Most High God, Whose blessing we invoke upon our arms, and we pray that no one who serves that cause will dishonour it by cowardice, inhumanity, or rapine. In this supreme hour the Irish nation must, by its valour and discipline and by the readiness of its children to sacrifice themselves for the common good, prove itself worthy of the august destiny to which it is called.

Signed on Behalf of the Provisional Government,

THOMAS J. CLARKE,

SEAN Mac DIARMADA, THOMAS MacDONAGH,
P. H. PEARSE, EAMONN CEANNT,
JAMES CONNOLLY. JOSEPH PLUNKETT.

# Dublin 1916
The French Connection

**W.J. Mc Cormack**

*Gill & Macmillan*

Gill & Macmillan
Hume Avenue, Park West, Dublin 12
with associated companies throughout the world
www.gillmacmillanbooks.ie

© W.J. Mc Cormack 2012
978 07171 5412 8

Typography design by Make Communication
Print origination by Síofra Murphy
Printed and bound in the UK by MPG Books Ltd, Cornwall

This book is typeset in Minion 11.5/15 pt.

The paper used in this book comes from the wood pulp of
managed forests. For every tree felled, at least one tree is
planted, thereby renewing natural resources.

A CIP catalogue record for this book is available from the
British Library.

5 4 3 2 1

*In memory of*

*Justin Keating (1930–2009)*

*Out of great affection,*

*And out of regret that we had not time enough to discuss ideas outlined in the following pages which would have been better for his criticism;*

*And (not least) because he once proposed that a statue of James Joyce should be erected in University College Dublin; then was threatened with expulsion for his trouble.*

*The cars came scudding in towards Dublin, running evenly like pellets in the groove of the Naas Road. At the crest of the hill at Inchicore sightseers had gathered in clumps to watch the cars careering homeward and through this channel of poverty and inaction the Continent sped its wealth and industry. Now and again the clumps of people raised the cheer of the gratefully oppressed. Their sympathy, however, was for the blue cars — the cars of their friends, the French.*

*The French, moreover, were virtual victors. Their team had finished solidly; they had been placed second and third and the driver of the winning German car was reported a Belgian. Each blue car, therefore, received a double measure of welcome as it topped the crest of the hill and each cheer of welcome was acknowledged with smiles and nods by those in the car. In one of these trimly built cars was a party of four young men whose spirits seemed to be at present well above the level of successful Gallicism: in fact, these four young men were almost hilarious. They were Charles Segouin, the owner of the car; Andre Riviere, a young electrician of Canadian birth; a huge Hungarian named Villona and a neatly groomed young man named Doyle.*

*James Joyce, 'After the Race' (December 1904)*

# Contents

# Acknowledgments

Advice and support has been generously provided by Ciara Baker, Ciaran Brady, Peter Caldwell, Conor Carville, L.M. Cullen, Denis Donoghue, Tom Garvin, Paddy Gillan, Andreas Hess, Carla King, Michael Laffan, Simon McCormack, John P. McCormick, Jason McElligott, Jon Marcus, Reinhard Mehring, Thérèse Moriarty, Michael Neal, Honor Ó Brolcháin, Proinsias Ó Drisceoil, Eve Patten, Jean-Paul Pittion, Kitty Shields, Stephen Stokes, Dennis Tate, Fergal Tobin, Patrick Wallace, Larry White, Theresa Whittington and Stephen Wilson.

Major Dublin libraries assisted with the efficiency and good cheer I have enjoyed for decades of research, despite recently imposed financial difficulties. Notable among these were the Central Catholic Library, the National Library of Ireland, the Department of Early Printed Books in the library of Trinity College, the Royal Irish Academy, and the Archives Department in the library of University College. Beyond the Pale, staff at the Cavan County Council Library, notably Katharine McLoughlin, provided valuable support. In London, staff at the German Historical Institute, the London School of Economics, and the Warburg Institute assisted my endeavours in the same spirit.

Fergal Tobin, of Gill & Macmillan, has not only supervised this book with exemplary care but has also allowed me to implicate him in the Introduction. My thanks, indeed.

# A Letter of Introduction

*Bill Mc Cormack*
*Monaghan*
*17 March 2011*

Dear Fergal,

Many thanks for your very positive response to the chapters that I submitted for your consideration. Your comment, that perhaps they need a less detailed introduction, is well taken. The book which you have agreed to publish arose from several kinds of source or prompt or unease, and the reader is entitled to know something of them.

First, **a personal debt** is being settled. Liam de Paor died on 13 August 1998. The following Saturday, while his funeral was taking place, a republican bomb exploded in the town of Omagh, killing twenty-nine people, not all of them Irish. It would be no less offensive than redundant to wonder what the author of *On the Easter Proclamation and Other Declarations* (1997) might have said. Approached by elements in the Fianna Fáil administration long before the Arms Trial (1971) to lend academic cover for illegal importations, de Paor regarded the militarisation of conflictual politics with abhorrence, reserving especially thoughtful condemnation for the sneak-bomber, the absentee warrior.

He and the present writer first met in the Seán Connolly branch of the Irish Labour Party (Dublin South-East constituency), regarded by head office as a troublesome refuge for intellectuals who often disagreed amongst themselves. That was late in the 1960s, yet before 'the north began ...', the venue Mrs Margaret Gaj's restaurant in Baggot Street where republican veterans, feminists, and Trotsky-ites had their tea. (In one evening Gery Lawless could spot more armed detectives across the road than would fill Croke Park.) Further upstairs, when the Labourites convened, de Paor enunciated brief but effective suggestions for policy, never unconscious of the latent tension between nationalist and socialist interpretations of history. In 1970 he published a Penguin Special embodying this thoughtful engagement under the title *Divided Ulster*.

The republican movement had already split into Official and Provisional factions, the former overtly, but not plausibly, Marxist in orientation. De Paor was un-seducible from constitutionalist politics. He prefaced *Divided Ulster* with an unexpected Old Testament quotation (the King James version), including the words,

> Be ye therefore very courageous to keep and to do all that is written in the book of the law of Moses, that ye turn not aside therefrom to the right hand or to the left.
>
> (Joshua, 23:6)

Bloody Sunday in Derry (January 1972) greatly assisted the Provisional wing, and the ghastly tit-for-tat decades of atrocity got under way. Inaugurated in one dimension by the Official IRA's stupid, immoral and desperately incompetent bombing of Aldershot (February 1972) — the victims six civilian canteen workers, and an army chaplain — these long years drained the Left of argument, methodology and morale. The Provisionals were not to be out-heroded; three children died in the bombing of Claudy village a few months later. It is difficult now to reconstruct the headlong simplicity which people vested in their pet option — Irish unity, UK integration, or whatever. I recall very clearly how de Paor advised against confusing any plebiscite with the complex, un-dramatic workings of democracy. I believe his relationship with the thought of Ernest Renan (1823–1892) might be explored through this apparently casual remark, particularly with Renan's discussion of the modern nation, the role of 'sacrifice', the shared past, etc. From that same period of French history, more particularly the 1870s, a martial 'literature' developed. In it Peadar Kearney found models for 'A Soldier's Song', composed in 1907 and thus unaffected by the formation of the Irish Volunteers and the soldiering of 1916.[1] In the pages that follow, however, the focus is concentrated on a later generation of French thinkers than Renan's.

There is then **a problem about commemoration**. Even by mid-2010, when a proposal to re-issue de Paor's work was mooted, the bugle calls to commemorative amnesia were audible — though the Proclamation's centenary still lay almost six years in the future. That was the summer when an official enquiry into the Claudy bombing (July 1972) strongly suggested the involvement of a rogue Catholic priest, provoked to action by what he knew of Bloody Sunday (January 1972). It was also the summer when the remains of Charlie Armstrong, who was disappeared in 1981 heading for Mass, were discovered at Aughrim More bog, County Monaghan. The issue of Provisional IRA responsibility was, Gerry Adams averred, 'a secondary matter' which brought to mind Pearse's franker admission that 'we might shoot the wrong people.' A long tradition for whoever 'we' might be, a tradition of unease, evasion and bad faith.

In contrast, nationalist movements regard their fundamental propositions as self-evident truths. It does not necessarily follow that these propositions are false, but it behoves enquirer and exponent alike to adopt a modest hermeneutics of suspicion. Likewise, terms of analysis which have been devised in relation to one movement are often resisted or ignored in regard to another. If Pearse invoked revolution, perhaps he intended a sub-set of what German historians term 'the conservative revolution', available in hard and soft versions. Preferring for the moment to use the term 'separatists', his most recent biographer has identified 'a longing for the small integrated communities where everyone had face-to-face contact and which they perceived to be under threat from a modern large-scale impersonal society.'[2]

Against this cosy assumption, a critique might be offered despite the fact that Theory is now more unfashionable than canasta or fondue. If there is a central point of principle, or 'theoretical' hypothesis, to be advanced, it might be this: no human project or achievement of any complexity can be fully understood on its own terms alone. In the words of a recent historian of the Dreyfus Affair (1893 onwards), 'revisiting historical cases rarely results in the reassuring closure of a new verdict that simply replaces the prior one.'[3] And this leads me to outline the fundamental difficulty in writing about the 1916 Rising — its double existence as historical event and as foundation myth, complicating commemoration in 2016 (see Chapter 10 below).

**Foundation myths** may be ancient or modern. The story of Romulus, Remus and the she-wolf is a good example of the former, telling how the city of Rome came into being, how it was essentially founded. Modern examples are more difficult to choose, because there are so many of them and because they are inevitably surrounded by a buzz of contemporary, 'non-essential' knowledge. The Boston Tea Party (1773) was steadily mythologised by American separatists from an early date, though only with the Tea Partyers of today has it acquired the dignity of farce. The Alamo (February–March 1836) might serve better — the heroic few, the cruel besieging enemy, the gallant reinforcements, sacrifice, defeat and triumph. This was an 'iconic' event in the Texan Revolution and, consequently, in the development of the United States as a transcontinental power.

Though there are other routes to Rome's origins — for example variants traceable through Virgil's *Aeneid*— they do not challenge the story of the two boys as a foundation myth. The logic of contradiction does not apply; the principals are semi-divine. With the modern instance, there are inevitably bothersome details — the Alamo's original establishment as a mission station, and the later aggression of Texas and the United

States towards Mexico and 'hispanics' generally. The twentieth century has its own examples to offer — the reception of Vladimir Lenin at the Petrograd railway terminus (February 1917) and the Beer-Hall Putsch in Munich (November 1923). In the first case, Leon Trotsky exploited a routine transport detail to produce a transfiguration, the revelation of a saviour shortly to become head of the first Soviet government; in the second, Adolf Hitler failed in proclaiming 'The National Revolution Has Broken Out', though later the incident 'became' crucial in the emergence of the Nazi Party and the Third Reich.

The Easter Rising provides a foundation myth for independent Ireland, in keeping with *some* of the features active in the examples cited. It is not an origin myth, because the constituent parts are already in place, awaiting the transfiguration which (in the Irish instance) is crucial. What is founded is the state, not the nation, not Ireland; and Pearse's anxieties about human generation are in turn motors of action disguised in natural (biological) garb. Not all republicans accepted the foundation myth. In a late address to an audience in Galway, the veteran Peadar O'Donnell differentiated himself from those who held that the War of Independence stemmed from Easter 1916. He argued that the Conscription Crisis of April 1918 created widespread popular resistance to British power in Ireland, upon which Dan Breen and his associates predicated their January 1919 attack on policemen. But O'Donnell was ever the iconoclast.[4]

Such modern myths as we have looked at cannot survive the logic of contradiction, and so their custodians prohibit any modification (however minor) or critique (however obscure). It is therefore necessary to devise an approach which may disinter hitherto neglected connections between the event and the myth. I have tried to do this by concentrating on a cultural dimension, for the most part French in origin and literary in form.

For the **French connections**, one could go back to the Jacobins of 1798, or even the marquise de Saint-Ruth at the Battle of

Aughrim (1691), as indeed Pearse did on several occasions. In brief, the present book investigates three kinds of contemporary influence on the Easter Rising of 1916. These could be named (i) retrospective nationalism, (ii) revolutionary syndicalism, and (iii) Catholic Revival literature. The three overlap, and cannot be regarded as French monopolies. Indeed, retrospective nationalism may have a longer Irish pedigree than French, though the centre of energy at the beginning of the century was Paris, not Dublin. The period of influence might be dated 1890 (or earlier) to 1914, but it is distinctly marked into two phases by the Entente Cordiale (1904) between the United Kingdom and France, the *annus mirabilis* of James Joyce. Some may wish to regard Joyce as an ornamental thread that runs through the Hiberno-European fabric I am trying to unfold. He is not the thread; he is the needle or, more bluntly, 'Kinch the knife-blade' (*Ulysses*, chapter 1).

One could look further back in French culture. Baudelaire's excavations of the modern city disclosed **Archaic modernity**. Such a *super*-stratum is not wholly at odds with the iconography of 1916 in Dublin, the figure of Iron-Age Cuchulain in a score of texts — poems and plays by Yeats, essays by Pearse, and also the art-work of Oliver Sheppard. On the last, Denis Donoghue has useful comments to make: 'on April 21, 1935 — Easter Sunday — Oliver Sheppard's sculpture "The Death of Cuchulain" was unveiled in the centre of the General Post Office in Dublin. It was not designed for the occasion or commissioned by a Government to celebrate, the following year, the twentieth anniversary of the Easter Rising, 1916. Sheppard created the sculpture in 1911/1912 ...'[5] So much for the unity of symbol and meaning. It is fitting that Cuchulain should be more recently appropriated by Ulster Loyalists, bent on keeping southern-style republicanism at bay.

Donoghue is keen to explore Samuel Beckett's first novel *Murphy* (1938) which, through one incident, might claim to commemorate 1916. A character named Neary has entered the

GPO to study bronze Cuchulain from the rere. He then assaults the heroic buttocks 'such as they are' with his head. A policeman arrives, and a friend of Neary's. The friend, carefully named Wylie, offers reassurance that no damage has been done. 'Not a feather out of her ... No blood, no brains, nothing.' Given the maleness of the hero and his assailant, the feminine pronoun remains detached — unless one includes in the brazen scenario 'a raven, signifying death' on Cuchulain's shoulder. Birds — farmyard chickens and mythical phoenixes — will recur in the pages that follow, also the theme of politicised sacrifice. Beckett has it skewered: 'Wylie ... had already seized Neary round the waist, torn him back from the sacrifice and smuggled him half way to the exit.'[6] But whose sacrifice — Cuchulain's, Pearse's, Sheppard's, Neary's? If there is an answer, then the answer is: Always Somebody Else. The archaic super-stratum flies over the heads of Hitler's storm-troopers, deaths-head *Standarten*, colossal Roman arches, the resurgent *fasces* held aloft. The past will last a thousand years.

One could approach this unpleasant challenge through a more abstract formulation. **Progressive regression** must appear to be an absurd contradiction though surely there are examples to be found in the history of more than one de-colonised state (Zimbabwe, for example, or Burma). And some modern foundation myths, like some classic foundation garments, draw attention to what lies behind.[7] If we now regard Edmund Wilson's *To the Finland Station* (1940) as a late and too-naïve endorsement of the useful myth engineered by Trotsky *after* February 1917, Wilson's early chapters still provide an astonishingly helpful commentary on the French historical writers of the nineteenth century — Michelet, Renan, and Taine — through whom 1789 was de-revolutionised and re-booted as a platform for expansive regression. Two of these historians featured in the French syllabus read by Pearse at the Royal University of Ireland, where other vital actors of the period — Joyce, MacDonagh, Geraldine Plunkett,

Thomas Dillon, the Sheehy sisters, Frank Skeffington — were educated.[8] Their outlook permeated bourgeois Irish Catholicism and, if Renan's attitude to Christianity rendered him unwelcome, his Celticism won him selective tolerance. On the topic of the nation as such, Renan had argued in 1882 that *forgetting* perhaps as much as memory is a constitutive force. He went on — 'and I shall even say historical error[s], form an essential factor in the creation of a nation; and thus it is that the progress of historical studies may often be dangerous to the [i.e. concept of] nationality.'[9]

We can go further back still, however briefly. The regression of which I speak was really the denial or abandonment of *progress*, a concept which has been traced, cautiously, even among the Greeks and Romans of old. In 1969, a significant year for Ulster, the Belfast-born classicist Eric Dodds delivered a public lecture on 'The Ancient Concept of Progress'. The argument is learned and intricate, referring to dramatic poets, naturalists, sophist thinkers, medical men and philosophers. But Aeschylus's play about Prometheus, and the mythic figure of Prometheus the bringer of fire, is central. Against it, Dodds pits the evidence transmitted by Hesiod (eighth century BC). Of these two sources, he can then advance the proposition, 'If we ask how the poet came to substitute the idea of progress for the Hesiodic regress, part of the answer must surely lie in the triumphant experience of progress enjoyed by Aeschylus and his generation.'[10] Of course, there were dour counter-views according to which Man was getting worse, not better, having fallen out of a once-ordained Golden Age or Lost Paradise.

What is relevant for the present context is an implicit model discerned by Dodds — Optimism about the Future vs. Exhaustion and Fears of Degeneracy. He goes so far as to suggest a parallel between certain Roman expressions of concern and twentieth-century anxieties — the former is 'crisis poetry', comparable to the literature of the nineteen-thirties.[11] Of the earlier Attic phase, one could advance broader and longer parallels with the Victorian age, the gradual inner collapse of confidence, the growth of irrationalism and authoritarianism and, through the Celtic Revival, a yearning for primitivist restoration. Pearse knew Michelet and Taine; Yeats knew Prometheus through Shelley though the latter was, in that appropriation, purged of his atheism and radical politics. Dodds knew Yeats and Yeats's late preoccupation with 'pollution' and eugenics. If regress fails to deliver restoration, then acknowledgment of fallen man's Original Sin may follow, not necessarily with the corpus of Christian doctrine still intact. Instead, Alfred Jarry's Savage God Rules OK.

These ideas were not debated in the *Freeman's Journal, The Irish Times* or the Gaelic Athletic Association. They circulated in different forms — learned (or esotetic) and more popular (exoteric). They emerged in local or antiquarian colour, notably through that burgeoning literature about Cuchulain to which Standish James O'Grady, John Todhunter and T.W. Rolleston also made important contributions. (Here we will note the great German sociologist Max Weber's early interest.) While Standish James O'Grady (1846–1928) spun out adventure novels, his cousin Standish Hayes O'Grady (1832–1915) worked the esoteric lode, a Celtic scholar to his refined finger-tips, president of the Ossianic Society, cataloguer of Gaelic manuscripts in the British Museum. Newer disciplines emerged. Alienism gradually gave way to psychology and psycho-analysis, whose terms raised implications for accepted ideas of free will — and hence of politics too. (Here we might note — for balance — the role of George Sigerson in the English transmission of Jean-Martin Charcot's ideas.) For its size, Ireland was not inconspicuous. In comparative literature and linguistics (H.M. Posnett), sociology of the ancient world (J.P. Mahaffy), philosophy and psycho-analysis (J.A. Wisdom), Irish non-literary thinkers cut paths and sometimes little roads into the dark grove of what was not conscious, obvious, reassuring. If most of the cited names tinkle faintly of a Trinity long gone, a clue might lie in its rival, the Royal University's preference for instruction over research, consistent with Cardinal Newman's priorities. Perhaps that preference was itself an exercise in distinguishing the spheres of learned and popular discourse, the latter raised a notch to satisfy a growing Catholic middle class, the former discreetly reserved for great minds like Newman's own or, short of that, the Jesuits. Like Prometheus, Joyce stole their fire.

Nothing was exactly clear-cut, black and white, at turn-of-century. Some of Joyce's instructors were English Catholics, some of Pearse's Irish protestants. A Trinity vice-provost, John Kells Ingram (1823–1907), had as a young man published 'The Memory of the Dead' back in 1843, its opening line eventually echoed in 'Who Fears to Speak of Easter Week?' (written by Sister Columba). Despite his academic success and the jibes of narrower minds, he insisted in 1900 that he had never disowned the poem. Instead, with prescience, he compared the potential for renewed republican/nationalist violence unfavourably with the United Irishmen's campaign. Professor first of Oratory, then English, then Greek, he was a leading figure in the advancement of positivism, having met Auguste Comte in 1855.[12] His younger brother, Thomas Dunbar Ingram (1826–1901), was emphatically *not* a Trinity man; from 1866 to 1877 he held the chair of Hindu law and jurisprudence at the President's College, Calcutta. Retired home, he was just the Unionist numb-skull to infuriate Gladstone.

By the early years of the new century, an Irish Catholic intelligentsia undoubtedly existed — Thomas Kettle, Stephen MacKenna, Eoin MacNeill, Fred Ryan, Fr George Tyrell are diverse examples (all male). And there was evidence of transferring energies — Denis and Aubrey Gwynn (both historians) converted to Catholicism. But political theory? No. While Donal McCartney and Ciaran Brady have recently examined in depth the work of W.E.H. Lecky, Anthony Froude and J.P. Prendergast, the results disinter no politics below what is latent in any Irish historiography from the Victorian age. Isaac Butt had been a practising lawyer; Parnell wasn't even that. Tom Kettle sat in parliament, wrote about Nietzsche, and held a university chair in National Economics. *The Open Secret of Ireland* (1912) demonstrates Kettle's familiarity with Bergson, Moritz Bonn, Alfred Fouillée, Michelet, Renan, Taine, Nietzsche, etc etc, and his own distinction (hardly original) between utilitarian England and cultured Ireland. As for political theory, he remained a captive of Home Rule nostrums.[13]

Both Connolly and Pearse published numerous articles and pamphlets rich in persuasive detail and original thought. Yet, when they and their co-signatories composed the Proclamation of 1916, it delivered familiar dicta and laudable aspirations. In their one gesture towards originality, they had to invent a Gaelic word for 'republic' — poblacht, modelled on ríoghacht (kingdom or monarchy).[14] One must sympathise with their fewness of words, given the haste and oppressive secrecy under which they worked. But perhaps the Proclamation was itself a heroic effort towards the exoteric popular enunciation (suitably veiled even from its evangels) of yet-secret doctrines. Orderlies of the Golden Dawn were loose-lipped demagogues compared to adepts of a Neo-Fenian Brotherhood. Using the ordinary language of political organisation, Liam de Paor spoke of the 1916 leaders forming a 'conspiracy within a conspiracy', with Eoin MacNeill in the outer circle, and Tom Clarke in the inner. Was there yet an inner-most? Is there?

The chapters which follow treat a cultural *milieu* contemporary with the maturing of ideas and individuals finally activated at Easter 1916; they do not trace the nativist pedigree of official vindication. Their substance lies quite outside the usual frame of reference, partly in being contemporary, not historical, and by being (for the most part) French. Maurice Barrès, Henri Bergson, Paul Bourget, Jean Malye, and Georges Sorel all outlived the doomed signatories. And if there is a tragic aspect to the executions, and conversely to the French view of Easter 1916 as a 'stab in the back', its memory refused to lie down. Instead it propelled the dynamic towards the defeated camp — the German Reich morphing into a hateful Dictatur-Theorie. While Edmund Wilson moved on to research his Part Two: Chapter 5 ('Karl Marx; Prometheus and Lucifer'), Irish veterans of 1916 were in cahoots with Hitler (see Chapter 10 below). Marvellous how regress keeps up with the leaders!

Irish republicans of the nationalist persuasion are condemned to look back on **the German future**. The inclusion of German right-radical thought may seem odd, but the point of Carl Schmitt's interest in Easter 1916 coincided with his interest in Georges Sorel (who was not essentially a nationalist). By 1998 a leading American critic of Schmitt's work could cite an interpretation 'now practically hegemonic in Europe, that Schmitt's whole intellectual corpus is fully motivated by a sometimes hidden, sometimes expressed Catholic political theology.'[15] The wonder is that he did not find a greater take-up in Ireland. Yet behind Schmitt, though half concealed, stands the admonitory figure of Nietzsche, whose impact in the Anglophone world drew in Synge and Yeats in contrasting ways.[16] From this brief digression, it should be clear that the French influences traced throughout the book are neither liberal nor left-ist in any convincing way.

**T.S. Eliot or James Joyce?** French and German influences or affinities, while more unexpected in their orientation than traditionalists would imagine, are likely to appeal beyond any suggestion of debts to English culture. These latter must await their apostate, who might begin by examining the prologue to, and wider effects of, the Catholic Revival in Victorian Britain.[17] Suffice it to say for the moment that the influence of Charles Dickens can be assumed in the household of James Pearse, and that of *A Tale of Two Cities* (1859) discerned in the tangled political rhetoric of Patrick, his son. Juxtaposition of 'the republic' and 'resurrection' gradually converges in the death of Sidney Carton, whose demeanour surely contributes to Pearse's imagined Robert Emmet.[18] While on the military-masochistic wing of English influence, one might propose Tennyson's knights of the round table (cf 'Morte d'Arthur') as an influence on Standish O'Grady, and then as models for Na Fianna, courtesy of Baden Powell.

This is to consider English literary history over half a century. The brothers Balfour — each had been Chief Secretary in Ireland — were serious investigators of philosophical and cultural topics impinging on Irish thought in the years just before the Great War, though they did not choose any topic specifically because it impinged or might impinge on the apple of our eye.[19] A thorough-going Unionist, A.J. Balfour worried that the Orange revolt against prospective Home Rule threatened the 'ordinary ties of social obligation' already endangered (he thought) by suffragettes and syndicalists.[20] Lloyd George distinguished adroitly between socialists and syndicalists at this time, though his concern was tactical, not philosophic. More immediate to the concerns of the 1916 poets and their colleagues was the contemporary French interests of a young man in the process of becoming English — T.S. Eliot (1888–1965) — inheritor of a Symbolist tradition not without impact in Ireland.[21] Among Modernist writers, I have discovered James Joyce to be the exemplary if laconic commentator, all the more so for being in Zurich when the Gaelic mini-Zeppelin went up. A student of the English language under his tutelage tackled Joyce about the Rising before the consequent executions were finished — 'nothing to do with' it. The student, it emerges, was a Hapsburg Imperial intelligence officer who insisted that 'the pen of this man should be made use of.'[22] At the time Joyce was awaiting publication of *A Portrait of the Artist as a Young Man*, whose central figure castigates the Fenian recruiter:

No honourable and sincere man, said Stephen, has given up to you his life and his youth and his affections from the days of Tone to those of Parnell, but you sold him to the enemy or failed him in need or reviled him and left him for another. And you invite me to be one of you. I'd see you damned first.

Joyce's position is not solely moral. His earlier summary of Davin's political and religious positions employs the term 'myth' first to make a negative aesthetic judgment and then to specify an amalgam of ideologies which had been fired at Easter 1916 —

He stood towards the myth upon which no individual mind had ever drawn out a line of beauty and to its unwieldy tales that divided against themselves as they moved down the cycles in the same attitude as towards the Roman catholic religion, the attitude of a dull-witted loyal serf.[23]

**American admonitions**. The notion that Joyce might be the author of a political critique deserves further attention.[24] A word might be said on another neglected angle — the influence of American thought on Irish nationalism. There is of course the loosely accepted assumption that democracy in the post-bellum Union augmented and consolidated the United Irishmen's legacy, principally through the Fenian movement and its transatlantic agency, Clan na Gael. In this scenario, the generation of John Devoy (1842–1928) is crucial, though the personal experiences and prejudices of John Mitchel (1815–1875) left a profound literary as well as ideological imprint. But to what American intellectual influences were thoughtful exiles open — transcendentalism, pragmatism, the idea of manifest destiny ...?

In the longer perspective, American historiography has models to provide. Bernard Bailyn's *Ideological Origins of the American Revolution* (1967) overturned many popular beliefs about the prelude to independence by analysing a vast tranche of pre-revolutionary pamphlets. In the present book, the examination of Catholic periodicals may produce a similar effect in the historiography of Irish nationalism and independence.[25] Bailyn, in his foreword, quoted Hugh Trevor-Roper — 'by our explanations, interpretations, assumptions we gradually make [the great event] seem automatic, natural, inevitable; we remove from it the sense of wonder, the unpredictability, and therefore the freshness it ought to have.'[26]

———

So, Fergal, I hope that the above paragraphs do the job you helpfully specified. As I wrote them, I remembered that we discussed the project together years ago, outside a *café* across from the Luxembourg Gardens in Paris. Some readers may be initially offended at the pigeon-holing of their foundation myth as a foundation myth, preferring to regard it as a self-evident truth, a fact of national history. The street we gazed across had been the familiar beat of the Gaelic scholar Richard Best, the classical scholar and neo-Platonist Stephen MacKenna, and the playwright J.M. Synge. None of these three great Irish minds would have been so great without their French experience. Down the hill, on the Carrefour de l'Odéon, the medical student J.A. Joyce argued with all comers of all nationalities until he became the maker of truth-laden fictions.

Finally, a word about two areas of undoubted importance to a full understanding of the conflicts embodied in Easter 1916, areas which could not be treated here without distraction from my chosen focus. The papal encyclical *Rerum Novarum* (1891) sought to reconcile church authority with 'true social rectification'.[27] Its influence in the debates between nationalism and socialism in the years between the fall of Parnell and the Easter Rising remains to be traced in detail, though at least one thoughtful young participant in the events of 1916 (Colm Ó Lochlainn) was influenced by it. Second, oddly enough, is the official neglect of the interaction of Gaelic literary and political material with the history of what is (again oddly) treated as a largely Anglophone occasion. There is no edition currently available of Pádraic Ó Conaire's *Seacht mBuaidh an Éirghe-amach* (1918), but then we have no properly edited text of Pearse's extensive works, and no biography whatsoever of Plunkett. Honor Ó Brolcháin, *16 Lives: Joseph Plunkett* (Dublin: O'Brien Press, 2012) appeared while the present book was at proof stage.

# Chapter 1
# Children of the Nation, or a Nation of Children?

*as my father I have already died, as my mother I
still live and grow old.*

Nietzsche

L iam de Paor's 1997 Preface began with the laconic
statement 'this is an essay on words.' And so it largely
remains though, I would suggest, it veered off in the book's
final sentences towards a problematic, different domain. He
remained always attentive to the interpretation and
misinterpretation of specific words in the Easter Proclamation,
taking particular care to indicate how attention to another
document (American, French or Irish) might illuminate the text
in hand. For example, analysing the Proclamation's fourth
paragraph, he quoted extensively from the Ulster Covenant of
September 1912.[1] His point was to argue that Pearse and Co. were
answering in positive and (they hoped) reassuring fashion the
Unionists' insistence on 'religious freedom'. The words quoted
from the 1916 document were:

> The Republic guarantees religious and civil liberty, equal
> rights and equal opportunities to all its citizens, and declares
> its resolve to pursue the happiness and prosperity of the whole
> nation and of all its parts, cherishing all the children of the

nation equally, and oblivious of the differences carefully fostered by an alien government, which have divided a minority from the majority in the past.

The positive dimension came down from the United Irishmen's vision of Irish independence and their ambition to unite 'Catholic, Protestant and Dissenter'. In 1916 substantial numbers of non-Catholics lived in Cavan, Donegal and Monaghan (soon to be 'border counties') but also in the decidedly southern counties of Wicklow and Cork, not to mention Dublin City in which the Rising was to take place. Reassurance was unquestionably in order. But the great block of non-Catholic residents on the island lived in what was to become Northern Ireland which, by various means, the Proclamation's designers were excluding from their enterprise, in practice if not in theory. Where 'religious freedom' was most anxiously, if belatedly, defended or sought, the Dublin signatories were in no position to deliver; which, by the ironies of partition, led to increased deficits of religious freedom north and south.[2]

What does religion mean in these two documents, if not Christianity in its conflicting versions? Admittedly, no specification is made in either the Ulster or the Dublin text and, given the peculiar Ego-Christ-ological interests of Pearse and Plunkett, not to mention the less fervent Catholicity of other signatories, this must be taken as an act of discretion on their part. Dublin goes for God twice (first and sixth paragraphs), Ulster once, but without any naming of denominations or creeds in either case. Given these silent concessions to the 'minority', how is the issue formulated in words?

De Paor calculated that the Proclamation amounted to 486 words, not including the signatures. This figure gives one pause to think how very brief it was and is, even if the conditions of treasonable typesetting under hostile war-time conditions are recalled. A tally of some notable terms, alphabetically listed, is revealing:

| | |
|---|---|
| arms | 5 |
| children | 4 |
| citizen/s | 2 |
| freedom | 3 |
| generation/s | 2 |
| government | 6 |
| Ireland | 4 |
| Irish/- | 13 |
| liberty | 1 |
| man (including plurals and compounds) | 4 |
| nation/al/hood/s | 7 |
| people | 7 |
| provisional | 3 |
| sovereign/ty | 3 |
| state | 1 |
| woman (including plurals and compounds) | 3 |

A number of comments arise promptly, the first and least significant being the predominance of 'Irish' as an emotive descriptor; this is a nationalist declaration, and no mistake. (In three cases the adjective forms part of an organisation's title, e.g. 'Irish Republican Brotherhood'.) Other terms naturally have a wider potential application, and indeed 'government', 'nation' and 'people' are used beyond their Irish instances, e.g. 'foreign people and government'. The Proclamation is formally addressed to 'the people of Ireland', and 'people' exceeds any other term for the entity (including 'Ireland'). In allowing for 'the ownership of Ireland', the Proclamation echoes the constitution (drawn up by Sean O'Casey) ratified by the Irish Citizen Army in March 1914, though the earlier document specifies both 'moral and material' ownership. We are here examining, and not merely listing, 12.5 per cent of the Proclamation's lexicon. Additional words will come under scrutiny in succeeding paragraphs.

'Citizen' is present in the 'Irish Citizen Army', and in only one further instance, significantly in the paragraph where the new Republic guarantees civil and religious liberty 'to all its citizens'. De Paor's point about the Proclamation's echoing the Ulster Covenant on this issue of religious liberty is reinforced when one recalls that the latter document also referred twice to 'citizenship', although no such term had legal validity under UK laws. Here it may be appropriate to add that, while 'the Provisional Government' of the 1916 document is most frequently taken to be an affirmative allusion to Robert Emmet's manifesto of 1803, de Paor in a lengthy footnote (see p. 17 above) listed the Provisional Government of Ulster's twenty-one members, the vast majority of them elected members of parliament.

'Nation/al' is more complicated than might be expected. Ireland's proposed 'exaltation among the nations' carries a religiose overtone which can be confirmed by reference to numerous Old Testament verses; maybe Plunkett had a hand in this formulation, though he was confined to a nursing home during much of the period in question.[3] Emmet had modestly spoken in court about his country 'taking its place' among the nations of the world, and the idea of exaltation may echo the language of early twentieth-century French 'integral nationalism' (as it will come to known). But continental matters remain for later treatment.

The nation in the Republican Proclamation has its own local problems, and these immediately precede the undertaking to cherish 'all the children of the nation equally'. Referring to 'happiness and prosperity', the signatories are clearly echoing French and American precedents. However, a fuller quotation suddenly reveals the Irish difficulty — 'happiness and prosperity of the whole nation and all its parts'. What are, in the text's inevitably makeshift terminology, the parts?[4] Connolly would doubtless have provided a social answer, that is to say, an answer in terms of class. (Or, rather, he would have, if he had not opted to subordinate Citizen Army objectives to those of the Volunteers.) But other possible answers, employing territorial (regional) or confessional (denominational) terms, could be formulated. The point is, the question got no answer in the Proclamation, except by way of an over-worked metaphor.

De Paor argued (persuasively, I think) that 'cherishing all the children of the nation equally' did not refer to children but to 'the people of Ireland', and he mentions the frequency of the noun in the Proclamation — 'summons her children to her flag', etc. Revelations during the last quarter century about the treatment of infants and young persons in the three states which indirectly stem from the Proclamation (the Irish Free State, Éire from 1937 to 1949, the republic of 1949 onwards) have understandably led protestors and campaigners to quote with outrage what many still take as a foundational document. But it is worth asking if this metaphorical use of 'children' is not part of a wider evasion concerning definitions of the nation 'and all its parts'.

Consider the four occasions:

1. 'Ireland, through us, summons her children to her flag'
2. 'supported by her exiled children in America'
3. 'cherishing all the children of the nation equally'
4. 'the readiness of her children to sacrifice themselves'.

In the first case, the age-old idea of nations and countries having a feminine-gender name led on to a more specifically female characterisation of the motherland and, more familiarly still, to La belle France, Little Mother Russia, Cathleen ni Houlihan, etc. It seems natural therefore that people, 'the people of Ireland', are the children of the Mother: of the four occurrences of the noun, three include the possessive adjective ('her'). But nature is a rare maker of constitutions. A categorical demarcation has been crossed in moving from feminine to female, especially at the time of the Easter Rising when suffragette agitation was at a height.

In moral and historical perspectives, the Proclamation achieves a very remarkable modern egalitarianism addressing itself to 'Irishmen and Irishwomen', claiming 'the allegiance of every Irishman and Irishwoman', and in referring to 'the suffrages of all her [Ireland's] men and women'. To isolate a word de Paor had no need to interrogate, preferring to describe the surrounding statement as that of 'a junta executing a coup',[5] let us take a first look at the neglected 'suffrages', an obtuse term even in 1916. What does it mean? Or, what does it mean *when*?

In 1916 suffragettes were still in the news, having stormed buildings in July 1912 when the Prime Minister (Asquith) visited Dublin. Suffragettism (a decidedly radical and activist movement) continued to be a damned nuisance for government during the War. Earlier, suffragism carried the flag of women's enfranchisement without the sharpened main-staff, the self-applied handcuffs, and (from the authorities) violently imposed forced feeding. The Proclamation's fluffy and antiquarian 'suffrages' goes even further back, despite the show of gender equality and democratic fair play. 'Suffrage/s' was a collective noun of the early modern centuries signifying prayers, especially for the dead. It also signified (in the sixteenth century) a vote given by the member of a particular collective body to elect another. Its more recent applications enter the language through an American usage of the revolutionary period (cf. de Paor generally), though *female suffrage, household suffrage*, etc were in circulation earlier in the eighteenth century. In 1916 it had a quaint ring, not the radical one complaisantly assumed. Irish Catholic responses to the Rising and its Proclamation sharply differed in their capacity to absorb the suffrage or feminist reference.[6]

The real adults, manoeuvred in these phrases, are simultaneously demoted to the level of ideal childhood through the repeated use of 'children' to connote 'the people'. The Proclaimers are adults and, by implication, so are the otherwise unaccounted-for Provisional Government. An authoritarian summons relates the leaders to the followers, modelled on conventional parental relations. By alluding to 'children', the document further avoids any specification of the nation's 'parts', whether in social terms (the urban worker, the strong farmer, the *rentier*, the holder of stocks and shares) or denominational ones (the Ulster Elimite, the enclosed Carmelite nun, the first-communicants, the Unitarian of 'Cromwellian' descent, the Jew, and of course the former Established Church élite). It is the more obscure examples which put the Proclamation under pressure, for the claim on every Irishman and Irishwoman's allegiance may be an exercise in quietly ruling *out* rather than warmly inviting *in*. De Paor, who was no programmatic anti-nationalist, detected 'a call to a jihad'.[7] Historic evidence of Presbyterian republicanism and the more recent contribution of individual Anglicans to the Gaelic language movement could be glibly cited, but these cannot add up to 'all the parts'.

The admission that the nation has parts, even if there is also a discernible 'whole nation', implies an internal complexity left unspoken. The Elimite, the nun and the Jew may be silently treated as children because, even less consciously, a domestic authoritarianism underpins much of the Proclamation's political unconscious, based on a nationalism in turn based on family relations, which are slowly achieving more emphatic formulations within Catholicism. Emigration had no doubt contributed to the image of those who had left in early youth, frozen at the age they were when last seen in Mayo, Tyrone or Queenstown. Pearse's originality and practical success as an educator cast an uncomfortable light on these issues, as if his professional work and political vision occupied separate spheres. Children do what they are told, and in the Proclamation's final deployment of the word, a readiness to sacrifice themselves is proudly noted.

I have written elsewhere about Pearse's rhetoric of blood sacrifice and its questionable pedigree in Irish republican tradition. Certainly Wolfe Tone was no martyr figure in his own mind, and his suicide (often denied) embarrassed Catholic followers. Cruise-O'Brien usefully drew attention to the importance in this ideological context of 'Cathleen ni Houlihan', Yeats's play of 1902, but was wrong to speak of 'its mystical glorification of the blood sacrifice of 1798', for the glorification and the theme of sacrifice *both* belong to 1902, not 1798.[8] Of a somewhat later event Marianne Elliott speaks of 'the cult of sacrifice' which she considered 'fundamental to [Thomas] Russell's psyche'. Russell had been out of Ireland for years — one of her exiled children — and experienced deep guilt at his inability to achieve the great goal when he returned. Emmet was a different matter. In Elliott's words, 'Unlike Tone, who was a deist and critical of established religion, Emmet's sincere Christianity was more amenable to the blood-sacrifice traditions of Irish republicanism, a tradition that he consciously helped create.'[9] Patrick Geoghegan recalls a detail from Emmet's father's rhetoric, a breakfast ritual in which he questioned his children, 'Would you kill your sister for your country? Would you kill me?'[10] But the elder Emmet is mobilising an ancient Roman virtue, exemplified in Lucius Junius Brutus (supposed founder of the Republic), very different from the early twentieth-century nationalism imbided by Pearse, though not without influence in revolutionary France.[11] However, contemporary influences are no less influential than so-called traditional ones. If bold Robert Emmet stands behind the Easter Proclamation, nodding in recognition of its Provisional Government, the hard-headed members of Ulster's Provisional Government were closer in time. The Proclamation's notion of time, including historic time ('God and … the dead generations' … 'six times in the last three hundred years …'), re-arranges these choral figures, with a consequent greater acceptance of sacrifice. In doing so, the victims are all the readier cast as children. Only the moment — a word repeated in the Proclamation with breathless rapidity[12] — holds apart dead generations and children.

In addition to some close-up of Pearsean details, one should not neglect a longer or broader perspective through, for example, a timely article of 1898. Written by two Frenchmen, and dealing with anthropological material, *Sacrifice: its Nature and Function* might be read as anticipating some ritual developments of the Dublin rising, even with regard to the posthumous Gaelicisation of Pearse as Mac Piarais and the earlier, more extravagant conversion of Charles William St John Burgess into Cathal Brugha: 'In the early Church the neophytes, after having been exorcised, were baptised on Easter Day. Then, after this baptism, they were given communion, and a new name was bestowed on them.'[13]

The Proclamation's tally of Irish rebellions — 'six times in the last three hundred years' — is clearly a rebuttal of its principal sponsor's anxiety about Irish manhood.[14] If it is assumed that Easter 1916 is final in the series, then little difficulty can be feared in listing five earlier instances. The Fenian Rising of March 1867 must be counted most recent, despite the activity of informers, the denunciation by a Bishop of Kerry, and the abject failure of military endeavours except the attack on Knockadoon's coastguard station. With a retrospective glance, one next finds Emmet's Dublin rising of July 1803, a one-day affair remembered for the brutal murder of a liberal-minded judge. Behind that the far more substantial, ideologically prepared, and widespread United Irishmen rebellion of 1798. Of the six assertions of Irish independence in arms referred to in the Proclamation, we have swiftly accounted for four (including 1916) within just 118 years. No less than 272 years remain to be examined, taking us back to c. 1616 when the Great O'Neill died in Rome.

It is an awkwardly long interval, between the Earl of Tyrone's death in well-watered papal exile and the deist Wolfe Tone's suicide in jail. Certainly rebellion broke out in October 1641, but it had nothing to do with Irish sovereignty and less than nothing to do with republicanism or democracy. Catholic and Royalist, at once savage and promptly libelled for excesses now thought utterly beyond execution, the Rising of 1641 was partly a forerunner to the English Civil War and partly an insular episode in the Thirty Years War of religion in Europe. Pearse & Co. need it if they are to prove a case about three hundred years of recurrent insurrection; but it would be stretching things to suppose that, among Rory O'More's priorities, cherishing 'all the children of the nation equally' ranked high. October 1641 is less a date for Irish politics than it is in European religious warfare.

One slot in the Proclamation's calendar of armed assertions on Ireland's behalf remains blank — or perhaps two, if supporters of Charles I are denied recognition as proto-Fenians and prophets of the Citizen Army. We should look forward from 1641, not back. Enter (left, is it?) Prince William of Orange in 1688. The wars of 1688–1691 constituted an Irish theatre of the more distinctly external conflict between Protestant and Catholic Europe (with, however, the Papacy on William's side) than the massacres of 1641. Again Irish sovereignty is not an issue, though sovereignty as such unquestionably is, not only in the English parliamentary appeal to a Dutch prince but also in the political treatises of John Locke. If Pearse & Co. in 1916 wished to invoke the Williamite/Jacobite wars as precedent to their own efforts, only two lines of historical argument helped: (1) Foreign (in practice French) support especially at the top of the military command; (2) Irish manpower especially at the bottom of the burial middens.

A schema of historic events implicit in the Proclamation looks like this:

1641 — the insurrection of October, notably but by no means exclusively in Ulster and the north midlands;

1688–1691 — Jacobite-Williamite Wars, with Louis xiv's army committed on the Jacobite side;

---

1798 — United Irishmen's insurrection, supported by revolutionary France;

1803 — Emmet's rising, partly planned with French approval, but unsupported by United Irishmen outside Dublin;

1867 — Fenian (IRB) risings in counties Clare, Cork, Dublin, Limerick, Louth, Tipperary, and Wicklow, aided by veterans from the American Civil War;

1916 — the IRB-directed insurrection in Dublin (with some incidents in Galway, Kerry and Meath), partly armed by the German Empire but without any foreign intervention.

The bar-line above indicates a distinction between those events which asserted defensive exercises on behalf of existing (English) monarchy and those of a proposed Irish republican variety. Elide the bar-line in the name of Pearsian tradition, and you perpetrate a blatant exercise in retrospective nationalism. Perhaps that ideological manoeuvre had been well established in Irish nationalist historiography before the twentieth century, but it drew strength beyond its own, notably out of French examples.

There is one episode, tiny in scale but huge in implication, yet to be located in (or near) the Proclamation — the Invincibles' assassination of the Irish Chief-Secretary and Under-Secretary in November 1881 with surgical knives. Those responsible were Fenians, or ex-Fenians, or Fenian associates. Such was the revulsion which followed the murders — Michael Davitt promptly offered to help Scotland Yard — that Pearse & Co. were never likely to invoke the Invincibles or even favourably allude to them. ('It shouldn't have happened,' in Gerry Adams's phrase.) That discretion leads one to consider more closely the broader avoidance of nationalist specifics in the Proclamation's claim to a historic continuity — no Emmet, no United Irishmen, no Patrick Sarsfield, just the contemporary (and conspiratorial) Irish Republican Brotherhood. At one level, an explanation may be built on the exigencies of type resources available to the compositors of the document who evidently had no numerals and so were obliged to avoid dates ('1798 ... 1803' etc.) But at a further level of interpretation, one observes the silent operations of a retrospective nationalism which surrenders no detail to the critique of sceptics or outsiders.

Elliott's account of 'the blood sacrifice' traditions of Irish republicanism has to be understood within the rhetoric employed by Pearse. Early in 1914 he delivered two public orations in New York devoted to Emmet. In the first, we encounter a phrase echoed in the Proclamation — 'an old tradition of nationhood'. The 2 March 1914 address in the Brooklyn Academy of Music also characterises the Irish people as children in sentences laden with pathos. Both addresses veer towards an identification of Emmet with Christ which still leaves room for the speaker humbly to associate himself with the rebel of 1803. The extent to which the Proclamation reworks the American addresses is limited only by an impossibility of recruiting the Redeemer, though Tom Clarke's insistence on an *Easter* rising will make up lost ground. In the 1940s Pearse was roundly denounced by J.J. Horgan in political terms and his imagery was eventually subject to critical rebuke by Fr Francis Shaw in the celebratory mid-1960s.[15] For his pains the Jesuit's critique, warning of blasphemy, was denied publication until 1972, by which time blood was again plentifully in evidence. When Pearse vaunted Emmet's death as 'a sacrifice Christ-like in its perfection', and claimed that he had 'redeemed Ireland from acquiescence in the Union', he was not drawing on the language of Myles Byrne, Michael Dwyer, Thomas Addis Emmet or even Thomas Russell. He echoed a contemporary exercise in hagiographic nationalism — the efforts by French right-wing radicals to transform the 'Maid of Orleans' into Saint Joan.

This decidedly twentieth-century campaign provided a model by which the early nineteenth-century Irish rebel is absorbed into timeless Fenianism. In New York, Pearse declared that 'the new generation is re-affirming the Fenian faith, the faith of Emmet.'

Alliteration apart, what is striking in this formula is its assumptions about Time. One of Pearse's obsessions was with generation as such, with the human species' reproduction of itself in successive periods. This was at once biological *Angst* and historical observation; he worried about the failure of his own generation in Ireland to attempt what Tone, Emmet and Mitchel had done in their time. On 25 December 1915 (Pearse's last Christmas), he signed off a little pamphlet called *Ghosts*. It opened cheerlessly:

> There has been nothing more terrible in Irish history than the failure of the last generation. Other generations have failed in Ireland, but they have failed nobly; or, failing ignobly, some man among them has redeemed them from infamy by the splendour of his protest. But the failure of the last generation has been mean and shameful, and no man has arisen from it to say or do a splendid thing in virtue of which it shall be forgiven.[16]

Inertia between 1691 and 1798, thanks to penal repression's helpful alibi. Closer to his own time, and to a less overt state violence, generation nonetheless leads into degeneracy. The New York formula had dissolved this linear succession to suggest a defining *moment* in which a total transformation of all that is or has been sordid and less than 'noble' will be effected. In the second paragraph of the first New York address, Pearse boldly expounded politics as faith:

> For patriotism is at once a faith and a service. A faith which in some of us has been in our flesh and bone since we were moulded in our mothers' wombs, and which in others of us has at some definite moment of our later lives been kindled as if by the miraculous word of God ...[17]

In August 1914 Pearse supplied an addendum to the American texts. He was happy to report a 'quick movement of events in Ireland' and the arming of young men. 'Blood has flowed in Dublin streets.' Then, using a term later to be familiar in very different circumstances, he affirms that 'the cause of the Volunteers has been consecrated by a holocaust.' What is noteworthy is not Pearse's somewhat exaggerated reflection on the Bachelor's Walk incident of 26 July, when British troops killed four people, having failed to impound Volunteer weapons; it is the specific biblical term 'holocaust' (Douay version; Genesis 22:2) when God directs Abraham to sacrifice his only son.[18] (God, of course, provides a surrogate ram, and thus *prohibits forever* the sacrificing of human beings.) What is more striking is Pearse's subsequent acknowledgment of a violence out-shadowing Bachelor's Walk:

> A European war has brought about a crisis which may contain, as yet hidden within it, the moment for which the generations have been waiting. It remains to be seen whether, if that moment reveals itself, we shall have the sight to see and the courage to do, or whether it shall be written of this generation, alone of all the generations of Ireland, that it had none among it who dared to make the ultimate sacrifice.[19]

With the Proclamation still uppermost in our minds, we notice the appearance here of some key terms — notably 'the [dead] generations'. This is the major theme. More significant, perhaps, is the minor theme, closely related — Pearse's emphasis on 'the moment ... reveal[s] ... that moment'. These words re-appear in the same order in 1916. Generation and moment, repeated failure and possible success. Not only in his martyrological pre-occupation with sacrifice does Pearse echo contemporary French thinking, but also in this choice of 'the moment' as the metonymy of time.

Pearse assumes that the formative or constitutive unit of Irish political action (indeed, of society, by implication) is generation, an assumption ripe with Social-Darwinian implications. The present generation, he fears, may not dare to make the ultimate sacrifice. But what generations do to enact the term itself is *to generate*, that is, to give birth to children, at some climactic moment in the hero's or martyr's case. In the last sentence of the Proclamation, the self-cancelling logic of Pearse's argument on behalf of the Irish Nation is disclosed in the presumed 'readiness of its children to sacrifice themselves for the common good.' The individual, in quitting childhood, became a dead adult, through a self-cancelling which ideally required a new philosophy of time. De Paor noted the bellicose rhetoric of August 1914, especially concentrating on the Germanic phrase 'Der Tag'.[20]

## Chapter 2
# The Phoenix as Dying Bird

*I should like to be in a crowd of beaks without words.*
T.S. Eliot (cancelled line in *The Waste Land*)

**Names Will Never Hurt**

Among celebrated dicta of nineteenth-century clerics, please note the declaration ascribed to a Bishop of Kerry — that hell was not hot enough, nor eternity long enough to punish the rebels of 1867. Antagonism between the Catholic Church and organised Irish nationalism had a long history, reaching back to the 1790s when the United Irishmen were thought little better than Jacobin infidels. The role of protestants such as Thomas Davis and John Mitchel among the Young Irelanders and Confederates of 1842–48 did little to re-assure the hierarchy, even if some parish priests also supported the movement. With the foundation of the Irish Republican (originally, Revolutionary) Brotherhood in 1858, the Church's concern was doubled, for the IRB was active both in North America and at home in Ireland. Like the United Irishmen, but unlike Young Ireland, it was a secret society of oath-bound members committed to military action. Though the attempted 'rising' in 1867 was a dismal failure, Bishop Moriarty left his flock in no doubt as to the ultimate condition of 'Fenians'.

The origins of any shorthand name are mixed. The IRB operated in part through Phoenix Clubs, relatively open associations which anticipated the 'entryism' practised later by British and Irish followers of Leon Trotsky. The Phoenix connoted indestructibility, survival of lethal force and, by a kind of transference, it became the eternal flame itself. These were values increasingly associated with the Gaelic language by the revivalists of post-Famine times. John O'Mahony ran Fenian Clubs in New York, distinct (being open) from the IRB; the names of these organisations skipped about.

Though the Gaelic revival movement aimed at re-establishing a vernacular, it also paid close attention to historical, literary, mythic and philological sources. Scholarly work, for example that of the Ossianic Society (founded in 1853), brought to Victorian attention the ancient saga and heroic material of pre-Christian Ireland. Oisin, after whom the Society named itself, was the son of legendary Fionn Mac Cumhail, leader of a warrior group known as the Fianna (to whom O'Mahony alluded, with his clubs). When this material — its written sources largely dating from the post-Viking era — was rendered into English in the nineteenth century it was generally termed Fenian literature; indeed the Society declared its objective to be 'publication of Fenian poems'.[1]

The poignancy — and potency — of this doubled usage can be traced in Douglas Hyde's early career. In 1877 he recorded a Fenian (i.e. IRB) meeting which occurred at Frenchpark, his clerical father's Roscommon estate; later he became an expert in Fenian (i.e. pre-Christian) textual studies.[2] As a professor in the Royal University, he jointly set an examination paper which Pearse would sit in the summer of 1899; one task required of students was to re-translate into Gaelic a passage (from Geoffrey Keating) which included the statement that 'they have not made a stoop for the virtues and good customs of the Old-English or of the Gaels who were inhabiting Ireland during their time ...' The examination papers generally required an extensive knowledge of early Irish history, though the English chronicler William Camden also featured in commentary. In 1899 Hyde published the authoritative and influential *Literary History of Ireland* in which he wrote of Saint Patrick's supposed unease while listening to stories of the 'ancient Fenians'.[3] By a pleasing coincidence, in old age Hyde, as the first President of Ireland, officially resided in the Phoenix Park outside Dublin, its name supposedly Gaelic, *fionn uisce*, or (spring of) clear water. By a less pleasing coincidence, it was in the Phoenix Park that the Invincibles, or ultra-Fenians, murdered Cavendish and Burke.[4]

Shimmering philology more than once spread its aura before emergent nationalisms, and not only in Ireland. But the crux of this particular textual exchange was the return of Oisin from the pagan Land of Youth (Tír na nÓg) and his encounter with the Christian missioner. W.B. Yeats drew on such material, including some from the Ossianic *Transactions*, for 'The Wanderings of Oisin' (1889; revised 1895), a narrative poem in the final (third) book of which the timely-ambiguous term is reiterated — 'The Fenians a long time are dead.'[5] As an acute editor has observed of this poem, dream and reality trade places — 'the dream is vibrant, clamorous, human, while the "reality" is a sodden oblivion.'[6] Much the same could be said of the Ireland sketched at the outset of Yeats's poem 'Easter 1916', and — with adjustments of class setting — of Eliot's 'Love Song of J. Alfred Prufrock' also.

Converted by Patrick in the scholarly texts, Yeats's Oisin reverts to paganism, a theme inseparable from the crisis of faith resulting from the geological and biological publications of Lyell and Darwin. The Fenians (IRB) occupied a more modest but threatened space, almost exclusively Catholic in social terms but highly suspect in their conspiratorial activities. In moving from the failure of 1867 to the triumph of failure in 1916, one cannot exaggerate the importance of two interlocking political themes — those of the Land War and of Parnell's quest for Home Rule.

Yet these in their turn cannot be fully appreciated without reference to external matters.

Although the celebrated term Home Rule provoked a crisis in British politics, its origins lay in the more modest Home Government Association of 1870, established in Dublin with the assistance of both Fenians and Whigs. Though the point was never clearly stated, it sought Irish representative control of those areas of government business loosely associated with the old Home Department. War between France and Germany in the summer of 1870 produced a wave of pro-French demonstrations across Ireland, in which the hand of the (Fenian) Amnesty Association has been detected, though a less ideologically charged Francophilia (hearth and altar, instead of throne and ditto) was more evident.[7] Between 1870 and Parnell's dramatic campaigns, the domestic metaphor of home rule was transformed in its emotive force by the Land War and cries of 'hold on to your homesteads'. That is to say, the eventual emergence of an owner-occupier small farm system produced along the way a new valency in the very notion of *home*. It was to be, as Michael Davitt predicted, a highly conservative social process and outcome.

Something similar was, unsurprisingly, taking place elsewhere. While the profound differences between France and Ireland should not be forgotten, Eugen Weber's *Peasants into Frenchmen* (1976) can still cast light on issues which climax in the Dublin of April 1916. His study of the extent to which sports contributed to a sense of national well-being in the face of cosmopolitan decadence could provide a framework for re-assessing the Gaelic Athletic Association in European terms.[8] Land and health, the soil and vibrant living — these were cardinal points of reference for ruralist conservatism in France and Ireland (and elsewhere), hostile to modernity, urban life and cultural diversity, but claiming to know (or even to be) the nation's soul.

Parnell scarcely troubled with such matters, yet the 'split' of 1890 was as divisive in Ireland as the Dreyfus Affair in France. The domestic aspect of his situation — a long-standing covert relationship with (English) Mrs O'Shea — in many ways encapsulated the struggle for power in the Irish countryside. Condemned by the Catholic hierarchy, Parnell retained the qualified support of some Fenians (not including Davitt), while seeking electoral support from urban voters, including workers. At the time, Henry Labouchère noted the Irish people's 'fetishism of Parnell', and a recent American historian has suggested that manliness in rhetorical performance and in violations of social convention constituted his principal appeal.[9]

In the Land War and the Parnell Split alike, Catholic clergy were powerfully influential, if not always consistent. On behalf of tenants who were parishioners, they could speak with authority about domestic conditions, hardship, and even oppression. They provided moral cover for acts that were unquestionably illegal. Quite how priests *represented* their flock defies exact definition, for they were neither appointed, nor chosen nor elected by any constituency. However, those who objected to the adulterer Parnell on moral grounds were often accused of abandoning the national cause in its time of greatest need. The implicit identification of Irish nationalism with 'actually existing' Catholicism raised problems for both the Church authorities and the party leadership. Rome condemned radical disturbers of the social order and, on the whole, Irish prelates took the pontifical view. British legislation, however, failed many a test of Catholic policy, especially in areas of education and married (i.e. home) life.

### French Relations

Church/state relations in Ireland were complicated by a strong feeling that no state possessed a legitimate existence, neither that embodied in Dublin Castle, nor that of Whitehall. Elsewhere the lines of conflict were clearly drawn. The government (1899–1902) of Waldeck-Rousseau was certainly radical — it included the first socialist minister in any European cabinet — and, in the words of one historian, 'anticlericalism was ... the cement which bound the different elements of the Republican bloc together.'[10] Religious orders were suppressed, driven into exile. Freemasonry infiltrated the French army. Though the government fell in 1902, a united socialist party (1905) came as an indirect consequence. Not all Republicans of course were radicals of the Left. Ethnographer, patriot, and 'homme politique' Louis Marin (1871–1960) is a notable exception. As a 'bourgeois republican' and later prostitutor of academic geography for politico-commercial purposes, he visited Ireland in 1898, researching workers' conditions.[11]

The presence of French intellectuals in Ireland during the *fin de siècle* years (loosely defined) arose mainly on a short-term basis. The most notable figure was the writer Guy de Maupassant (1850–1893) who visited his cousin Florimond Alfred Jacques de Basterot (1836–1904) at the latter's north Clare retreat. The novelist-politician Maurice Barrès (1862–1923) also came, apparently on more than one occasion.[12] There too another Catholic novelist, Paul Bourget (1852–1935), turned up as early as 1881, conveyed on one occasion from Gort railway station to de Basterot's Parkmore (now Duras House) by the grandfather of Brian Lynch, latter-day poet, novelist, playwright and sometime Government Press Officer; Bourget's 'Neptune Vale' specifies a date by reference to the Invincibles.[13] No well-wrought fiction by the standards of Flaubert or Joyce, it ends in sentimental evasion, though at its heart there occurs the brutal killing of a farmyard cock which owes a debt to Yeats's folkloric induction. The dying bird's blood is sacrificed on the ground 'to keep the dead from coming back when a house was haunted ... *they will avenge themselves.*'[14] In 1927 an unforgiving ousted peasant of Mayo, scourge of both church and republic, deliberately revived memories of 1882 to critique the *status quo*: 'James Carey, who planned the Phoenix Park murders, and hanged his accomplices, used to go to Holy Communion in the morning as a preparation to give the murder signal in the afternoon.'[15]

The dying bird is specifically a cock or cockerel. It may be risky to treat symbolic in the political or ideological realm a detail attached to a solitary fictional character and isolated action, and all the more questionable if the author is a French visitor and the matter under investigation a self-definingly Irish insurrection. However, the longer argument under way in these pages involves two strands that are already intertwined in 'Neptune Vale'. One is the powerful ideology of sacrifice which will play centre-stage in the rhetoric and manipulative strategies of Pearse, Plunkett and (even) Connolly in the prelude to and direction of Easter 1916. 'Without shedding of blood there is no redemption', says the Citizen Army leader whom de Paor classifies as a 'last minute Fenian', while also suggesting that the conversion is Tertullian's — 'credo quia absurdam'.[16] Emphatically, the origins of this ideology are not to be traced in the Fenians of 1867 or in the thought of Wolfe Tone. Far from it. They are French nationalist, neo-Catholic notions, and contemporary with Pearse and Plunkett's coming of age.[17] And the second strand, relevant here, is the literary form itself and its negotiations with the folk. If Yeats may have helped Bourget over the stile and into the farmyard at Duras, to specify a motif associated with a deranged tenant determined to curse the foreign inheritor who would sell to the local usurer, he certainly will help MacDonagh, Pearse, Plunkett and the other minor poets of 1916 — help, and reflect. 'Did that play of mine send out / Certain men the English shot?'[18]

Bourget should not be written out of a narrative taking *fin de siècle* conversations in Duras House on to the contested streets of Dublin. His affinities with Nietzsche, and even a debt incurred in that quarter by the prophet of Zarathustra, have been noted. In *The Case of Wagner* (1888), Nietzsche asked, 'what is the mark of every *literary decadence*?' In reply, he wrote:

That life no longer resides in the whole. The word becomes sovereign and leaps out of the sentence, the sentence reaches out and obscures the meaning of the page, the page comes to life at the expense of the whole — the whole is no longer a whole. This, however, is the simile of every style of decadence: every time, there is an anarchy of atoms, disgregation of the will, 'freedom of the individual', to put it in moral terms — and when expanded into political theory, 'equal rights for all'.[19]

This pronouncement had been prompted by Bourget's *Essais de psychologie contemporaine* (1881–83), specifically Bourget's treatment of Charles Baudelaire.[20] These had commenced publication shortly after the period of fictional action narrated in 'Neptune Vale', symptomatically defined by the novelist with reference to the Invincible murders, and indicate the author's outlook in relation to his Irish visit. The commendation of decadence as a 'disgregation' — the word derives from thermodynamics — of the will is echoed in György Lukács' laconic condemnation of the late nineteenth century. 'Every written work, even if it is no more than a consonance of beautiful words, leads us to a great door — through which there is no passage.'[21] French symbolism of this period inflects Yeats's poetic practice ('words alone are perfect good') and that of Eliot ('There will be time to murder and create').[22] In an incipiently violent interpretation of literary culture, it has been exemplified when a word 'becomes sovereign.' Bourget's *Le Sens de la mort* (1915; in English as *The Night Cometh*, 1916) mixes religiously motivated self-sacrifice, the Great War, the medical profession and potassium cyanide in a plot too readily 'solved' in the end. The aesthetic and the anaesthetic blend unconvincingly. The Dublin-based Jesuit quarterly *Studies* reviewed *Le Sens* before the year was out.[23]

In keeping with this insight, Easter 1916 has even been considered as a work of art in itself, or the city which is its backdrop taken as a dramatic tableau (not without Wagnerian analogues).[24] In Pearse's anxious pre-insurrectionary resolutions, guilt about success, succession, and generation spurts from the page — so that, in the apocalypse, blood will the sovereign cleanser. The deranged Harriet Corrigan of 'Neptune Vale' would punish the worldly young French aristos who determine to sell their birthright in Ireland, punish them in the same act as will protect the dead from the torment of returning as ghosts to their former property. 'They will avenge themselves,' she insists, with suitable ambiguity. Or, modifying the terms of Maule's curse in Hawthorne, we might render this as 'God will give [them] blood to drink.'[25] The blood in 'Neptune Vale' is cock's blood, echt-volk perhaps, or fíor-Ghael, thanks to Yeats. But it melodramatically unites the emblem of Old Gaul and the betrayal of Christ.[26] Having awkwardly dredged up the Invincibles, Bourget, in the end, may have wrought his urn well, post-textually. By 1916 the right-wing agnostic had acknowledged Holy Church, and the somewhat Marxist Connolly had adopted Pearse's holy invocations. At least one contributor to *The New Age* suggested a conservative motivation behind Connolly's choice, without going so far as to suspect a Conservative Revolution in Ireland.[27]

The French novelist, unlike the old aristos in his Irish story, returned. In August 1895 Bourget and his wife visited Coole Park, and admired the last photograph taken of Parnell in life.[28] Gregory's *Our Irish Theatre* recorded some of the details in 1913, placing de Basterot central, and describing 'the old Count' as her late husband's close friend, a man much preoccupied with questions of race. He was generous to the poor of north Clare while in residence. Yeats, on the other hand, and in George-Moorish temper, noted that the Count was 'paralysed from the waist down through sexual excess in youth.'[29]

This was no casual ultra-Celtic holiday caprice; the de Basterots held Irish land since the 1820s, and had intermarried with the O'Brien clan, even establishing some links to the Martyns of

Tullira. When the vicomte embarked on a journey from eastern Canada to Peru, he opened his journal 'Duras 5 août 1858', providing no account of Dublin or Liverpool as he travelled through these large cities. His interest in the Americas is principally focused on native peoples, though he notes the Irish presence in New York (numerous, attached to the Democratic Party) and in Mobile ('Irlandais dègénérés et malpropres'). In the original drafts, Eliot's *The Waste Land* opened with nervous sardonic vignettes of the Boston Irish. For de Basterot, the rebellion of 1798, the figure of Robert Emmet, and the inescapable fact of mass immigration come to mind. He also cites J-A Gobineau's *Essai sur les races* (1855). Southern landscapes (or seascapes) remind him of the west of Ireland, as described by the 'vieux bardes de Connemara'.[30] De Basterot is a mid-nineteenth-century French traveller in America, repeatedly employing Ireland as a point of reference.[31]

Close to his north Clare abode, in the vicinity of Gort, Gregory (1852–1932) held court, with Edward Martyn (1859–1923) an eccentric but talented neighbour, devoted to Catholic liturgy and Henrik Ibsen. Martyn's distant cousin and ardent Francophile George Moore (1852–1933) raised his rents further north in Mayo, but the literary circle of which Gregory's Coole Park was a symbolic focus was steeped in French culture and political debate. (Sir William had been a major figure in public administration.) Initial discussions which led to the foundation of the Abbey Theatre took place at de Basterot's Parkmore.

If one fails to disinter any specific programme behind Bourget's interest in the West of Ireland, there is a general pattern no less important. From different backgrounds, professional and social, de Basterot and Marin were both ethnographers, one preferring exotic cultures, the other concerned about industrial development and its implications: Ireland constituted an opportunity for casual fieldwork, solidly Catholic in the south and west and yet part of the almighty United Kingdom, borderline primitive, borderline imperial. British anthropologists, notably A.C. Haddon (1855–1940), studied Irish evidence from a different professional and intellectual background. Yeats's future biographer, J.M. Hone, studied de Basterot and Gobineau, yet another anthropologist.[32] Even after the vicomte's death on 15 September 1904, his extended circle continued to make little marks on the score-sheet of Catholic taste in Ireland; Duras eventually passed to the Ebrill family, and Mary Ebrill contributed short stories to *The Irish Monthly*.[33]

We shall encounter several names as unfamiliar or obscure. A striking number are of women. Mary Ebrill contributes to the broad background as a minor literary figure, a practising Irish Catholic of Huguenot origins. Her woollen merchant family is commemorated in a stained glass window in the Redemptorist church, Limerick. George Ebrill taught at the Catholic University's medical school in Cecilia Street, Dublin, where he met Joseph Mary Plunkett's future brother-in-law (and in-arms), Thomas Dillon, a bomb maker in 1916 and later a distinguished professor of chemistry.[34] Another of Dillon's protégés was Jim O'Donovan who resumed his explosive career in January 1939 (see Chapter 10).

Other kinds of French connection were simultaneously operative. When Mungret College (outside Limerick) opened in 1882 as a Jesuit institution, a Joseph de Maistre was named as one of the lay governors. He was not the famous author of that name, though clearly related. When Rodolphe, comte de Maistre (1789–1866; son of the author), died near Turin, a notice to this effect appeared in an Irish newspaper.[35] One might wonder why. Two links emerge. Mary O'Byrne (1831–1900) married Joseph de Maistre (1825–1861) who was almost certainly the Mungret governor; a wealthy land-owning Catholic, in 1866 she had built an elaborate monument to her family at the parish church in Saggart, County Dublin. Patrick de Maistre (1899–1911) was the short-lived grandson of Joseph and Mary. Later in the century — indeed persisting into the new one — Stephanie de Maistre, resident of Cork, contributed short fiction to a number of pious magazines, including *The Catholic Bulletin*. Oddly enough, she fails to appear in any de Maistre genealogies, nor did she register in the Irish censuses of 1901 or 1911.[36] The *fons et origo* of these minor ornaments on the Irish scene was the Savoyard diplomat-author Joseph de Maistre (1753–1821; father of Rodolphe). His writings, against the French Revolution or in favour of the Spanish Inquisition and wholesale capital punishment, established God through his universal Church as the Absolute in all earthly disagreements.[37]

Beyond Stephanie de Maistre's transient stories in *The Irish Monthly* and elsewhere, the family effected a more ideologically focused engagement with an emergent readership. Xavier de Maistre, younger brother of the old count, wrote fiction which attracted attention in the English-speaking world, serving as a French text for Cambridge examining boards in the 1880s. 'La Jeune fille de Siberie' was also chosen for the Irish Intermediate School syllabus in 1889, and an edition published in Dublin for that purpose by Brown and Nolan. The same story was translated into Gaelic as late as 1958.[38] In 1905 a selection of texts (in the classical languages, Gaelic, and modern European languages) drawn up for scholarship candidates in agriculture by the appropriate government board included a second story of Xavier's — 'La Leprose de la cité d'Aoste'.

De Maistrean fiction, whether Xavier's or Stephanie's, conformed to a model of reassuring sentiment and orthodoxy. Nothing done in their name achieved the pervasive intimacy of the well-placed IRB-man at his Gaelic League class, Dineen's *Foclóir* in one hand, ballot-paper for the Ard Craobh in the other. Yet a filament of Bourbon Restoration ideology had taken root in Ireland, perpetuated through editions of the old count's *Saint Petersburg Nights*, from the original French edition of 1821 through the translation of 1851 and onwards. James Joyce read something of de Maistre's in 1895, under the resisted influence of his Jesuit educators; one likes to think it was 'Eclaircissement sur les sacrifices' (1810). The family's Irish attachment had been secured by marriage; when countess de Maistre died at the beginning of the twentieth century, she left property in at least three counties (Galway, Longford and Tipperary). In *The Irish Times'* view of things, the reigning comte was her only son.

The originating de Maistre may have attracted a degree of Irish attention, but he was becoming far more influential in Spain, France, and (later) Weimar Germany. Two English translations of major works had appeared early in the 1850s, the work of a Scottish-born priest of Irish background, who later preached at a requiem mass for the Young Irelander Thomas D'Arcy Magee.[39] The count's ideological stock was bolstered by the publication in the late nineteenth century of youthful texts which he had never released in print — these including some thoughts on freemasonry. Even the Church of Ireland saw fit to invoke him in passing. In 1901 at a veterans' church service at the Royal Hospital, Kilmainham, the primate scarcely rejected the de Maistrean edict that war implemented the Divine Law. Pearse echoes the sentiment in November 1913: 'bloodshed is a cleansing and a sanctifying thing', though there were many sources, French and German as well as British, for this bellicosity.[40] Who, we might ask, is sanctified, the perpetraters or the victims, or the berveaved? Newer and more trenchant forces at work in France hitched de Maistre's star to their wagon; in 1907 the Institut d'Action francaise organised seminars on his thought.[41]

In Ireland, the sphere represented differently by Mungret College and Stephanie de Maistre — that is, education, including that of women — conveyed a more effective delivery of contemporary French Catholic thought. Teaching orders such as the Saint Louis nuns (founded 1844) established primary and secondary schools in Ireland — the Saint Louis initiative began in 1859 at Monaghan. The Holy Ghost Fathers (founded Paris, 1703) opened Saint Mary's College for boys (Rathmines, Dublin) in 1890. These enterprises were missionary in spirit, that is, they confronted a hostile or ignorant culture and undertook to instil religious enlightenment against the prevailing protestant, complaisant or imminently secular establishment. Recalling the 1930s, the poet Thomas Kinsella has described thunderous political sermons delivered by Oblate priests in Inchicore, then one of Dublin's more industrialised inner suburbs.[42] Their altar had been built by James Pearse (1839–1900), monumental sculptor and father of the Proclamation's signatory.[43]

Oblates in Inchicore, novelists like Barrès and Bourget in Clare or Galway, visiting professors in the Royal University — it does not amount to a comprehensive French Catholic ideological presence in Ireland. The little western concentration has more obvious links with the literary revival of Yeats and Gregory than with the militant nationalism of Pearse and Plunkett, though the latter owes the more specific debt. In his youth, Bourget had mocked at the ease with which well-known killers could receive Holy Communion twice a year on this 'Catholic and murderous island.'[44] His return to the Church, and his novel of 1902, *L'Etape* [The Staging Post], propose contrasting examples for his attentive Irish readers, the novel powerfully suggesting that an ascent from peasant class to professional bourgeois is ill-advised in one move, and contrary to doctrine.

Fenianism was not simply a response to the suffering, bureaucratically intensified, of the Famine: it was *rooted* in emigration to America, in dislocation from the native land. Its organisational arrangements owed much to European continental models of conspiracy.[45] That post-Famine Ireland in all its exposed gauntness appealed to French intellectuals is a conundrum awaiting decipherment, though an examination of literary (more exactly, *lapidary*) style may be predicted as a necessary component. The classifications blur and leach into each other. The 1916 Rising was, in some important respects, a literary occasion, partly on terms of causation which bothered Yeats in old age. MacDonagh, Pearse and Plunkett were poets of some talent, if not in the same league as the author of 'Man and the Echo' and 'Under Ben Bulben'. But the militancy that Pearse exemplified differed from the tradition that he invoked; the New Nationalism mixed politics, culture and religion in a fashion which Wolfe Tone, James Fintan Lalor and even John Mitchel would have found incomprehensible. And binding these central ingredients was a fourth — violence taken as regenerative in itself. France after the Dreyfus Affair was the *locus classicus* of revolutionary conservatism; its 'redemptive anti-Semitism' was no joke. The literary wing, or Catholic Renaissance, was 'the more remarkable for the fact that it began from almost nothing.'[46] When the Church in Ireland did embrace the defeated rebels of April 1916, it was of some importance that contributory French ideas and anxieties had circulated in late nineteenth-century Ireland, especially in journals which blended literature and piety.

# Chapter 3
# Baptising the Neo-Fenians

*A man suffers martyrdom only for the sake of
things about which he is uncertain.*

Ernest Renan, 1884

*The Irish adore a successful man or an executed
man (the latter for preference); but a fiasco they
never forgive.*

G.B. Shaw, 30 April 1916

## Baptism and Blood

Fenianism, insofar as one could posit its active existence in 1890, was in part compromised by the New Departure (1879) when Parnell, Davitt and the Irish-American John Devoy agreed to yoke the constitutional and conspiratorial movements together.[1] It was also affected by social change, especially in the countryside and country towns, by the growth of a Catholic middle class with its own version of nationalist complaint and compensation, and by the arrival of owner occupiers where previously there had been tenants at risk of eviction. The ageing Fenians, to experience a phoenix revival, needed something new. Jealous of clerical influence, and for the most part *petit bourgeois* in social background, they were unlikely to pick up the silken thread of de Maistrean thought in Ireland. Mary O'Byrne and her wealthy siblings were no Fenians.

The generally accepted view is that the Irish Republican Brotherhood recovered under the mantle of Sinn Féin (founded 1905).[2] The two organisations differed in many ways, not least on economic issues. Sinn Féin's doctrine of self-sufficiency embraced cultural and commercial activity with equal zeal. Nor was it indifferent to possible models deriving from the continent. Arthur Griffith, its founder, published *The Resurrection of Hungary: a Parallel for Ireland* in which he elaborated a vision of national independence under a dual monarchy. The pamphlet's success — it even gets into Joyce's *Ulysses* (1922) — probably contributed to the mistaken but widespread view in 1916 that the Easter Rising was the work of Sinn Féin, whereas the publicly committed forces were those of the Irish Volunteers (with Eoin MacNeill officially in command) and the Irish Citizen Army (actively led by James Connolly).[3] The tiny inner council, which planned the Rising, was of course dominated by the IRB in a brilliant entry-ist *coup*. Of the fourteen men executed in Dublin after the Rising, eight were Fenians — Eamon Ceannt, Thomas J. Clarke, Con Colbert, Thomas MacDonagh, Pearse, Plunkett, John MacBride and Seán MacDermott. Two others (Edward Daly and Michael O'Hanrahan) were the sons of Fenians active in the 1860s. Connolly, though he sat on the secret Military Council organised by Fenians, does not appear to have taken the oath, then or earlier.

The Council may have recalled David Moriarty's words of condemnation, though it was unlikely to have considered if his attitude had been shaped by his years as rector of the Irish College in Paris. In the days before the Rising, Count Plunkett was despatched to Rome in search of a papal blessing upon the action about to be taken by his son and the other signatories. The ancient Fenians never sought clerical approval, and were not disappointed. Count Plunkett's mission indicated several distinct changes of Irish allegiances since 1867.

The first in the scale of its unmentionable implications for the future was the strength, including military strength, of Ulster Unionism. In planning the Easter events, the IRB military council effectively conceded the partition of Ireland; there was to be no action in Belfast (Connolly knew how promptly civil war would engulf the city's proletariat); the Belfast man Denis McCullough (1883–1968), who headed up the IRB's Supreme Council, was therefore kept in the dark about the Dublin plans: as notional President of the Republic he was deceived about its declaration. Admittedly these Dublin plans in practice turned out to be more or less the only ones which led to insurrection, due to the failure of Casement's attempt to land arms in Kerry and to MacNeill's general success in countermanding publicised calls upon Volunteers to 'exercise' at Easter. Nevertheless, the negative impact was to compound difficulties raised by the Ulster Question. Four important and highly active men, each sidelined by the signatories and their Proclamation, hailed from Ulster — Bulmer Hobson, Roger Casement, Denis McCullough, and Eoin MacNeill. In practice, the North would not begin, or join in.

Separated in their final action from the United Irish traditions of Antrim and Down, the signatories tilled the ground for a partition rapidly installed in 1920–22. The IRB's kidnapping of Hobson just before the Insurrection had no local sectarian basis — Hobson came from a Quaker family — and it can hardly have been done to impress the Pope.[4] But it inevitably draws attention to the apparent Catholic monopoly among the leaders of 1916. Fenians though most of them were in strict and sworn fidelity or by intimate association, all these men — including Thomas Ceannt (executed in Cork), and Roger Casement (executed in London) — were Catholics, in stark contrast to the roll-call in Yeats's 'September 1913' — Emmet, Fitzgerald, and Wolfe Tone.

The Irish Volunteers and Citizen Army were led into combat on Easter Monday at very short notice. All concerned invoked the traditions of 1867, 1803, and 1798, accepting those events in Old Nationalist and insular terms. Contemporary British labour agitation, the Paris Commune (1871), the emancipation of American slaves, the abolition of monarchy and aristocracy in France — played little or no part in supportive rhetoric for the resurrectionary hour. At home the extension of parliamentary franchises had served to emphasise what some historians have termed 'ethnogenesis', that is, the construction of new social entities in which religious and political identities (also a new word) were fused. Ulster Unionism was protestant unionism, largely as a consequence of popular electoral engineering. Catholic separatism, though less concentrated territorially and far from hegemonic, did not lag far behind. However, nationalist tradition had to contend with those distinctly non-Catholic heroes such as Tone, Emmet and Mitchel, choosing a variety of means to do so, sentimental, violently sentimental, and the downright mythic.

Comforted in this connection by G.N. Plunkett's strikingly non-Fenian mission to Rome, the rebels of Easter (or those few who knew anything of the mission) occupied an unprecedented vantage point in the teleology of Irish separatism; they would have God on their side at last. This achievement in its most persuasive — that is, Roman — form had called for economies of truth in a few details. Thus, while it was helpful to invoke Emmet as a noble protestant antecedent, the fact that Thomas MacDonagh's mother (Mary Parker, 1843–1908) had been a Unitarian was better left unspoken; much the same could be said of Connolly's wife (Lillie Reynolds, a protestant native of Carnew, in Wicklow).[5] If Tom Clarke was senior Fenian on Easter Monday, through whom the IRB got an Easter rising, his father had been born into the Church of Ireland, a native of Leitrim. The Pearse Brothers presented less direct inheritances of non-Catholicity, perhaps; biography remains discreet, even when Joe Lee contributed important notices to the *Dictionary of Irish Biography*. James Pearse, father of Patrick and William, is invariably described as a Londoner or an Englishman, with little reference to denomination. Ruth Dudley Edwards, however, specifies Unitarianism, later atheism.[6] Whatever about his religious practice while the famous children were growing up

— and there is no doubt of their mother, Margaret Brady's, Catholic allegiance — one must suspect that James Pearse's first wife, Emily Susanna Fox (died 1876, aged 30), was a protestant of some sort.

James Pearse's first household is rarely mentioned in accounts of his sons by the second wife. However, details unearthed by Ruth Dudley Edwards and (more recently) by Joost Augusteijn deserve close consideration in any attempt to evaluate the cumulative problems facing Church and would-be State at Easter 1916. The issues were no less disruptive for being rarely admitted. If Pearse was head of the Provisional Government, its imminence fast-forwarded to the Papacy, then the father's origins and religious orientation can no longer be passed over in virtual silence. James Pearse was unquestionably English, not in itself a stumbling block. In a late essay, Freud pointed out the occurrence of foreigners, or persons of recent foreign extraction, as charismatic leaders of their host nationality, instancing Napoleon and Disraeli. However, not only was James Pearse English (with Patrick and Willie thus half-English *by blood*, a talisman Pearse revered passionately), he had also been an atheist or at best a Unitarian whose late attachment to the Catholic Church smacks of commercial opportunism. Dudley Edwards refers to 'certain Catholic stone carvers … objecting on religious and racial grounds to church-work being given to him' in the late 1870s, and that was after the family had been received into the Catholic community. Some time about 1870, all of them were so received, suggesting that baptism had taken place earlier, but under a different church's ordinances. Emily Susanna had seen to it that her first two children were christened in the Church of Ireland, with James making no effective objection if any.[7] Still under pressure from professional rivals who were by now his co-religionists in name, James Pearse found it advisable to obtain a priest's formal testimony to his conversion. From distant Belfast, Fr Pius Devine (1838–1912) wrote: 'I recollect well your sensible objections and difficulties whilst you were under instructions and the clearheaded manner in which you saw the answers as soon as they were proposed to you by me.' And a few lines later, 'I wish you every success in your business and if you continue to give in future the satisfaction you have given in the past I have no doubt you will. If anything comes in my way to suit you, you shall certainly have the preference.' In a word, James Pearse's Catholicism was 'cerebral'.[8]

By the time of Fr Devine's testimony, Mrs James Pearse was dead, and likewise at least one of the couple's four infants.[9] The survivors were Mary Emily (1864–1944) who married in 1884, and James Vincent (1866–1912) who does not appear to have remained in Ireland. Their father's second marriage, and the coming of half-siblings, may have made for uncomfortable relations. James and Margaret (née Brady; his second wife) took additional responsibility for two orphans, sending one (Mary Kate Kelly) to boarding school; she later married a Fellow of Merton College, Oxford. James Pearse died in Birmingham, while visiting his brother. It is difficult to assume these lives into the Gael.

After Pearse read the Proclamation 'from the steps of the General Post Office' — there are none — Dublin was not myth-making in its enthusiasm. Even a sympathetic observer such as the poet James Stephens was horrified by the speed with which a Citizen Army occupier of Stephen's Green killed a truculent citizen trying to retrieve his cart from a barricade.[10] Some Dubliners in Sackville Street may have associated the Pearse Brothers with the colony of mainly English (some non-Catholic) craftsmen that had grown up in the Brunswick Street (formerly Moss Lane) area between the river and the college, from about 1860 onwards.[11] No ephemeral shift in the city's artisan employment. The Rebellion was not automatically or axiomatically a nativist expression of ancient traditions, nor was the Dublin populace inclined to imagine it as such. Its considered response to the upheaval was to indulge in opportunistic looting, as the mischievous Sean O'Casey reminded a born-again audience ten years later.

The outraged witnesses to 'The Plough and the Stars' were, by implication, the outraged or contemptuous witnesses to Easter 1916 and its Proclamation. The passage from looting to hooting was made possible by several administrations of collective baptism in the course of which the old Fenians' anti-clericalism would be absolved and the intrusive Unitarian, Anglican, and (frankly) English affiliations of some signatories' immediate forebears would be washed away. Naturally, the social framework in which this re-alignment of religious and political attitudes was possible deserves recognition as a necessary preliminary condition — the greater electoral importance of the Catholic majority, the greater confidence of the Catholic professional classes, the implicit division of the political domain into a southern moiety where the Catholic population predominated, and a northern one which could be cynically written off with lavish gestures of hand-wringing. Here, what is under closer scrutiny is the ideological framework.

The campaign to baptise Fenians involved three very different approaches, pastoral, propagandistic, and commemorative, adopted by different Catholic agencies. Even before the fighting had ended, Capuchin friars (a division of the larger Franciscan order) were at work tending the wounded and dying, comforting those whose lives were thrown into confusion and uncertainty, and establishing routes to the ultimate spiritual care of the leaders in the hours before their executions.

In examining the response of the Catholic press, one should start with its most intellectually dignified organ. *The Irish Ecclesiastical Record* (founded 1864 by Paul Cullen) devoted a good portion of each monthly issue to articles on canon law, church history and liturgical practice. Irish material as such did not occupy a prominent position in what was unmistakably a *Roman* Catholic publication. Some French contributors and topics featured, e.g. Ernest Daudet on 'Two Saints of the Middle Ages' (July 1916), and the Rt Rev. John S. Vaughan on 'Charles Joseph Eugene de Mazenod' (April 1916). From the latter we learn that the founder of the Oblates visited Ireland in 1857. Alongside these learned pieces, little or nothing about political events in Ireland in 1916 is recorded. The opening article in the first issue of 1917, Very Rev. James McCaffrey's 'The Catholic Church in 1916', deals at length with European and American matters but, when it finally turns to Ireland, no reference is made to any named Irish individual; indeed Asquith (as Prime Minister) is the only named public figure. This restraint in the business of naming names will stand in stark contrast to the tactics adopted by *The Catholic Bulletin* on the topic of Easter 1916.

The *Record*'s political stance was loftily judicious, to a degree that confirmed the worst Fenian suspicions. When McCaffrey finally got to grips with the Insurrection, his tone was diplomatic and distant:

> When at last the explosion, that all prudent men could have foreseen, took place, an opportunity for statesmanship presented itself such as had not arisen for centuries. All parties were sobered both by what had been and by what might have been. Had there been a man at the head of affairs with the courage to announce that the only prudent course to take, in view of the events of Easter week, was to abolish autocratic rule in Ireland ... he would have done much to relieve the tension in Ireland.[12]

Such prudence was replicated in silence by other contributors. When Dom Benedict Steuart wrote on 'Sacrifice and Oblation' in the July issue — by this date *The Catholic Bulletin* was a cauldron of 'martyrs' and sacrifices — he made no allusion whatever to the heavily theologised vocabulary of Irish politics, preferring to concentrate on biblical scholarship, the attitude of the protestant reformers, and official Catholic teaching. It is only in June 1918 that *The Irish Ecclesiastical Record* took up the immediate issue. In 'The Conscription Crisis in Ireland' Fr P. Coffey listed the various stages of Irish political change, including 'the rise of the Sinn Féin policy to abandon parliamentarianism', a topic addressed at much the same time by William O'Brien, MP.[13]

The *Record* boasted on its cover that it appeared with episcopal sanction, but a consequent reluctance to score easy points was not shared by other journals carrying an imprimatur. *The Catholic Bulletin and Book Review* (founded in 1911 and published in Dublin by M.H. Gill as a commercial undertaking) is best known through the campaigns of Fr Timothy Corcoran SJ (1872–1943) from the early 1920s onwards.[14] Its first two numbers had appeared simply as *The Catholic Book Bulletin*, and the change of emphasis does nothing to discount the importance of literature and popular reading in the coming crisis.[15] During the first four months of 1916, the *Bulletin* maintained a number of serial articles on the 'Reunion of Protestants with Rome', also 'Poland's Experience of Imperialism', together with incidental poems and pieces of short fiction. The May and June issues were conjoined, as a consequence of April's insurrection; the editorial was represented by three blank pages to show up official state censorship. Another page, blank but for a title 'Dublin — May, 1916' and signed Gobnait ní Bhruadair (Lord Midleton's sister), probably was intended to carry a poem. Further blanks occurred later in the issue. Under the heading 'The Martyrdom of a Nation', extracts from a Saint Patrick's Day sermon delivered in Rome by Mgr Michael O'Riordan evaded censorship by concentrating ostensibly on the condition of Irish Catholics during the eighteenth century.[16] But the term martyrdom was already achieving a contemporary usage, unconnected with matters discussed later in the May–June issue under the heading 'Ritual Murder among the Jews'.[17]

The July issue closed with a lengthy set of biographical notes, entitled 'Events of Easter Week', illustrated with nineteen portrait photographs. The *Record*'s avoidance of personalised rhetoric was not shared by the *Bulletin*. Those commemorated were Pearse, William J. Pearse, The O'Rahilly, Eamonn Ceannt, John MacBride, Thomas MacDonagh, Plunkett, James Connolly, Michael Mallin, Thomas J. Clarke, Edward Daly, Seán MacDermott, Micheal [sic] OHannrachain, Cornelius Colbert, J. J. Heuston, Peadar Macken, Richard O'Carroll, Sean Connolly, John O'Reilly, Thomas Weafer, Sean Bernard Howard, Peter Paul Manning, Philip Walsh, and Thomas Allen. Nowhere in these notices was the Irish Republican Brotherhood mentioned, nor the term Fenian employed, doubtless to protect those in danger of arrest or prosecution.

For contrast, one might look at the June number of *Studies*, a Jesuit quarterly which published scholarly articles on Celtic literature, reflections on contemporary affairs, theological material and a wide-ranging book-review section. No Irish periodical with a Catholic readership could ignore the Rising for long, but the Jesuits were reluctant to follow *The Catholic Bulletin* into a propaganda frenzy. The Jesuits, as a militant arm of the universal Church, did not find nationalism always to their taste, especially if it addressed the lower orders in society. Accordingly, the first post-Rising *Studies* opened with a photo-insert account of 'The Reconstruction of O'Connell Street' which happily drew attention to the Rising's prime location but also to the authorities' promptness in repairing damaged buildings.[18] The treatment of rebel leaders was equally discreet; what began with an account of Thomas MacDonagh developed into a four-part series on 'Poets of the Insurrection'. MacDonagh had been a lecturer at University College Dublin (a Jesuit stronghold) and as such provided a more comfortable starting point than Clarke, Connolly, or Pearse. The event was to be classified as a literary loss, if possible.[19] In the same issue, two further articles extended the parameters of the Jesuit engagement with resurgent Fenianism, both contributed by members of the Society of Jesus — Lewis Watt on 'Suarez on the Sovereignty of the People' and Joseph Darlington (on whom

Joyce's Dean is based) on 'Mrs Pankhurst and the Poor'.[20] The
universal church had historic and philosophical resources
applicable to matters raised in the Proclamation, while it also
concerned itself with social deprivation and the claims of women.
Francesco Suarez (1548–1617), a Jesuit philosopher, anticipated
notions of international law and, in political theory, refuted the
Divine Right of Kings. By implication, the noisy disorder of
Sackville/O'Connell Street and Boland's Mill had already a
sufficient answer in Church teaching, tradition and authority.

In many ways, the most intriguing pages of *Studies* in June
1916 are devoted to book reviews. Several publications about
Austria or the larger Hapsburg empire are treated in a notice alert
to the war engrossing Central Europe. France is certainly not
neglected, though a review of Gobineau's *Inequality of Human
Races* (the translation of 1915) is unexpected. A volume of *Pages
Choisies* by Emile Boutroux provides an opportunity for noting
the capacity of orthodox Catholicism to live with modern science.

Burbage's pursuit of ritual murder among the Jews of Russia
continued in the August issue of *The Catholic Bulletin*,
which again closed with 'Events of Easter Week'. By photograph
or biographical note, the following were commemorated:
Thomas Kent, Richard Kent, William F. Burke, Patrick Shortis,
John Traynor, Francis Macken, John Keely, Patrick O'Flanagan,
John Costello, Edward Ennis, Henry Coyle, John Hurley, Joseph
Byrne, Patrick Farrell, Charles D'Arcy, and Patrick Whelan. It is
striking that little or no detail of the men's employment is given.

The 'Poets of the Insurrection' continued in September's
*Studies* with Cathal Ó Braonáin's essay on Pearse. A few pages
later, Virginia Mary Crawford's 'War and Literature in France'
surveyed the attitudes and achievements of Barrès, Bourget,
Claudel, Alain-Fournier, and Madame Marcelle Tinayre.[21] But
once again the book-review section contains some of the sharpest
intellectual comment. A.J.R. concluded his unimpressed epitome
of Sorel's best-known work with the flat comment 'there is a good

deal of unnecessary violence in these and similar reflections' (p. 461). The reviewer proceeded then to Robert Hunter's *Violence and the Labour Movement* (1916). C.O.B. (probably Ó Braonáin) commended MacDonagh's posthumously published *Literature in Ireland*, and A.J.R. returned to chide Bertrand Russell for failing to appreciate economic factors in *Justice in War Time*.

A plodding narrative of Irish Catholic journalism as it responded to the events of 1916 may benefit from a Shandyan digression. Mrs Crawford (1862–1948), who wrote on 'War and Literature in France' for the Jesuits, was no meek purveyor of orthodoxy. As the erring wife in the Crawford vs Crawford & Dilke divorce case of 1885–86, she had been at the centre of the scandal which destroyed Sir Charles Dilke (1843–1911), leader of the radical Liberals, a friend of Gambetta, and an erstwhile English republican. Though technically an adulteress, she won the sympathy of W.T. Stead (editor of the *Pall Mall Gazette*) and other acute minds. He employed her to write and interpret for him and, in the latter capacity, she met the French adventurer General Boulanger (1837–1891) on at least one occasion, in June 1889 and perhaps again in 1890.[22] As a consequence of Stead's introducing her to Cardinal Manning, Mrs Crawford converted to Catholicism, became a tertiary sister of Saint Francis at the Mill Hill convent in London, and briefly entered conventual life in 1892.[23]

Closer to present concerns, perhaps, was Stead's recommending Crawford in 1895 to the novelist George Moore, who employed her as a research assistant until his death in 1933. (He left her £500.) While contributing to *Studies* in 1916, she was aware of Moore's imminent publication, a novel called *The Brook Kerith* which relates a very heterodox account of Jesus' non-relations with Saint Paul.[24] In politics she was a Labourite, the first woman elected to London County Council, and an activist in social welfare circles linked to the Catholic Church in Britain.[25] Finally, she is sometimes credited with introducing the (previously)

French terminology of feminism and feminist into English usage.[26] Digressions have a point to make, even in *Tristram Shandy*, and the point about Mrs Crawford in 1916 is a demonstration that the native/foreign distinction is never universally applicable. Well, almost never. Francis Mulhern once observed of a prominent figure in 'Irish Studies' that he was incapable of discussing nationalism except in nationalist terms, a mentality in evidence throughout *The Catholic Bulletin*'s coverage of 1916 and after. Yet even it had an ulterior project, the reconciliation of advanced nationalism with the Church.

Accordingly, the final pages in the *Bulletin*'s September number commemorated Roger Casement (executed 3 August in London), Francis Sheehy Skeffington, Cornelius Keating, Daniel Sheehan, Charles Corrigan, J.J. O'Grady, James Quinn, Richard O'Reilly, George Geoghegan, Patrick Doyle, James MacCormack, and John Crenigan. In some of these cases, the presumed Catholicity of all individuals required qualification. Casement, it was well known, had been born into a Protestant family, though he had also been conditionally baptised a Catholic; nothing about Skeffington's religious beliefs could be admitted to the *Bulletin* which did, however, record his embarking on a hunger-strike in 1915. Sheehy Skeffington's killer, John Bowen-Colthurst, also had shot dead Thomas Dickson and Patrick James MacIntyre. These two journalists were not listed by *The Catholic Bulletin*, perhaps because they were loyalists (in Hanna Sheehy Skeffington's term) and unworthy of commemoration. Bowen's summary execution of seventeen-year-old J.J. Coady outside Rathmines church also failed to register, because to commemorate him would involve mention of the two loyalist journalists (one of them a cripple).

Of Cornelius Keating it was said that 'his uncle was one of the Volunteers who went to fight in defence of Pope Pius IX, and within that historic decade his relatives were prominent among the "stout-hearted Fenians of Caherciveen".'[27] James Quinn 'sprang from a Protestant family, and was brought up in that religion but, before his marriage, embraced the Catholic faith.'[28]

In three issues of *The Catholic Bulletin*, appearing between July and September, more than fifty 'martyrs' had been listed and commemorated. October brought memoirs of Casement contributed by various readers, together with notes on William MacDowell, John Owens, John Francis Adams, James Corcoran, Daniel Murray, James Byrne, Edward Walsh, John Dwan, Andrew Cunningham, William Maguire, John Kealy, Thomas Rafferty, Patrick Derrick, and John Healy. The age of some victims was astonishingly low, a point on which the obituarist made little or no comment, either in protest at the involvement of very young persons in violent action or in commiseration at their early death. John Byrne was 'about nineteen' and John Healy was only fifteen ('killed at Byrne's Corner, Phibsboro, while carrying despatches … last words, ten minutes before his death, were "God bless the Volunteers".')[29]

*Studies* in December limited its treatment of the April events with Peter McBrien's tribute to Plunkett (Poets of the Insurrection III) and a return to the 'Reconstruction of O'Connell Street', this time an article by R.M. Butler. In *The Catholic Bulletin*, the editor looked forward to completing the records of those who had died during, or just after, Easter Week. Gerald Keogh (aged twenty, 'son of a Fenian') had been sent late on Easter Monday by Pearse to the Plunkett family's encampment at Larkfield for 'a contingent of fifty men'. (On his way, he went to confession in Clarendon Street church.) Returning with two others (not fifty) he was 'shot dead in front of Trinity College' and buried temporarily in the College grounds.[30] Fred Ryan (aged seventeen), initially a Volunteer but later a member of the Citizen Army, was shot near Stephen's Green; 'Fred was a member of the Sodality attached to St Audoen's, High Street.' Peter Wilson 'got Confession on the golf links' near Finglas. Jack O'Reilly, who appears to have been on good terms with 'his Dusky Majesty the King of Tonga', died of pernicious anemia after release from military detention.

The December 'Events of Easter Week' appeared below a traditional church-art nativity scene. The text and illustrations provided less biographical material, but emphasised the family structure of the lives commemorated. Photographs of widows and their children predominated and, where the available image had not included all the children, an insert was provided. Groups represented were families of the O'Rahilly, James Connolly, Thomas Clarke, Michael Mallin, Eamonn Ceannt, Thomas MacDonagh, Seán Connolly, John F. Adams, George Geoghegan, Richard O'Carroll, Henry Coyle, Thomas Allen, Andrew Cunningham, James Corcoran, A.J. Byrne, William MacDowell, Philip Clarke, Patrick Doyle, William Maguire, Patrick O'Flanagan, Frank Sheehy Skeffington, Edward Walsh, and one or two single individuals. For Christmas, the Easter martyrs were represented as the Holy Family, Skeffington included. Nothing was permitted to suggest a fiasco. No sign of Mary Emily Pearse, Protestant half-sibling of the executed Pearse brothers.

Although the 'Events of Easter Week' continued to appear in the *Bulletin* throughout 1917, the essential work of baptising the Fenians had been completed by December. In part, this was achieved by avoiding on almost every occasion any use of the term Fenian, except in a genealogical context, and by substituting a biographical summary in place of the events highlighted in the serial title. These summaries were highly selective, especially with regard to secular activities. The naming of schools attended or sodalities joined implicitly established religious conformity; sometimes a priest's opinion of the individual underscored personal virtue. Whereas Yeats would name a few of the executed in 'Easter 1916' and also celebrate 'Sixteen Dead Men', the *Bulletin* constructed so numerous a tally as to suggest — and gradually to construct — popular approval.

'Reunion of Protestants with Rome' resumed publication in January 1917, the emphasis as ever placed on insurmountable difficulties. 'Events of Easter Week' diverged from its previous concentration on those killed. 'We are glad to be able to publish this month brief biographical notices of Count Plunkett and Prof. MacNeill, both significantly associated in a recent revision of "Early Christian Art in Ireland".'[31] This was a breath-taking appropriation of recent publishing history, for *Early Christian Art in Ireland* by Margaret Stokes (died 1900) had been issued in 1887 by the commercial firm of Chapman and Hall, and revised by Count Plunkett in 1911 under the imprint of His Majesty's Stationery Office. The Count's involvement in the events of Holy Week 1916 is nowhere mentioned. 'This is not the time to speak of what a living man said and did for Ireland when Ireland's manhood was tested to the utmost tension. But this we know, that the members of the Plunkett family have proved worthy of one another and of their race.'[32] G.N. Plunkett's career in the museum service is detailed, together with his early sojourn in France. 'Here he forgot the English language, earning French, Italian and Niçoise, but remained in feeling intensely Irish.'[33] His education by the Jesuits is noted with approval, but reference to Trinity College whence he proceeded after Clongowes is conspicuously absent. Plunkett's association with Home Rule is acknowledged though he also kept in touch 'with the more advanced party.' The account of John (more usually Eoin) MacNeill is equally tactful, concentrating on his immense academic learning and devotion to Irish and Gaelic affairs. 'The time is not opportune to discuss his connection [sic] with the Irish Volunteers.'[34] And, indeed, in January 1917, neither man was at liberty — the Count and Countess being involuntarily exiled to Oxford, and MacNeill in prison. *The Catholic Bulletin* was effectively providing a life-line of publicity for them and for a greater number of imprisoned rebels less distinguished by name.

The February issue dealt with women involved in Easter Week, not so much activists (though Constance Markievicz is treated) as widows and mothers, signifying family solidarity. Maud Gonne (divorced widow of John MacBride) was not mentioned, though her mother-in-law is pictured. Considerable effort was required to demonstrate the Catholic faith of some women. Markievicz is quoted as stating that she 'became a Catholic at the College of Surgeons', that is, under fire in the late stages of her military career. In connection with Grace Gifford (Plunkett's widow) it is asserted that she 'was received, after long preparation, into the Catholic Church on the 7th April, 1916.' An unnamed nun reports however that Mrs Plunkett 'is still getting the instructions required by a convert and [she is] eager to learn and practise all that is necessary to make a good Catholic.' Grace Gifford Plunkett never quite fitted the pious/patriotic role assigned her; the remarks already quoted, and others more verbose, indicate the difficulties encountered in assimilating all concerned into a confessional unanimity.[35] Her sister, the widow of Thomas MacDonagh, later committed suicide, an act inadmissible in the Catholic ethos of the Free State.

*Studies,* being a quarterly publication, was able to distance itself in 1917 merely by allowing one number to omit any overt reference to Easter 1916. Nonetheless the June number reverted to the essentially literary perspective adopted at the outset. 'Poets of the Insurrection' was extended to include John Francis MacEntee (1889–1984), who had not been killed or executed and who (as Seán MacEntee) many years later would become a deeply conservative minister in de Valera's cabinet. Belfast-born MacEntee served to represent, if only through poetic feebleness, the northern moiety so brazenly ignored at Easter. Arthur Clery contributed an appreciation of Pearse, MacDonagh, and Plunkett, indicating the harmony of literature and Catholic belief. A more exotic diet was provided by Mrs Crawford in 'Péguy and His Circle' and by M.R. reviewing Paul Bourget's new novel *Lazarine.*[36]

These French literary names, clustering in *Studies* and evident in less concentrated form in *The Irish Monthly*, will recur below in a broader consideration of the European ideological context in which *Dublin 1916* should be considered. Absent mediators across the gap were the novelists George Moore and James Joyce, whose *Brook Kerith* and *Portrait of the Artist as a Young Man* both appeared before the end of 1916. Suffused with time, like inertia about to storm the door Lukács observed in its impenetrability, Eliot's 'Love Song of J. Alfred Prufrock' had appeared in *Poetry* (Chicago) in 1915, and the volume *Prufrock and Other Observations* followed early in 1917. Stephen Spender compared Eliot's treatment of the word 'time' to a Beethoven motif, though Bergson was closer to hand. For local periodicals formally linked to the Irish Catholic Church these heresiarchs scarcely existed; instead pious verse by Count Plunkett appeared everywhere, before and after the Insurrection.

G.N. Plunkett had been hastily sworn into the IRB early in April 1916 and, while this exercise may have been designed to safeguard the Fenians while the new recruit headed for Rome, the late date of his taking the oath was typical of other, more active leaders in the Rising — de Paor classified both Pearse and Connolly as last-minute Fenians. By February 1917 Count Plunkett had been elected to Westminster in a North Roscommon by-election, and a wholly new phase of the republican struggle was under way. He did not take his seat, and may on that ground be regarded as the founder of absentionism. In a different perspective, the by-election at once demonstrates the authorities' willingness to maintain democratic procedures in wartime, and the victorious party's willingness to recognise (and exploit) these procedures. By late 1917 *The Catholic Bulletin*'s treatment of Easter Week had been relieved of some burdens imposed by military censorship, and it even began to relate local events such as 'The Defence of Mount Street Bridge'. In the September issue, 'we suspend our narrative of the Events of Easter

Week to tell briefly the story of the great and revered Bishop of Limerick who has just passed away.'[37]

A contributor to the *Dictionary of Irish Biography* credits the *Bulletin*'s first editor (J.J. O'Kelly, 1872–1957) with creating an important source for future historians of the Rising, though one might add that no attention is paid to Catholics whom the rebels killed, whether British or Irish, military or civilian.[38] Certainly, in the immediate aftermath, O'Kelly had to avoid any narrative accounts of 'Events', and so devised the quasi-obituarial format as a means of communicating rebel politics to his very large readership. The avoidance of detail about Protestant or English kinship might be excused in the circumstances, but its larger implications in relieving the Fenian tradition of its anti-clerical legacy, and in imposing a Catholic uniformity among the rebels, ignored important historical realities.

Quite openly, the *Bulletin* pursued the objective of demonstrating the identification of Catholic practice and republican Irish nationalism. In 1916, and across the island, very many Irish Catholic families had sons or brothers serving in the British forces, having been encouraged since 1914 by John Redmond to enlist. It could not be assumed that public opinion would favour the rebels, even after the summary executions of Pearse and the other leaders some of whom were little known outside Dublin. Consequently, successive numbers of the *Bulletin* repeatedly noted clerical relatives or the involvement of rebels in religious societies.

Let us take the list for August 1916, sixteen names in all. Three of these (the Kent brothers) had not been active in Easter Week at all, but were implicated in the killing of a policeman in County Cork on 1 May. Their mother was 'sister of Very Rev. Canon Rice of Mitchelstown,' but no spiritual details of the late policeman are provided.[39] W.F. Burke was 'cousin of the popular story-writer Fr Fitzgerald O.F.M.'[40] Patrick O'Flanagan was 'a member of the third Order of Saint Francis.'[41] Of the remaining eleven, seven were stated to be members of sodalities. The economic base of these individual lives — as tradesmen, labourers, clerks, domestic servants, farmers or whatever — is elided under the repeated listing of confessional activities.

The years following Easter 1916 remain open to various interpretations, including the republican insistence that the War of Independence was a renewal of Pearse's initiative. Present purposes do not require any extensive comparison of rival views, but it is important to stress that G.N. Plunkett's success in the North Roscommon election of 1917 marked an acceptance of parliamentary politics as a means to the goal of independence. Whether the Mauser and the ballot-box played in total harmony must be doubted. Some gunmen, who ran a constant risk of violent death, thought of the politicians as careerists and compromisers; some elected representatives feared that armed resistance could be mistaken as an end in itself, without political substance. The War of Independence was conducted along lines utterly different from those adopted by Pearse and Connolly; from the outset (January 1919) it was a guerrilla campaign fought in rural areas as well as urban; it constituted a national effort, at least in territorial terms.

Republican dismissal of majorities in Dáil Éireann (1921–2) and in general elections (June 1922, and August 1923) may be accounted for in local terms, but a wider European perspective of the early 1920s saw the growth of anti-parliamentarianism in Germany, Italy, and elsewhere (see Chapter 7 below). When Dáil Éireann met in December 1921 to debate the settlement negotiated in London, the authority of Easter 1916 and the Proclamation was little if at all invoked, despite the numerous veterans present. On the second day of substantive debate one finds three or four occasions when an allusion is made. These deserve attention as indicators of a presumed relationship between the Rising and the War of Independence. What follows are four discrete excerpts from that day's (15 December) debate on the Treaty; they do not constitute a continuous sequence of contributions:

DEPUTY SEAN ETCHINGHAM: I wish to refer to the question of the letter of credentials that the delegation got to present to the British Cabinet or delegation. It was not clear whether it was ever presented or not. There was a difference of opinion, and I think it is important. I am given to understand that if they represented the Irish Republic there, they could not, if they had full powers to sign an agreement or treaty, they could not do anything that would in any way break the constitution of the Government they represented.

DEPUTY EAMON DE VALERA: To say the Republic was given away because the name Free State was brought forward is to say that words were changed. We are not dealing with words now. We are dealing with certain facts. I hold that Ireland as [*recte* is] an independent State, and we as the Parliament and Government of that State, had a perfect right, if it wished, to make with the nation at war with it a treaty which would be consistent with its position and a treaty of that kind we tried to draw up.

THE SPEAKER [EOIN MACNEILL]: The only vote that can be taken is for or against the Treaty — ratification or non-ratification. If a vote were to be taken on this document what would it mean? I remember on one occasion in the early history of the Volunteer movement, before the Volunteers started, The O'Rahilly and Seán Fitzgibbon came to me and I explained the position and they reproached me with being an opportunist and I admitted I was and I have remained so since. Some of you may remember at a later stage, though few know so much about it as I do, that an attempt was made to bring the Irish Volunteer organization under the authority and control of the British War Office. You may remember there was a great deal of talk about that.

DEPUTY KEVIN O'HIGGINS: It has been said that to ratify this Treaty involves an abandonment of principle, that it is a betrayal of the principles of the men who died for independence in the past. When a country went to war in a just cause, or when an unjust war was forced upon it, must it continue that war? Has it no right to make terms? I submit that the men who went out in 1916 went out in the spirit that a military victory was out of the question and that they had to take terms in the interests of the nation that fell short of independence. Does anyone submit they would have fought on for a recognition of Irish independence? Are we to be denied that right to make terms in their name today? If the principle of Irish nationality is not immortal then it has died many deaths because the chiefs of the Irish clans swore allegiance to Henry VIII, the members of Grattan's Parliament sat in allegiance to the King of England and from 1800 we have been sending members to sit in the English Parliament at Westminster; and yet when Pearse went out in 1916 and proclaimed a Republic would anyone say he was acting dishonourably because the Irish chiefs gave allegiance to Henry VIII, because Grattan's Parliament sat in allegiance to the King at the time, or because John Redmond and his Party took an oath to the King of England? Parnell in his fight for freedom took an oath to the King of England. The struggle was a constitutional one and Parnell said no man had a right to set bounds to the march of a nation or to say thus far shalt thou go and no further. We who stand for this Treaty stand for it in the full truth of Parnell's dictum (applause).

Etchingham was, in effect, simply reminding fellow deputies that an Irish Republic had been proclaimed in April 1916 — there had been earlier Ur-Fenian declarations also. His objective was to achieve this in actuality. In one striking respect, the Dáil exemplified a precept built into the Proclamation — universal suffrages for women and men alike, but no invocation of its authority was heard. De Valera, who had been sentenced to death in 1916, likewise insisted that there *was* in existence there and then an independent Irish state (again, by mute virtue of the Proclamation), and his objective was to ensure that nothing in any agreement jeopardised that achievement. Professor MacNeill, who had been deceived by Pearse and the 'dissident' Volunteers' Military Council, contributed a detail of history which nobody sought to clarify or contest. It was left to Kevin O'Higgins, often regarded as the strong man of the pro-Treaty element, to invoke Pearse by name. His challenging submission to deputies went unanswered — 'that the men who went out in 1916 went out in the spirit that a military victory was out of the question and that they had to take terms in the interests of the nation that fell short of independence. Does anyone submit they would have fought on for a recognition of Irish independence? Are we to be denied that right to make terms in their name today?' This, however discreetly, was a rebuttal of sacrificial politics.

To invoke Pearse was challenging; invoking Parnell was even more dangerous, for deputies were soon accusing each other of fomenting a split in their ranks. The ensuing Civil War did not really end until May 1926, exactly ten years after the final post-Easter executions, when de Valera established a republican political party under the name Fianna Fáil. The Fenians were back in (somewhat constitutional) business, with O'Casey's new play to mock their pedigree. As for the intensified valorisation of Gaelic, one permanently hostile commentator mocked its religiose pretensions — 'The philological resurrection is dangerously slow.'[42] The synthesis of politics and literature, often thought central to Pearse's insurrection, had sundered. In its place commemoration offered an alternative, in which the two elements sought to neutralise each other.

Right at the end of the 1920s, an energetic and talented friar, Fr Senan, established *The Capuchin Annual,* a journal that ran for decades. One of the editor's major interests was religious art, including the contemporary; another was celebration of Pearse and (to a much lesser extent) his fellow signatories. Each issue, up to and including the twentieth anniversary of the Rising in 1936, included at least one item devoted to Pearse or (in 1933) his mother. A list, followed by some quotations and comments, is instructive:

No. 1 (1930), pp 30–41: Milo McGarry, 'Memories of Sgeoil Eanna'

No. 2 (1931), pp 188–197: Desmond Ryan, 'Five Portraits of P.H. Pearse'

No. 3 (1932), pp 110–114: Louis J. Walsh, 'P.H. Pearse'

No. 4 (1933), pp 91–97: Desmond Ryan, 'Margaret Pearse'

No. 5 (1934), pp 181–185: Alfred Denny, 'A Memory of Patrick Pearse'

No. 6 (1935), pp 217–224: Eamonn O'Neill, 'Patrick Pearse; Some Other Memories'

No. 7 (1936) — a more substantial but dispersed treatment, including (pp 160–162) photographs of the Pearse family [select], a reproduction of the National Museum's copy of the Proclamation, signed by the printer/typesetters, and colour reproduction of Somhairle MacCann's painting of Pearse's cottage in Connemara ('Teach an Phiarsaigh', p. 215).

Among identifiable contributors, Desmond Ryan was to prove the most enduring historian and advocate. Like Milo McGarry, he had been a pupil at Saint Enda's School (Sgeoil Eanna). Walsh was a district justice and minor novelist. Denny summarised the issues at stake:

I think I am right in saying that 1916 ended the scandal of the open separation between the revolutionaries and their [sic] Church, which had existed since 1867. The brown robed Capuchins and the other priests who comforted the last hours of the doomed men were the first to bridge the gulf. Pearse in the last days, sent word to Connolly that he prayed to God that the wounded leader should die a Catholic, in the faith of his childhood. Connolly replied that already Pearse's prayer had been answered and that he would die, not only as an Irishman, but also as an Irish Catholic.[43]

Two matters, and not just the one formally stated, were settled in this paragraph. Yes, the mutual distrust of the Church and the IRB was dissolved, not just by the Capuchin friars who risked their lives in the Dublin streets but also by *The Catholic Bulletin*'s sustained and unhesitating hagiographical zeal from May/June 1916 onwards. There is an arguable view that the Plunkett family achieved the concordat, Plunkett swearing his father into the IRB for the principal purpose of despatching him to Rome. The story of Pearse's concern for Connolly's orthodox submission is not glossed with anything like the political analysis it deserved, but its importance in 1934 can be gauged from the inclusion in the same *Annual* of a piece entitled 'Christ or Communism?', written by Fr James of the Capuchin Order. That Connolly's son, Roddy, had become a stalwart of the Moscow-affiliated Irish Communist Party remained unmentionable. Instead, a self-authenticating apostolic succession was emphasised. McGarry remembered how 'Pearse's addresses to us in the study hall grew more intimate. Emmet's death before a Dublin crowd became his favourite theme.'[44] It seems that even the wooden block upon which Emmet was finally decapitated had a central place in Sgeoil Eanna's reliquary.[45]

The impact of these annual commemorations is hard to exaggerate. Fr Senan, a shrewd businessman for all his unfeigned piety, issued each number at the beginning of December, so that it appealed strongly to a religious and republican constituency in search of thoughtful Christmas presents. A huge advertising section testified to the *Annual*'s capacity to draw in funds which helped to finance colour illustrations (usually of religious painting, but not excluding Pearse's cottage.) Occasionally, the editor included a certificate stating the size of his print-run — 15,000 copies for 1934; 20,000 the following year.

A striking feature of both *The Catholic Bulletin* and *The Capuchin Annual* in their treatment of Easter 1916 is the reliance on prolific illustration, a feature more recently of *The Field Day Review*. Within the extensive portfolios of images, a further preference for portrait photographs can be detected. Though the Rising had involved the capture of numerous buildings and attacks on others, little interest is shown in these locations, apart from the GPO. The birthplaces and homes of the leaders are likewise neglected. One could debate cause and effect. Given the social class from which most combatants came, simple 'mug shot' snaps and grander pictures of family occasions were readily available. Photographs of permanent objects, including houses, would have been thought extravagant at that socio-economic level. The range of images available was already biased towards the representation of individual persons, intensifying the project's martyrological dimension. Text was economically used, *The Capuchin Annual* preferring brief memoirs of one individual by someone who had known him in life. These strategies again intensified the aura of martyrdom, by encouraging identification between the reader and the subject, not as substitution (the living for the dead) but as implying an identity of beliefs, values and interests.

The 'higher' cultural responses preferred text. Again, class factors were operative. Portraits in oil were uncommon among Citizen Army men and women, and hardly less so among Volunteers. William Orpen's painting of Casement in the dock is clearly an exception, arising from the very public forum in which he was condemned. Sean Keating's iconography of nationalist struggle — rarely lacking an ironic dimension — paid little attention to the events and personalities of 1916, but concentrated instead on the War of Independence, a predominantly rural landscape, and *typical* ('Men of the South') representations. Jack Yeats's art of the period is too complex to analyse here, though he too focuses on the War of Independence rather than retrospections of the Rising.[46]

The late 1930s brought W.B. Yeats back to 1916, notably to the controversy surrounding Casement. 'The Statues' must rank among his most complex meditations on the relationship of history to art, though it evokes Pearse and Cuchulain, not Casement. He became circumspectly involved in the publication of W.J. Maloney's speculative account of *The Forged Casement Diaries* (1936).[47] As a poet, he could be by contrast reckless, at least with metaphors. The two poems about Casement are not memorable performances. But, after some flummoxing about the Kerryman's self-awarded title, the first stanza of 'The O'Rahilly' ends in a concentrated welter of major themes:

He wrote out that word himself,
He christened himself with blood.[48]

## Chapter 4
# Pearse, France and *The Irish Review* (1911–1914)

*Du siehst, mein Sohn, Zum Raum wird hier die Zeit.*

Richard Wagner

*the very point where my past expires in a deed.*

Henri Bergson

### Pearse, Anthologist of the Self

A recent study of 'the Irish factor' in European affairs has pointed to a 'dramatic deterioration of Franco-Irish relations between 1899 and 1914, especially after the signing of the Entente Cordiale in 1904.'[1] The implication that a closer British alliance with France automatically produced an Irish counter-reaction deserves critical scrutiny with, however, the proviso that Paris might have taken sophisticated steps to neutralise or even re-enchant Hibernian attitudes. Culture may emerge as a trump card, at least in the relatively short game. Personal preferences and crude political objectives may re-emerge in transformed colours. Tom Kettle in 1912 even envisaged Ireland as a 'culture State'.[2]

The attitudes and circumstances within which Connolly and Pearse operated in the years preceding the Rebellion altered several times and in different directions. Grave financial difficulties in the old family business, James Pearse and Sons, led to its closure in 1910, with the consequence that the only source of income was the school, Saint Enda's, which effectively absorbed the debts, the domestic furniture and the siblings into its risky but valuable experiment. The acquisition of a large eighteenth-century house provided excellent accommodation for pupils and, more important for Pearse, what he saw as a direct link with Robert Emmet. His identification with the doomed rebel of 1803 became all the more intense through their sharing the same rooms, walking the same paths, and contemplating the same landscape — give or take a hundred years. The discounting of time past, or compacting the interval into moments of ideological ecstasy, deserves as much attention as the Christological images employed by Pearse to bring Emmet to Pearse alive in the latter's own presence.

Pearse's career as a fervent republican took a promising turn in 1913 when he was inducted into the IRB, despite the reservations of some less romantically attuned members. His credentials, and indeed his bank account, benefited from a lecture tour of the United States in March 1914, when he spoke repeatedly about Emmet as a model. A little constellation (Ursa Minor?) of recurrent images developed — blood on the streets of Dublin, Emmet before a Dublin crowd, the gallows, etc — in which a peculiar ambiguity, or moral double-perspective, can be discerned. The metropolitan focus is often underestimated in assessments of Pearse's long-term plans; it was present from an early stage, evidence of a modern sensibility against the tradition of 'hillsiders' and 'men of the west'. Blood on the streets should not rank among the ultimate goals of republicanism, though its occurrence is a given intermediary. What happens in Pearse's ruminations on violence is not a distinguishing between means and ends, neither a scrupulous or callous distinguishing. It is a gradual, implicit, semi-unconscious abolition — or, more sympathetically, *elision* — of the distinction, the elision itself arising from, or facilitated by, the discounting of time past, the temporal relationship between means and ends whether in the past or future.

Pearse's understanding of the relationship between rural Ireland and the metropolis involved a similar exercise in projected history. The traditional habits, beliefs, and practices of the Gael — no one else lived in the countryside, we are to accept — will redeem Ireland from the modernising and urbanising influences of Britain (little reference to New York, Chicago, or Paris) through closeness to owner-occupied Nature, the fertile soil, the elements, etc. But the redemption depends on a successful re-enactment of Emmet's (failed) urban insurrection, which the wily United Irishmen of rural Wicklow had wisely left to unfold — into disaster. Pearse earnestly located Saint Enda's among woods and hillsides, but the Hermitage which had cosseted Emmet now lay not far off the Rathfarnham tram-line. His cottage, a crib of re-birthable Gaelic antiquity, looked across Galway Bay towards the de Basterot property at Neptune Vale, where Yeats or Gregory inducted Bourget into the magic of Anglophone Irish folklore.

Pearse's image of Emmet before a Dublin crowd is likewise contradictory, shimmering, ambiguous. A classic icon of the late nineteenth century showed a green-clad hero in the dock, surrounded by accusers and prosecutors (not forgetting his own lawyer, an informer, a Judas); he defies his enemies, he makes his famous speech.[3] But Pearse's preferred image is Emmet under the scaffold, in the open, in the street, surrounded by the crowd (or, is it mob?). He cannot say whether the onlookers are mutely sympathetic, cowed by the red-coats, or crudely mocking (Next week, Give us Barabbas). Pearse's 'Ecce Homo' conflates the 1803 trial and the execution of some days later, allowing for an indeterminedness of attitude in the implied onlookers. There are regular attendees at such Dublin spectacles; there is horror, pathos, leering curiosity, diligent journalism. What kind of audience will he, Patrick Pearse, have when his moment of re-living Emmet's death finally comes?[4]

'Ecce Homo' was a traditional theme and scene in classical art, endlessly imitated and reproduced. A contemporary re-working by the Hungarian painter Mihaly Munkácsy (1844–1900) had been exhibited at the Royal Hibernian Academy in 1899. It was written up by a fellow student of Pearse's at the Royal University, James Joyce, in an undergraduate magazine. Munkácsy occupied various transitional positions in European arts at the end of the nineteenth century; Munich trained, he had missed the boat to Paris; moreover, his painting techniques and materials resulted in physical deterioration of the canvases. Joyce was a fair, though remorseless critic. Specifying the moment in Christ's *passion*, he insisted, 'I use the word in its proper sense,' as if anticipating his fellow student's later and far looser indulgence of that vocabulary for political ends.[5] And the two knew each other personally if not affably, Pearse giving Joyce a few lessons in Irish Gaelic which the future novelist decided not to pursue. The Ecce Homo positioning of Emmet by Pearse is not just some eccentric foible of a neurotic ideologue striving for historic resonance; it is a contribution, more kinetic than aesthetic, to contemporary debates involving the young Joyce, the late Friedrich Nietzsche, and a score of French Catholic intellectuals. Nietzsche's autobiography, *Ecce Homo*, appeared posthumously in 1908. Pearse graduated in Modern Languages (including French) in 1900. Ciaran Brady has observed in conversation that, behind Pearse's Gaelic short fiction, Alphonse Daudet (1840–1897) presided, with *Lettres à mon Moulin* (1869) in his hand, published ten years before An Piarsach was born.[6]

By contrast, one of Plunkett's favourite authors was G.K. Chesterton (1874–1936) whose two best-known novels, *The Napoleon of Notting Hill* (1904) and *The Man Who was Thursday* (1908), fascinated that member of the Military Council as contemporary fables. Pearse's English reading is less well documented. Yet there is a well-known piece by Chesterton (collected in 1900) which approaches the Ecce Homo scene from an oblique angle and through an early moment in Christ's passion. The Donkey presents himself as a 'tatter'd outlaw' whom men may scourge, yet he keeps his secret still. With characteristic Chestertonian sentimentalism, the speaker keeps his secret (like any good conspirator) but also sells it on the market-place, dismissing the mockers with a term Pearse will use in his climactic speech at O'Donovan Rossa's grave (1 August 1915):

> Fools! For I also had my hour;
> One far fierce hour and sweet.
> There was a shout about my ears,
> And palms before my feet.[7]

It may seem highly improbable that Pearse or Emmet Redivivus recalled Chesterton while addressing the vast crowd in Glasnevin Cemetery, many of them armed. Yet there are pointers. The entry into Jerusalem is echoed in Pearse's unfinished (and undated) autobiographical sketch where his own childish imaginings of riding Dobbin, his wooden horse, into 'many a battle' are promptly followed up with his sister's 'triumphant entry into cities'. Chesterton's pious ballad is straight-forward enough, orthodox before *Orthodoxy* (1908) and well in advance of his Catholic conversion (1922). The notion of a '*far* fierce hour' may be credited to an indulgence in too much alliteration, yet it attempts to acknowledge the believer's renewed encounter with Christ's passion, by admitting the historic remoteness of the biblical events while also relating them as spiritual experience in the present. Pearse's battle was not of the same metaphysical or spiritual consequence, yet he could declare, 'As it took the blood of the Son of God to redeem the world, so it would take the blood of Irishmen to redeem Ireland.'[8]

Fortunately, we do not have to rely on the gyrings of local interpretation, endlessly parroting what is to be interpreted and so endlessly postponing that intellectual engagement. On Pearse's messianism the American William I. Thompson remains unequalled, and one might note the failure of Walter Benjamin's

Irish fans to relate it to the German's concept of messianic time.[9] However, S.F. Moran has bravely opened a route towards a psycho-analytic understanding of Pearse, while simultaneously indicating intellectual parallels between Irish republicanism of the 1916 period, military or cultural, with contemporary French thought. Much of this relates to Freud's then emergent Oedipal theory, applicable to Pearse's relations with his English father, with local father-surrogates (notably Tom Clarke), and with historic or mythic identifications (Emmet and Cuchulain) where father/son relations were central. Moran's book succeeds as an antidote to the hero-worshipping attitudes of Desmond Ryan which have found numerous adoptive agencies. It also indicates, without imposing, the advisability of keeping Pearse's sexual character in view alongside his tendency to dispose of bodies in ideal plans, educational, domestic, and military. For present purposes, more may be gained by employing a less overtly Freudian approach. In terms of ego-psychology, Pearse combines an unusual determination with an equally unusual imperception of real surroundings. Without the citable and over-exciting example of the Great War, these two aspects could never have come into an extreme engagement.

One might begin with an ethical or moral instance. When Pearse observed (ruefully, let's hope) that 'in the beginning we might shoot the wrong people', what one wants to add in the margin is an insistence that it is not those people who are wrong, but the shooting of them. The urge may be academic, prissy, but its underlying concern is with the distinction between the subject-ego and its objects (egos in themselves); it is not simply a moral scruple about agency in the familiar problem of 'being in the wrong place at the wrong time.' Pearse's ego was unevenly matured or, to use a branch of physiology, he had great distance vision, but poor lateral capacity. Perhaps Freudian explanations are valid, but they restrict our understanding to domestic and inherited zones. Leaving aside Pearse's treatment of children in the classroom and in his own writings, two distinct questions, his relationship with other people does not consistently concede their equal status as thinking and sensate adults. He was universally recognised as a prude, in effect relegating 50 per cent of the population to a lower level of acceptance and recognition. It might be counter-argued that he was advanced and promoted within the Irish Volunteers and the IRB, and thus taken as a reliable, fully-functioning human being, indeed one gifted beyond his peers as a speaker, a writer, and propagandist for the cause. These organisations, however, were exclusively male (unlike the Irish Citizen Army). In the case of the IRB, those truly in charge — Clarke, MacDermott or, later, Michael Collins — were willing and capable in the exploitation of a 'useful idiot' (Lenin's middle-class intellectual) male or female. The feminist or suffrage aspect of the Proclamation cannot be ascribed to Pearse.

Others for Pearse were weak ancillary egos, necessary but not real in the sense that he was real (and Emmet with him). These others were different, and thus disposable under unfortunate circumstances. They were not separate; they were deniable sub-agents of the identity ego. Hence the pathos of his invocations to Ireland and 'the Gael'. Whatever the psychological origins of such a mind, its practical implementation of the most fundamental structures of action — Time and Space, then being re-oriented by Einstein but, before August 1914 at least, regarded as reliable — deserves close examination in a wider context than that of Irish nationalism, its historiography and rhetoric. Yet where is one to find material for any comparative enquiry in this field?

### The *Review* as Serial Personality

In many convincing ways, *The Irish Review* exuded post-Edwardian confidence and, with it, 'normalcy' — the American neologism works politely as a sign of underlying unease. It published respectable young English authors such as Eleanor Farjeon; it recruited lucrative advertising[10] from its apparent twin *The English Review* whose second editor, Austin Harrison (1873–1928), took an interest in Irish affairs. The first volume of *The English Review* (under Ford Maddox Hueffer) published Joseph Conrad, Norman Douglas, John Goldsworthy, Gerhart Hauptmann (in translation), Thomas Hardy, Henry James, Leo Tolstoy (in translation), H.G. Wells, etc. Though prose fiction was its strength, the first volume also included three poems by Yeats. The second volume published Britannicus on 'The Dominance of the Irish Question', and F. Norrys Connell's obituary for J.M. Synge. This latter was immediately followed by Camille Mauchair on 'Le Roman français contemporain' (in French). George Moore makes two appearances in the early years, with an 'overture' to *Hail and Farewell,* and with a scenario to 'The Apostle', a forerunner to his novel *The Brook Kerith.*

Relations between the two *Reviews* deserve further investigation, and preliminary remarks must suffice for now. Harrison, who had worked as a journalist in Berlin, became staunchly anti-German, preaching liberal reform at home and military preparedness everywhere.[11] After the War, his *Review* became more conservative or conservative-radical; before the end of 1918 Harrison had begun to publisher Major Douglas's economic theories which would appeal so powerfully to Ezra Pound. Under Harrison's successor, it published a commendation of Carl Schmitt's essay on Catholicism and representation.

The city in which *The Irish Review* was launched could boast a lively cultural scene (a phrase then happily unknown.) Late in 1911 the Gaiety Theatre played Casimir Markievicz' 'The Rival Stars' while, at the Abbey, Yeats's 'Countess Cathleen' was revived in a revised version. The Dublin Orchestral Society included a good deal of Wagner (excerpts and arrangements) in its last concert of the season, also playing Mozart and Goldmark. When the Wagner centenary came round eighteen months later, an anonymous but appreciative critic balanced the pros and cons: 'Wagner was merciless in controversy, and he raised up enemies to himself wherever he went ... but his music grows and grows in popular favour, and now even here in our unmusical Dublin a bit of Wagner crowds the cheap places at the Sunday concerts.'[12] What was to unfold in Ireland, between 1911 and 1921, was effectively an ideological battle to fill the cheap places, to draw the lower middle class into this cause or that, social revolution, imperial retrenchment or nationalist separatism. In the *Review*'s third number, George Moore characteristically raised the stakes by contributing (in French) a rebuke to a relative in religion — 'La Réponse de Georges Moore à son Cousine Germaine, une Carmélite Depuis 23 ans quit lui a demand de Brûler ses Livres'. Joyce, the arch-heretic, never appeared in its columns.

As *The Irish Review* advanced from issue to monthly issue, it gave increasing evidence of a fratricidal ambition, not — perish the thought — to murder Harrison at his London desk, but (in Wolfe Tone's terms) 'to break the connection with England, the never failing source of all our political evils.'[13] The British condition of that moment deserves notice, if the Irish one is to be fully appreciated. In the words of Sam Hynes, 'No doubt a connection exists between imperial expansion [in the eighteenth and nineteenth centuries] and the intensity of national insularity [that grew with it]; as the British Empire expanded, England withdrew from political and cultural contact with other European nations.'[14] A shrewd participant in English literary modernism, Virginia Woolf suggested that 'in or about December 1910, human character changed.'[15] Pearse, who did not live to read her essay, might justifiably have protested at the identification of English conditions and human character. Bloomsbury, however, was remote from Connemara, and not much in touch with Dublin. On the other hand, the larger London sphere echoed to the names of Shaw, Wilde, Yeats, even Synge and, by 1923, Joyce.

Ireland suffered from a double insularity, making it seem provincial to Shaw, and potentially to Yeats a primitivist outpost of tradition. Ireland's relation to the United States was more openly plebeian than anything Henry James might convey to his English neighbours. And Ireland's relation to Europe or, at least Catholic Europe, changed subtly during the mid- and late-Victorian years, well in advance of December 1910. *The Irish Review* began inside Edwardian assumptions, and soon found itself in choppier waters. Meanwhile, the very concept of a periodical [publication] deserves attention in an historical moment secretly informed by Albert Einstein, Sigmund Freud, Max Weber, and a dozen others unknown to the average Irish Volunteer.

In this latter perspective, one should recognise that the Easter Rising was predominantly the work of men and women whose sense of what they were doing achieved full expression in terms of insular national tradition. For any wider consideration Ireland, in the Proclamation's sketchy external references, drew more heavily and confidently on 'her exiled children in America' than on 'gallant allies in Europe', military or other. But the leaders (or most of them) were certainly conscious of intellectual developments elsewhere, and nowhere is that more clearly evident than in the pages of *The Irish Review*. Its readership was broadly based, and its thematic range wide enough to include pictorial art and (in theory at least) the sciences, whereas other organs (whether edited by Connolly or Pearse, in particular) addressed themselves to very specific audiences — the working class, the Gaelic revivalists, etc. The *Review*'s leadership (or most of it) was made up of what the French had recently come to term 'intellectuals'.[16] MacDonagh was a literary critic, poet, and university lecturer; Pearse was a lawyer by training, a poet, playwright, and translator; Plunkett was a poet and editor, with scientific interests in radio technology and electrical theory. There were intermediary cases among the Separatists — Willie Pearse was a school-teacher, sculptor and actor; Connolly, though principally a trade union organiser, wrote some drama, also articles on historical and cultural topics. On the other hand

Tom Clarke, Sean Heuston, Sean MacDermott and John MacBride were *not* intellectuals, despite the last-named spending quite a time in Paris. Eamon Ceannt was probably not an intellectual either, though he played the bagpipes at a papal audience. The French did not use the term without a sneering undercurrent and, in this mood, one might modify an old phrase to define the intellectual as a person who can play the bagpipes — but doesn't.

In a television series devoted to the seven signatories of the Easter Proclamation, Professor Declan Kiberd observed acutely that several of them had written for *The Irish Review* — well, several of them edited it, and self-publication was the trademark of their outlook. More germane to an interpretation of their activities, literary, political and (very soon) military, is to note the very considerable quantity of non-Irish (*extra*-Irish, in one sense of the term) material in the *Review*, very specifically French material.

The August 1911 issue included the first part of Maurice Bourgeois' lengthy study of Bergson. The author listed recent English translations of the philosopher's works, without reference to T.E. Hulme's translation of the *Introduction to Metaphysics* because its publication lay two years ahead. Hulme's literary circles in England included a number of Irish poets, Joseph Campbell, Desmond Fitzgerald (who would fight, or at least serve, in the GPO), and John Todhunter. Bourgeois did not flatter Dublin's consciousness of the wider world. 'The thinking community in Ireland must ... become acquainted with the life and work of this great French genius.' For encouragement, he repeated (without endorsing) the opinion of the reigning Minister for Education in Paris, that Bergson was Irish, perhaps by descent! Certainly readers of the *Review* were given every encouragement to familiarise themselves with Bergson's thought, as Bourgeois' account ran to three lengthy instalments. The initial emphasis, naturally enough, falls on Bergson's central preoccupation. In Bourgeois' words, 'Abstract Time is but a "bastard" transposition of space, and that is why we conceive Time as a line.'[17] One of the central figures in publishing *The Irish Review* had, if anything, anticipated Bourgeois' advice; in January 1911, Plunkett began to read *Time and Free Will* (1889), translated the previous year.[18] This is the work in which Bergson commenced his study of time as *durée*, which is not to be translated with the English abstract noun 'duration', but understood as signifying the personal and subjective basis of time, irreducible to scientific formula. Calvin Bedient has valuable things to say about Bergson and Yeats.[19]

In September the theme is Bergson's relationship with George Berkeley who, at that time, had not won Yeats's devotion. Bourgeois maintained his determination to make Ireland hospitable to his countryman's thinking: 'sound empiricism — a thoroughly Irish trait — based in Berkeley on introspection, in M. Bergson on intuition, naturally explains their vehement reaction against ready-made concepts such as Matter (with Berkeley) and Time (with M. Bergson).'[20] What then follows is a summary of arguments about American influences, though no reference is made to William James's Ulster ancestry.

In his final contribution to the series, Bourgeois advances the case for locating this new philosophy closer to art than to science. (Bergson had written a short monograph on laughter or, indirectly, on comedy.) Writers mentioned in this connection include d'Annunzio, Maeterlinck, Mallarmé, and Novalis, with the composer Debussy, and several painters including Puvis de Chavannes. Towards the end, it is noted that 'Bergsonism has also its replica in the ethical and sociological thought of today,' and the names of Maurice Barrès and Georges Sorel duly follow.[21] We shall hear more of these. A forthcoming book on Bergson by Fr George Tyrrell is mentioned — no reference to his Irish birth — before Bourgeois concludes with the hope:

that in Ireland with whose genius M. Bergson's sound realism is so much in keeping, some great thinker will soon appear who may possibly find a solution of the Irish problem in this resourceful French philosophy.[22]

Bourgeois was no stranger to Ireland. He was researching a biography of J.M. Synge (died 1909) and preparing to translate several of the plays. He spent time in Dublin, getting to grips (or nearly) with the Synge family. Recommending Bergson to the Irish, he did not speak from one side of the proposition only. Some basic practical links between France and the literary revival (Gaelic as well as Anglo-Irish) indicate an audience for an alternative cultural commentary which was more than self-gratification. *John Millington Synge and the Irish Theatre* appeared in 1913, but did not attract notice in *The Irish Review*. Bourgeois' translation of 'The Playboy' did well in France where Moore's wicked suggestion that 'The Well of the Saints' had plagiarised a work by Georges Clemenceau fell on deaf or flattered ears.

Like hundreds of others, Pearse had studied French at what was by now UCD. Shortly after graduation he threw himself into organising the Gaelic League's publications committee, proposing to model its programme on French or German textbooks and anthologies. Later, as editor of *An Claidheamh Soluis*, he chose to represent daily factual news through quotation from continental newspapers.[23] It would be silly to take these strategies merely as a boycott of English goods, though no doubt a related emotion throbbed. There was a positive capacity to mediate between Irish and French experience, partly through a shared Catholicism in the majorities, partly through the influence of French orders in Irish schools, and partly through the prestige of France and its long tradition (and some very recent traditions) of culture and historical reflection. Thomas Davis had celebrated the exiled Irish soldier's valour at Ramillies (1706) and Fontenoy (1745); *The Irish Review* took up more urgent business.

The New Year opened with 'The Renaissance of Alsace-Lorraine' (by P.J. Sheridan). March's issue also echoed Bourgeois' closing sentiment: in 'An Appreciation of the Situation' an Ulster Imperialist (very likely a British Army officer) argued that 'the Irish Question has been prematurely forced into the front place just now, not by anything that has happened in Ireland, but by the condition of British political parties resulting from the 1910 elections.'[24] In his first paragraph the anonymous writer had declared, 'military phrases are so common nowadays in Irish, or at any rate Ulster, politics that I make no apology for using one as the title of this article.' He then proceeds to distinguish between the 'General Idea' and the 'Special Idea' as written up in peacetime martial exercises or war-game-playing.

French influence in Ireland is traceable in articles less sharply focused on politics, for example Ellen Duncan's review of 'Modern French Pictures at the United Arts Club' (May 1912) and Thomas Bodkin's 'Modern French Poetry' (October 1912).[25] With Alsace-Lorraine sometimes providing a bridge-head, Germany features also, as in Sheridan's article on Home Rule in the German Parliament (December 1912). German influence was traced, for example, in a piece signed Batha MacCrainn and entitled 'Ireland and the German Menace' (September 1912), but also approvingly and in unexpected places. The reviewer of James Stephens's fantasy-novel *The Crock of Gold* heard echoes of Nietzsche's Zarathustra.[26] Such fiction could also be the vehicle for irreverent political caricature, gently disguised. Just before the great Labour upheaval Stephens, in a Hadean short story called 'The Threepenny Piece', described how 'that young seraph, Cuchulain, walked about like a person who was strange to himself,' which surely mocks Pearse. In a disturbing image, the story had earlier echoed the famed Bishop Moriarty who damned the Fenians: '"I hate those sinners from the Kingdom of Kerry," said the Chief Tormentor, and he sat moodily down on his own circular saw; and that worried him also, for he was clad only in a loin cloth.'[27]

By mid-1913 *The Irish Review*'s centre of gravity had decidedly shifted into a more explicitly political role, counterbalanced uneasily by Stephens's whimsy. July had opened with 'Ireland, Germany and the Next War', signed by Shan Van Vocht or (in reality) Roger Casement. An Sean Bhean Bhocht had been a traditional feminine characterisation of defeated but resilient Ireland, especially the Ireland that had waited for French revolutionary assistance in the 1790s. Percy French had revived the term for a comic exercise, and now Casement reclaimed it, not to reinforce a French connection but to build a tactical alliance with Wilhelmine Germany, the occupation of Alsace-Lorraine notwithstanding.

The same issue brought Jean Malye's first contribution, a lengthy exposition in French of Maurice Barrès' *La Colline inspirée* (1913), a romano-celtoid novel in which the landscape of German-occupied Lorraine is central.[28] The critic Emmanuel Berl has emphasised how remote from the actual working society of his native province Barrès' fiction is — 'Who would realise … that he is describing a metallurgical countryside? He has seen the *mirabelliers* and neglected the blast-furnaces.'[29] The Proclamation, in its concentration on essentials, found no more room for any reference to industrialised Belfast or even the existence of trade unions.

In 1916 the young Eliot would devote an entire lecture to Barrès' fiction (including *La Colline inspirée*) in an educational extension programme heavily weighted with French right-wing texts.[30] Malye, a shadowy figure who claimed to have been Barrès' secretary at some undisclosed moment and who later worked as an editor among Parisian publishing houses, sounds the Celtic note on more than one occasion, for example recommending *La Revue des Nations* as the 'organe de la Ligue Celtique Francaise'. Among French poets of this tendency, Malye mentioned Alexandre Mercereau, now remembered as a writer on art, if remembered at all.[31] Yet *The Irish Review* also kept mainstream

English literary history in short-sight view. The August 1913 issue carried an elegant flyer for MacDonagh's *Thomas Campion and the Art of English Poetry*, forthcoming.

If Easter 1916 was positively memorable, one cause of this was the gender-egalitarianism inscribed in the Proclamation. *The Irish Review* published quite a number of women writers, including Maud Gonne (once). The fullest treatment, however, came from France and remained in French, untranslated.[32] The journal's bilingualism may be a tribute to its sophisticated audience, though one suspects that the editors (soon to don Volunteer uniform, though not yet sworn Fenians) had little time to commission translations.

The autumn crisis brought in James Connolly, who stressed the value of sympathetic strikes in Labour's conflict with Capital, and made no reference to Sorel, France, or Syndicalism. A supporting article by James Bertram took a decidedly internationalist stance, again without reference to France. 'Appeals to prejudice, so frequently utilised as a weapon against Labour, have failed to divorce Irish from English Trades Unionism. The real union of the two democracies dooms all such attempts to failure.'[33] Comradely unity across national divisions would not long survive the guns of August, and that collapse surely contributed to the pressures (or prejudices) urging Connolly into alliance with the bourgeois nationalists. Back in the mid-1880s, and a moment when a few on the French Left considered using General Boulanger as a stalking-horse, Friedrich Engels had warned of the likely consequences — leading to a general war in Europe and the breakdown of proletarian internationalism. His advice was heeded. But in 1914 and in 1916 no Engels existed and, in any case, Connolly's internationalism came from the American syndicalists (he learned some Italian in New York) rather than first-hand experience of France or Germany.[34]

Unionist Ulster's defiance of Home Rule led southern nationalists to create a defensive formation, the Irish Volunteers, whose manifesto appeared in the *Review*'s December issue. In effect, it had lost its interest in being non-partisan, and the word politics would replace science in its sub-title. Nevertheless articles on matters the Proclamation would serenely ignore appeared in considerable number, especially on the land question (November and December 1913; February 1914). Afforestation, national insurance, and the condition of Irish migrants in America, also figured. On armed resistance to legislated Home Rule, Moritz Bonn (who was in Ulster at the time) observed much later that 'Mr Bonar Law and Lord Carson, not Benito Mussolini, organised the first private armies to revolt against democracy.' And recalling the 'orderly revolution' inspired by the Ulster Solemn League and Covenant, he thought it 'more imposing than the triumphant march of the Nazis.'[35] The Edwardian age was well and truly gone; Armageddon hoved into sight.

Edward Martyn, in a rare appearance, closed the last year of international peace with reflections on Wagner's last opera.[36] Sometime president of Sinn Féin (in its pre-guerrilla days), and an earlier participant in the Duras House talks, Martyn shared a theatrical space with Plunkett in Hardwicke Street. Regarded as eccentric by many, he had a good claim to be acknowledged as the intellectual leader of Irish lay Catholics of the upper echelon, a novelist, dramatist and patron of the arts. *Parsifal* (1882) is Gotterdammerung toppling into decadence, a condition which alarmed and excited Martyn. Wagner, who had profoundly influenced an entire generation in the British Isles (including George Moore and Bernard Shaw), now embodied the enemy, not as fiendishly in the public mind as Nietzsche, but his presence was all the more disturbing for its erotic sonority.

*Parsifal* cast a curious spell on the 1916 leadership, especially those who edited or extensively contributed to *The Irish Review*. The opera is suffused with allusions to Easter (the Holy Grail used at the Last Supper, the Holy Spear used to pierce Jesus' side on the cross, etc.) Indeed it is a heterodox foundational score of the 'blood sacrifice' ideology behind 1916; a condition of spiritual poverty is represented in bodily decay (putrescence indeed) to be remedied only with the touch of a weapon. Shimmering philology had made another of its contributions to misunderstanding when Wagner gave his hero the name Parsifal in the belief that it contained a Persian element meaning 'guileless fool', a characterisation Pearse variously used of his heroes and (without the adjective) his enemies also. 'Pearse made a metaphysic out of foolishness,' as part of his semi-conscious messianic identification.[37] For Plunkett, the descent of a white dove at the opera's close — reintroducing the symbolism of John the Baptist — merged with a favourite private symbol in his own poetry.[38]

Ireland gave birth to no Wagner, though Standish O'Grady strove to incorporate ancient myth in works of fiction which have seemed to this reader almost as long as *The Ring*. W.I. Thompson speaks of O'Grady's narrative technique as Wagnerian *entrelacement*, and quotes a speech of 1899 — 'we have now a literary movement, it is not very important; it will be followed by a political movement, that will not be very important; then must come a military movement, that will be important indeed.'[39] Other sons of rectoric Big Houses did not follow O'Grady into Valhalla. Moore employed certain Wagnerian techniques in novels more sophisticated than O'Grady's, and dealt with the world of opera in *Evelyn Innes* (1898) and — indirectly — in its sequel *Sister Theresa* (1901), the latter perhaps less sublimely indebted to his friendship with Virginia Crawford. A less-remembered early contributor to the Literary Revival, Tipperary-born T.W. Rolleston (1857–1920) rivalled O'Grady in building fiction around the archaic figure of Cuchulainn, while also publishing on Wagner. Rolleston, whose illustrated *Parsifal* (in execrable lofty verse) appeared in 1912,[40] did not contribute to *The Irish Review*.

By reduction, one comes to look at Pearse's 'The Singer' in this light. Written late in 1915, it cobbles together elements from Yeats

('The Countess Cathleen') and Synge ('Riders to the Sea') in a chamber-folk style laden with unspeakable dialogue — 'Is it to sit up all night you did?'[41] MacDara, the hero, is the older son of Máire ni Fhiannachta; her Christian name suggests Christ's mother, and her 'surname' the ancient and pagan Fenians. MacDara had been obliged to leave home because of 'trouble' he was fomenting. Now returned, he is recognised as an inspirational itinerant Singer widely admired. He had undergone a prolonged crisis of faith: 'I felt inclined to run through the villages and cry aloud, "People, it is all a mistake; there is no God."'[42] But the Gael's Zarathustra has seen the error of his ways. His father presumed dead, MacDara has decided to become first Emmet, then Christ. Or perhaps the other way round: 'I seemed to see myself brought to die before a great crowd that stood cold and silent; and there were some that cursed me in their hearts for having brought death into their houses.' Or, 'when my mother stood up to meet me with her arms stretched out to me, I thought of Mary meeting her Son on the Dolorous Way.'[43]

'The Singer' is a weak play, a drab statement of intentions. Fr Padraic Brown, writing an introduction to Pearse's drama in 1917, was in no doubt (he wrote from Maynooth). 'The ideas of sacrifice and atonement, of the blood of martyrs that makes fruitful the seed of the faith, are to be found all through these writings.'[44] *The Catholic Bulletin*'s message had not been lost on the future monsignor, though imagery of seed and fruitfulness oddly reflects the structural and narrative anti-sexuality of the play. There is a widow and also an orphan girl, the latter losing the only two young men in her life. What remains are two old men, and MacDara's disturbing recollection of an incident in his wanderings, 'I gave to the little lad I taught the very flesh and blood and breath that were my life. I fed him on the milk of my kindness; I breathed into him my spirit.'[45] Compacted without content, this is a self-obit — 'I gave ... my life.' Total art, secreted literally in the totalitarian as its end and means, is a lethal mirage dreamed of by Mussolini, denounced by Benjamin: its avatar was Wagner, as Nietzsche perceived at the time of his apostasy in 1888.

One detail from *Parsifal* will do. Towards the end of Act One, Scene One, the aged knight Gurnemanz is leading the holy fool Parsifal on what is in effect a quest for the holy grail, though the youth does not even know what the grail is. As they travel, Parsifal observes, 'Ich streite kaum / doch wähn' ich mich schon weit.' [I scarcely tread, yet seem already to have come far.] Gurnemanz offers an explanation in up-to-date terms, 'Du siehst, mein Sohn, / zum Raum wird hier die Zeit.' [You see, my son, time here becomes space.] It is by no means a clear explanation, except that it implies that time has passed beyond the mere measurement of stage-time. That on occasion time and space share a material identity, or at least are capable of that identification, anticipates Einstein's revolutionary theory of relativity (1905). In more obvious terms of characterisation, the aged knight and the young innocent are drawn together by the imminent success of the quest. This movement-towards will prove ultimately triumphant in overcoming the curse blighting the land. In Gurnemanz' earlier words: 'Alas! How it grieves my heart to see the liege Lord of a conquering race in the pride and flower of his manhood fall a slave to his sickness.' In the 1880s, O'Grady had written of Ireland under a 'stupefaction', its will paralysed, 'supine under the fanning of gigantic wings'. His source had been the story of Cuchulain who defended Ulster when it lay under 'a great enchantment'.[46] Pearse is more likely to have read O'Grady than listened to *Parsifal*, though one should not underestimate Wagner's infiltration of the Anglophone public sphere. He can be assumed to have known Rolleston's versions of Cuchulain, and to have been aware of Rolleston's assemblage of ancient Parsifalian material. Adorno's comment on *Parsifal*, and on Wagnerian music generally, may yet prove valuable in deciphering the manifest declarations of Irish nationalism. Perhaps 'Wagner's orchestration is inseparable from the idea of the human body;

some of his theatrical figures seem to be instruments of the orchestra that have become flesh and blood ...' and he proceeds to discuss *Parsifal* in detail.[47]

Martyn, of course, knew nothing of an Easter plot, for its conception lay several years in the future, made possible by the outbreak of war in Europe. Neither he nor Wagner had the last word in *The Irish Review*, which closed with its November issue. Jean Malye featured more or less at quarterly intervals throughout 1914: in January providing a 'Chronique de France', much of it devoted to puffing a new journal, *L'Art de France*; in March describing 'Le Mouvement Philosophique en France', in which Emile Boutroux (1845–1921) and Bergson figured, scientism was denounced and the Celtic note played yet again; in July–August assessing 'Le Home Rule et la France'.[48] All of these pieces appeared in French, evidently without editorial adjustment. The last concluded — ironically in the light of Casement and Plunkett's subsequent German contacts — "La France aidera l'Irlande a prendre sa place parmi les grandes nations, à devenir une nation européëne.'[49] The author of these words would later serve in his country's Washington embassy as *Major* Jean Malye.

It is worth looking at this French undertaking in the context of statements made less than two years later in such contrasting places as *The Irish Monthly* and *The Irish Times*. (These will be examined in more detail in the pages which follow.) On 1 April Joseph Hone smuggles a commendation of Georges Sorel (also on Eliot's list) into the columns of Ireland's stuffiest newspaper; in the April number of M.H. Gill's respectable and largely parochial magazine, a contributor will quote the novelist Maurice Barrès calling for sacrifice in time of crisis. 'Let us give our blood and some greatness of soul to the cause.' The Easter Rising owed something to both Sorel and Barrès. Earlier, Bourgeois had looked for 'some great thinker' to apply Bergson in Irish circumstances. By 1917 the French government set up a Bibliotheque et Musée de La Guerre, with the same Bourgeois becoming head of the English section. Within months of the insurrection, or by the time the Somme was finally over, French interest had altered focus.[50]

One drastic textual placement of the Easter Proclamation would treat it as a later than final, brief and unashamedly illegal issue of *The Irish Review*. Although such characterisation would risk irritating traditionalists by appearing to deny the document its status in the annals of Irish republicanism, there may yet be benefits to reap from a consideration of the two. Of the seven signatories, three were notable contributors to the magazine — MacDonagh, Pearse, and Plunkett. A fourth (Connolly) contributed though not repeatedly. Another of those executed (the non-intellectual MacBride) might be thought represented by his ex-wife, who contributed just once. Two of the above (MacDonagh and Plunkett) acted as joint editors. Finally, Plunkett (who had far more capital behind him than any of the others) was the *Review*'s proprietor in its final stages. Among the signatories, only Clarke and MacDermott (the IRB hard-men) were not implicated in the magazine. The Kiberdian case is unanswerable, but also unremarkable. The original founder, David Houston (died 1932, in Bracknell), was so outraged by the German sinking of *S.S. Lusitania* (May 1915) that he decided to enlist either in the British Army or the local Veterans' Defence Corps.[51] He was not on the scene in 1916, though he had cultivated the Celtic tiger-cubs. Bourgeois made plain his attitude as a Frenchman to the Easter events; they constituted treason against the Allies, amounted to a 'coup de poignard' (or, we might say, stab in the back).[52] Major Malye can be assumed to concur. The legacy of *The Irish Review* was not more unanimous than the response of political contemporaries.

In London, its original model naturally responded to the Easter Rising with horror. Major Stuart-Stephens contributed three articles in successive numbers of *The English Review* claiming that, in 1909 and with W.T. Stead, he had met a deputation of three Sinn Féiners, and further claiming (in 1916) to have warned the British authorities of all that would unfold.[53] Mid-war the London journal continued to publish a good deal of French material, some of it literary, some of it 'morale-boosting'. In the present context, a significant though infrequent contributor was Christopher Dawson.[54]

## Chapter 5

# Joe Hone Introduces Georges Sorel to Dublin, March 1916

*In Ireland the Counter-Reformation was
established before the Reformation had made any
real headway.*
        John J. Silke, citing R. Dudley Edwards (1935)

T he specialist disciplines which the academic profession gave
rise to unquestionably contributed to a more exact
understanding of their areas of concentration — economic
history, history of ideas (including literary history) and so on.
However, there was a concomitant isolation of each area or
discipline from others with which it might have had greater
interaction. To take a local example, *Irish Economic and Social
History* (founded 1974) has published many valuable contributions
to the study of economic and commercial factors in human history,
while remaining comparatively incurious about the range of
materials — cultural, religious or pedagogic, to take three examples
— which might be expected to feature under the heading of social
history. More fundamentally, by NOT being *An Irish Journal of
Economic and Social History*, what we got reinforced a
presupposition of national focus. There were few articles on topics
such as French demography, steel production in Germany, Spanish
agriculture — to look no further than western Europe. In fairness,
one should add that a comparative perspective was constantly latent.

Providence, more historian than historical actor in any vigorous sense, has provided an ironic coda to this strict arrangement by allowing for occasional instances of discontinuous influence. If one says that the great German school of Celtic Studies, founded under romantic auspices in the eighteenth century, 'led' Moritz Julius Bonn (1873–1965) to investigate the economic history of Ireland, with specific reference to English colonialism and to the place of agriculture in that nexus, the appearance of a pathetic fallacy (in the verb 'to lead') should not blind one to the intellectual and practical engagements which developed between the German economist and leading figures of 'the Celtic Revival' — Constance Gore-Booth, Augusta Gregory, Horace Plunkett, T.W. Rolleston, G.W. Russell (AE), and W.B. Yeats.[1] When war broke out in 1914, the novelist George Moore (1852–1933), an acerbic foe of British jingoism during the Boer conflicts, expressed his revised position through unjustified criticism of the Celticist Kuno Meyer (1859–1919), founder of the Dublin School of Learning. Elements of the French press alleged the complicity of German scholars in 'Boche Barbarism'.[2] Roger Casement's decision to seek arms in Germany for his fellow rebels should be read in a similar light, a task of interpretation to which Bernard Shaw (who was no nationalist) was better suited than Arthur Conan Doyle, despite the latter's Catholic Irish ancestry.

Although familiar accounts of the events in Dublin during Easter Week 1916 allude to a meagre German military contribution (old guns, not young soldiers), and a much greater provision of cash and morale by Irish Americans, little had been written about an ideological debt owed to foreign influences or — to dilute the phrase for a moment — external affinities. Explanation of this near silence can be found in the official creed of the Irish Republican Brotherhood, with its repeated invocation of a long native tradition, traced with some confidence back to the 1790s (and, more vaguely, to the seventeenth century), culminating in the Rising led by Connolly, Pearse, Plunkett, and other signatories to the Proclamation. The commemorative endeavours of 1966 were naïve when not opportunistic, always excepting the rigorous historiographical work of F.X. Martin whose preferred specialised field was mediaeval. Fr Martin, of course, was not alone though he was generally ahead. In *On the Easter Proclamation and Other Declarations* (1997), Liam de Paor brought his knowledge of American constitutional history to bear on a text too often regarded as beyond compare, but the more significant portion of his book analysed the patchwork multiple authorship of modern republicanism's founding charter.

Another exception to the general pattern was provided in 1994 by Sean Farrell Moran in *Patrick Pearse and the Politics of Redemption*, which advanced a blunt Freudian analysis of Pearse's domestic background more boldly than it pointed to continental right-wing analogies in the political field. Few if any have trodden the same path, while the lively mechanism of self-vindication in republican argument has preferred to drive Casement under scrutiny in a context liberally or blurredly stretched from the Congo to the Amazon basin.[3] A sexual dimension, in Pearse's case and Casement's, can be left aside here and now, while the contemporary European radical right is admitted to clearer view. It had never been completely excluded, even while its position on the left-right spectrum was obscured. Strangely — but then history might be defined in terms of its intimate strangeness — it took Margaret Thatcher to convince inmates of the British Isles that the term 'radical' was no exclusive property of the Left.

———

Events in Europe were reported in Irish newspapers as a matter of course but usually with an underlying concern for the interests of the United Kingdom or (when a difference arose) for those of the Catholic Church. *The Irish Times* paid less attention to the

latter than the *Independent*. In October 1910 a revolution in
Portugal drove the king into exile, and major industrial unrest in
France brought the mobilisation of troops to avoid a general
strike. *The Irish Times* had an editorial line to meet the demand.
It approved Premier Aristide Briand's use of the word 'revolution'
to indicate what might result, detailed the breakdown of rail
services, and proceeded to a broader analysis. 'The present
conflict is not, like all its predecessors in France, an attempt to
change the Government of the State, but one to sweep away the
State itself.' The magnitude of this threat was rendered all the
greater because 'the ideals of the organisers are almost unknown
in this country.' Yet it was clear to the writer that something other
than Socialism was at work:

> The Syndicalists, as they are called, will have nothing to do
> with the Socialist ideal of the State or collective ownership. To
> them the State is the great enemy, and anarchy is their object
> rather than democracy. The French Syndicalist philosophy
> seems to mark the ultimate stage of social degeneration of
> which Socialism is an earlier symptom. It represents the entire
> dissolution of the elaborate system of mutual independence
> which we call civilisation … etc etc.[4]

Much of this was designed for consumption by holders of
international stock, residents of outer Rathmines, pillars of the
establishment all. It detected (but did not pursue) a
philosophical, as distinct simply from a tactical, motive behind
the French condition. Nowhere does the press seek out the
origins of articulate syndicalism, its proponents or authors.

In February 1912 a coal-miners' strike commenced in
Derbyshire and became more widespread the next month. Union
leaders urged troops to mutiny rather than open fire on strikers.
On 30 April Arthur Balfour presided at a meeting of the
Sociological Society in London when Graham Wallis read a paper

on syndicalism. The main speaker dealt with 'the control of industry', but Balfour was keen to establish that the Syndicalists (by implication, he referred to France) had found 'a new philosopher' in Henri Bergson. *The Irish Times* duly reported the views of a former Chief Secretary.[5] When a massive industrial strike broke out in Dublin a year and a half later, syndicalism was occasionally referred to, though without any reference to Bergson or Georges Sorel. Transport was a focal point in the struggle between employers and unions because, in Ireland as in France, all industrial production relied on a network of roads, railways and shipping companies. R.S. Tresilian, secretary of the Dublin United Tramways Company, insisted that his company had no issue with trade unions as such and dealt with them in the ordinary course of bargaining. '[We] do object to have any dealings with an Association which is worked on syndical principles.'[6] It was left to a magazine primarily concerned with literature and the arts to explore Bergson's thinking and its possible relevance to Irish conditions. As for Sorel, the founding proponent of syndicalism, his Irish debut awaited its impresario.

Though *The Irish Review* was striking in its attention to French culture, and receptive to French contributors, it was by no means alone in Ireland on that account. As we have seen, the religious journals kept in touch with developments among the faithful in Europe and, beyond the ranks of the churches, there were individuals alert to contemporary ideological and literary shifts of taste and direction. Nowadays it is usual to staff this consciousness by naming poets, novelists and painters notably (in rough chronological order) Sarah Purser, Patrick Sheehan, George Moore, Oscar Wilde, W.B. Yeats (a near-monoglot), J.M. Synge, James Joyce, Evie Hone and so forth. Sheehan, exceptional in many regards (he was a Catholic priest long interested in German romanticism), earns special attention for 'The Monks of Trabolgan; a Story of the Future' (1905) which features a German naval landing in Cork Harbour.[7]

There were other avenues to Paris and Berlin, through journalism and politics, and through scholarship including Celtic Studies. Nor was the traffic one-way. The morning after Saint Patrick's Day 1916, *The Irish Times* printed a routine 'Publications Received' column, listing twelve items under various headings. Given events unfolding in Europe, even relatively neutral categories reflected preoccupations with the War and the United Kingdom's role in it. Fiction, for example, included *Notes from Blighty*, by Dorothy de Vere. Censorship was coming into force everywhere, partly administered from London by George Mair, enigmatic husband of Molly Allgood, the late J.M. Synge's intended. Under 'Political and Economic', the columnist mentioned a work on *British Income and Property* (by J.C. Stamp), and *Reflections on Violence*, by Georges Sorel, translated with an introduction and bibliography by T.E. Hulme, and published earlier in March.[8]

The inclusion of Sorel's explosive hymn to the transcendent value of revolutionary violence might be regarded as an oversight by the paper's editors, even if it was not among 'Books Relating to the War'. Originally published in 1907, *Reflections* had been translated by a tough-minded English minor poet, and issued by the respectable London house of Allen & Unwin. Its author, born in 1847, had resigned as an engineer in the French state's employment to become a man of political letters, a mercurial ideologist, and a prophet of syndicalist revolution. To some he was the prodigal heir to Marxism, by him renewed in its moral vigour and purged of 'scientist' accretions; for others, he would become a proto-fascist, an irrational champion of myth (newly defined) as the engine of all genuine change.

More unexpected than the mere listing of Hulme's translation was the anonymous review of it appearing on 1 April in the same newspaper. The writer — I will suggest Joseph Maunsell Hone (1882–1959) — opens predictably enough by observing that 'there can be no doubt of the timeliness of the appearance of the clear translation by Mr Hulme of M. Sorel's "Reflections on Violence".' Indeed, he ignores the book's original appearance seven years before the Great War began, preferring to treat at length the courage of an (unnamed) soldier recently awarded the Victoria Cross. 'To the reviewer this is one of the strangest phases of the war, and it is one that M. Sorel does not face.'

It is hardly surprising that the War should loom large in any treatment of violence in 1916, but *The Irish Times* review is noteworthy for its attention to German claims on a *Kultur* deeper than that of the Allied powers. 'The Germans and the Hungarians hold that they possess a civilisation superior to that of the nations by which they are surrounded.' No reference to Belgium or France, and scant acknowledgement of Britain — apart from a dismissive allusion to Mill's *Principles of Political Economy* (1848). 'There we found the English philosopher contemplating a state of society which was stationary, in which there should be no great changes. To M. Sorel such a stationary state of society is at the antipodes of his thought. Violence will prevent stagnation, and will render the progress of mankind capable of wonderful expansion.'

It would be risky to attribute the review to Hone simply because he had studied Franco-German relations from a perspective not unkind to the German position, or because he would manifest a considerable anti-English animus in the years to come.[9] Reference to Sorel in Hone's Introduction to *The German Doctrine of Conquest* (1914) by Ernest Seillière (1866–1955) does little more than enlarge the possibility.[10] So the question of authorship may continue open for the moment. Whoever wrote up the *Reflections*, noting its non-reference to the Great War, may have made that observation on the basis of contact with Hulme.[11] At the end of March Sorel wrote to a colleague, noting that the English edition had appeared and reporting that he had been asked by the translator 'to add a letter on the war. [He] did not dare write it, not knowing at all the true state of opinion in England ...'[12] The reviewer could be thought to reflect this private refusal by Sorel.

Before returning to consider the general significance of Sorel's name emerging in *The Irish Times* of spring 1916, we might consider one further detail suggestive of Hone's involvement. In 1911 Daniel Halévy's biography of Friedrich Nietzsche had appeared in an English translation by Hone and with an introduction by Tom Kettle, MP for East Tyrone. Of Zarathustra Kettle wrote that he 'is a counter-poison to sentimentalism, that worst ailment of our day.'[13] Mr Duffy, of 'A Painful Case' (completed 1906) is a suburban-domestic Zarathustra powerful, not in heroic self-denial, but 'in denial'. The years immediately following would see large quantities of public counter-poison at work — in 1913 (Dublin), 1914 (all over Europe), 1916 (Dublin again). The book was published by the London house T. Fisher Unwin, which (having become George Allen & Unwin) issued Sorel's *Reflections* in March 1916. Beyond sharing a publisher, there is Halévy's central role in the initial publication of Sorel's work, acknowledged in the first book-version by a long letter from Sorel to Halévy which serves as a preface in all subsequent editions.

There is another substantial issue to be addressed immediately — the absence from the review of any reference to Marxism. This might be partly explained in terms of respectful or self-imposed wartime censorship, but it might also provide a clue to the subterranean influence of Sorel's *Reflections* in the months (perhaps longer) leading up to the Easter Rising. Sorelian doctrine held that revolutionary action should take the form of a spontaneous general strike by workers' associations (*syndicats*) inspired by fervent myth. (The question of success or failure was deemed bourgeois.) Behind this scenario lay the rejection of historical determinism, any belief in progress, future happiness, or the inevitability of change. Society (and indeed Marxism itself) was degenerate, with deep pessimism the only heroic outlook to be adopted. The general strike would come spontaneously from the anger of workers bound, either in a single union (as with American syndicalism), or in a combination of general unions (like the Irish Transport and General Workers' Union), not from craft unions or parliamentary lobbies. What was locally termed Larkinism was also seen as an Irish manifestation of the wider syndicalist cause.[14] But by 1916 Jim Larkin was in America, his place in Dublin taken by James Connolly. The recurrent term used in Sorel's 'Letter to Halévy' is *deliverance.*[15] And in the text proper, Sorel draws extensively on Nietzsche.[16] Eliot in 1916 noted the fundamentally religious character of Sorel's politics.

Nothing could be further from the dialectics of classic Marxism. Deliverance requires an abject, fatal or parlous condition from which one may be delivered only by a superior intervention. (Consider the Israelites in Pharaonic Egypt, or Daniel in the Lions' Club.) Sorel's recourse to the history of primitive Christianity, to the thought of Pascal and Calvin, even to quotation from John Henry Newman, is no cynical injection of popular opium. The general strike will be an eschatological event, hardly a social one. Nevertheless, Sorel maintains a steady chain of references to nineteenth-century socialism. The reviewer, by contrast, utterly avoids deliverance, Jesus, Jaurès and Marx. Writing for an Irish paper, he signally ignores Sorel's extended reference to C.S. Parnell, which arose from views expressed in 1905 by Charles Bonnier, a French socialist. Sorel, it might seem, assumed Parnell's responsibility for the Phoenix Park murders, declaring that 'a few acts of violence, controlled by a parliamentary group, were very useful to Parnellian policy.'[17] Hone also remains silent about the one Irish 'agitator' whose syndicalist activities in 1912 and 1913 had been noted by French newspapers, the unmistakably left-wing Jim Larkin.[18]

However, the *Irish Independent* is not to be neglected in this birds'-eye view of press coverage of syndicalism, even if its proprietor was Larkin's Public Enemy Number One. At the height of the 1913 Lockout, William Martin Murphy's paper published a letter (signed 'H') under the headings SYNDICALISTS' TACTICS: How the Worker is Duped. The text is worth considering in its entirety, with some footnotes added:

> Sir — According to the Address of the President of the International Syndicalist Congress, as reported in yours of yesterday, the principle of Syndicalism is (inter alia) concerned "not only with the idea of extracting benefits, but ultimately doing away with capitalism entirely."[19] Now, on the authority of Sorel, the great apostle of Syndicalism, and the leading man of the movement, Syndicalists are not at all really concerned with "extracting" any immediate benefit for the workers. Their principal weapon, the general strike, is merely intended as a "blind," or, as Sorel has it, "a myth, intended to fire the imagination of the worker and bring about solidarity."[20]
>
> The idea is to first engineer the general strike (led up to by the "sympathetic strike"), and then prolong it until the workers, driven to desperation by starvation, break out in rioting, and then, say the Syndicalists, their (the workers') revolutionary zeal being fired, they will be easily led on to attack the whole fabric of society.
>
> TO PLAY THE FOOL[21]
>
> Of course, the workers are not told that they are being asked to play the fool. You don't find much revolutionary zeal amongst men who know they are fighting for "a myth".[22] The workers are led into the fight entirely ignorant of the fact that their objective has no place in the Syndicalist programme.[23] Social anarchy is the goal at which Syndicalism aims, and Socialism has fashioned the weapons that are being used.
>
> Under the thinly veiled pretence of remedying the evils of the present industrial system, Syndicalism is organising its forces for the revolutionary outbreak which, starting under another name, it hopes to bring about, and Socialists, who

pretend to condemn its methods (not its policy, mind you) are aiding and abetting it. The main function of both Socialist and Syndicalist demagogues is to stir up the feelings and passions of the workers, and then use them for their own ends.

Study the strikes of the past few years, and they show the workers not so much as antagonists of capital as enemies of society at large.

Such is the doctrine which is now being openly preached and practised in our city.

H.

Dublin, October 1st, 1913

One should be wary of assuming that the letter published in the *Irish Independent* of 2 October 1913 was written by the same hand who contributed a notice of *Reflections on Violence* to a different Dublin paper thirty months later. Nevertheless, H displays a familiarity with Sorel before the *Reflections* were translated which must have been rare enough in 'our city'. Indeed, his allusions to Sorel's letter to Halévy might be thought evidence of a familiarity with the latter also, in which case Joe Hone's translation of work by Halévy becomes relevant to any attempt at identifying H. The background to H's contribution is, significantly, the widely international gathering of syndicalist organisations in London, involving Britain, Europe, and several parts of America north and south, then in session. The immediate engagement of the Irish Transport and General Workers' Union (deemed or branded syndicalist by many) in a major struggle with employers was noted at the Congress. H's letter, with its localist final emphasis on 'our city', is a thrust against internationalist politics or agitation. This is entirely consistent with the *Irish Independent*'s line: on 29 September 1913 an unsigned article had characterised Dublin workers as 'the unwitting tools of the "internationals".'[24] In November the *Catholic Bulletin* offered its own irresistible choice, between Gaeldom and socialism.[25] In seeking to cut off Irish workers from the support of their fellows across the globe, the employers' newspaper had a manifest class interest. In offering 'Gaeldom' as an alternative to class-politics, the new voice of zealous Catholicism also sought to protect its own values, traditions, and investments against radical change, even though the Church had contributed to the decline of Gaelic as a vernacular language in the nineteenth century. All in all, 'identity' offered the most attractive bulwark against the inroads of modernity, democracy, and imminent secularism. It was not an entirely new strategy; back in the sixteenth century the absorption of what historians call 'the Old English' into an amalgam-Irishry served to hold a line (not a strong one) against the Reformation. Ernest Renan, a shrewd observer of the Celtic world, observed that it was the unceasing vigilance of the Irish for the fame of Duns Scotus (1265?–1308?) that made him an honorary Irishman, an enterprise conducted amid highly conflictual Renaissance debates about religious belief and the history of philosophy.[26] Scale things down, and the same process can be observed in the making of Padraic Mac Piarais, Cathal Brugha, and Eamon de Valera.

By January 1914 the *Irish Independent* could report a poor attendance at a pro-syndicalist meeting in Dublin's Antient Concert Rooms. Loiterers at the door were admitted free, and 'two Indian students wearing turbans, Mr Sheehy Skeffington and Mr G.E. [sic] Russell were prominent in the reserved seats.' Hanna Sheehy Skeffington distributed suffragette literature outside.[27] People went to political meetings for reasons ancillary to whole-hearted support of the organisers and their stars. Some went with a critical interest, others with the intention of advertising different opinions. The paper's teaching of late 1912 — that syndicalism was anti-patriotic — was perhaps bearing fruit.[28] In a materialist-inclined analysis of the period between 1912 and 1916, the outbreak of war did more to fracture international solidarity among workers than any newspaper or political lobby could have hoped for. The war had its causes too.

# Chapter 6

# Sorelian Myth, and 'Suffrage of the Dead' (Barrès)

*We could be failures. Terrible favour, terrible grace.*

Charles Péguy

At the level of press coverage, Sorel's vicarious arrival in time for the Easter Rising was not a unique contribution by the French Right. *The Irish Monthly* of April 1916 carried a lengthy article about the political career of novelist Maurice Barrès, drawing together his talents as populist and his devotion to the renewed cult of Jeanne d'Arc. When Barrès opposed the rehabilitation of Alfred Dreyfus (on grounds including crude anti-Semitism) he was 'Deputy for Les Halles, a crowded and by no means aristocratic arrondissement of Paris where he got the votes of seven thousand citizens, the greater number of whom had never read his books nor even heard of them.' The novelist, we might interject, had followed Boulanger in his youth (as did Lucien Millevoye, Maud Gonne's lover, the father of Iseult Gonne); the ability to attract popular support is no guarantee of a democratic politics.[1]

But the *Monthly*'s correspondent had issues more urgent and more historically charged. Pearde Beaufort's article concludes with a rhetorical flourish:

Unconquered and hopeful Maurice Barres keeps the national spirit alive. Blessed Joan left the mystic woods of Domremy to lead the armies of France to victory. Maurice Barrès also chose the active life because France called him. His own words tell us why. 'Our fathers failed once, our honour demands that we accomplish the task, we must consecrate our lives to winning back the exiles. Let us give our blood and some greatness of soul to the cause.'[2]

This passage carefully mixes verifiable fact and ideological desire in its effort to bring the past into the active present. Joan had indeed been beatified before the opening of the Great War, and so was rightly called Blessed. The invitation to transfer Joan's legendary qualities on to a contemporary leader has its Irish analogue in Pearse's cult of Cuchulain, another hero who rescues his people (of Ulster, ironically) at time of dire crisis and general stupefaction. Barrès' emphasis on the failure of 'our fathers' also has its echo in Pearse's obsession with redeeming the Irish past from the sin of (anti)revolutionary torpor. Barrès' exiles have never moved, but they are captive in Alsace-Lorraine; Pearse's 'exiled children in America' confirm in their description the anxiety of generation already noted. But there are limits to the analogy. The Pope who beatified Joan had also condemned L'Action Francaise, of which Barrès and Sorel had been occasional confederates. When Pearse and his followers gave (or took) blood, absolution was on tap.

It is perhaps time to revisit Joe Hone's possible authorship of the review. Throughout a long introduction to Seillière's *German Doctrine*, Hone had sprinkled continental names like paprika on savoury dumplings — Gobineau, Pierre Lasserre, Mario Morasso, Albert Sorel, Tolstoy and other incompatibles. For Georges Sorel he went further, listing him among 'social mystics' and explicating the central doctrine of the *Reflections*: 'when Sorel asks the working class to go to battle for the *myth* [original emphasis] of the general strike, a mental construction, he means that mystical experience has the virtue of a tonic ...' The original words had been written before the guns of August proved, at least for *Irish Times* readers, the reality of Hun aggression. A candidate for identification as Sorel's reviewer in April 1916, Hone had studied the *Reflections* two years earlier before any translation was available, and had related its central theme to German 'doctrine'.

What does the review say about the Ireland in which it appeared, on the eve of a small-scale but transformative outbreak of violence? After all Maunsel and Co. had published Connolly's *Labour and Irish History* in 1910, and would issue Sean O'Casey's critical *Story of the Irish Citizen Army* in 1919. (Between these two classics of the Left, the company also published Pádraic Ó Conaire's fictional response to Easter 1916, *Seacht mBuaidh an Éirghe-amach.*) Is it legitimate to regard Hone's silence on the Marxist background to Sorel as evidence of the manner in which the *Reflections* were already affecting Irish ideological re-alignments? His introduction to Emile Montégut's little book (1915) on John Mitchel fits neatly between work on Seillière and Sorel.[3] Independent of Hone, Bergson had been mentioned more than once in earlier despatches, nor was the least significant of them Bourgeois' citation in *The Irish Review* of 1911, quickly followed by the longing for a 'great thinker' to solve the Irish problem through Bergsonian philosophy.[4]

While the events of Easter Week have been often chronicled in detail, the months preceding the Insurrection remain unclear in many important regards. A distinctive feature would prove to be the alliance of Eoin MacNeill's Volunteers with Connolly's Citizen Army. It is well known that Connolly was abducted by IRB plotters in January 1916, as part of their secret undermining of MacNeill's authority: one interpretation suggests that the inner circle feared Connolly would precipitate violent conflict with the State before plans for German support could be perfected. (De

Paor refers modestly to Connolly's 'syndicalist tendencies'.[5]) An escalation of deaths among enlisted working-class Dubliners might have projected the Citizen Army, rather than the IRB, to leadership of the proletariat: after all, the IRB had largely stood aside in 1913.[6] From a different angle, it is also suggested that Connolly intended a hopeless ('spontaneous') proletarian uprising with a view to drawing the cautious but larger middle-class Volunteer body into supportive action. Either way, Sorelian doctrine or something like it was abroad, even though the result could never achieve the proportions of an Irish general strike. If Connolly had quasi-Marxist credentials, Pearse was happy to add a myriad mythic references, Christian and Cuchulainoid, republican and Iron Age simultaneously.[7]

As with other IRB arcana, documentation will prove difficult. Indeed one has to accept that a degree of unconscious absorption of contemporary political thought worked even on the highly tradition-conscious IRB. Certainly there was an avenue of intellectual contact between Pearse and France in the shape of *The Irish Review* (1911–1914), eventually owned and edited by Plunkett, one of the IRB abductors who negotiated a rebellion timetable with Connolly. The *Review* even had a Paris address (c/o F Tennant Pain, 18 rue Favart), with a press agency representing *Black and White, The Connoisseur*, etc.

Connolly's syndicalism was more direct or practical, building on his early engagement with labour activity in America, his familiarity with Scottish conditions, and his later efforts in both Belfast and Dublin to advance trade union militancy. The years before 1914 were rife with conflict, strikes and lock-outs. The term 'syndicalism' was introduced to Britain in 1910 by Tom Mann, and by 1912 an Industrial Syndicalist Education League was publishing a paper called *The Syndicalist*. The young Ramsay MacDonald tried to allay fears by insisting that there were two kinds of *syndicat* in France, the larger devoted to 'proper' trade union concerns. Referring to a House of Commons debate of

27 March 1912, he characterised the more alarmist reactions to news of syndicalism as a 'charming revelation of the ordinary Englishman's mind under the influence of a bogey'.[8] He also made the customary link between Sorel and Bergson, referring to Arthur Balfour's article in the *Hibbert Journal*. Arthur Lewis, publishing in the same year, devoted more space to the threat of direct action and 'the general strike'. He was also inclined to take up the religious idiom of the *Reflections*, and offered to improve on it. For him, syndicalism was a form of Messianic politics. However, 'the Christians have spoiled the idea with their false spiritualisings. It is the idea of a man who is destined to come, at the right moment, in order to revenge the wrongs done to the poor by the prosperous wicked. But he will not come until the right moment, when the poor have become ready for him and understand the wrongs and rights of their class. He comes not at first to bring peace but to bring a sword.'[9] Some of this will feature shortly in Pearse's rhetoric.

The sword took centre stage from August 1914, later swathed in less chivalric devices like barbed wire and mustard gas. The Anglo-French *entente cordiale* had no time for insular critiques of continental theory and, to the west, the vast majority of the Volunteers rallied to John Redmond and support for the war. Studies of Irish syndicalism, few in number, have tended to concentrate on the years after 1916 and on the trade unions, without giving thought to the influence of French ideas on the Easter Rising itself.[10]

Hone's review of 1 April, if we accept it as his, demonstrates how Sorel's revolutionary text of 1907 could be presented without any Marxist or even socialist coloration. Some of Connolly's admirers have conceded that his decision to join Pearse and Plunkett marked a similar elision. One review doesn't make a summary argument for spotting external influences behind the GPO. But the enshrined accounts of Easter 1916 deserve to be re-examined in wider contexts than the national.

There is little sense in proposing that Hone followed Connolly's example of January 1916; he displayed little or no interest in working-class conditions or agitation, though he did pseudonymously edit the writings of James Fintan Lalor. His interest in Lalor and John Mitchel was not, at heart, nationalist. Nevertheless, Hone's drift was decidedly to the right, his greatest achievement to interest W.B. Yeats in the philosophical side of Italian fascism. Sorel's notable post-war success also came in Italy where Mussolini and the intellectuals of his movement acknowledged the Frenchman's influence. Robert Michels, Gaetano Mosca and Vilfredo Pareto — though larger minds — were not immune.

S.F. Moran's approach to these questions in 1994 may have been cautious but it was supported by a close reading of the *Reflections on Violence*, indicating that for Sorel the effective myths of revolution are not 'descriptions of things but expressions of a determination to act.'[11] This determination was not directed simply at the complacent-coercive status quo, but was urgently required to overcome the degeneration of bourgeoisie and 'official' socialists alike, a moral terminology inscribed by Sorel in the second chapter of the *Reflections* — 'Violence and the Decadence of the Middle Classes'. Faced with such a comprehensive alliance of foes, the heroic proletariat could not assume victory. Instead, in Moran's words, its driving myth 'serves no ideology that needs expression or apology, it exists as an explanation of will, it brooks no academic differences or analytical equivocations that render it meaningless or impossible, and its essential truth is affirmed when it is suppressed or persecuted.'[12]

This theme founded itself upon theological fundamentals, not upon casual metaphor. 'The curse of primal sin lies upon a people. Personal sin brings doom to their doors; a youth, free from the curse, akin with them through his mother but through his father divine redeems them ...'[13] As a doctrine, it remained peculiar to Pearse, though other future leaders of Easter 1916 used his formulaic notion of a redemptive cadre. In May 1915 MacDonagh prematurely assured a friend in America that 'We have done more for our generation, thank God, than any of the men of of [sic] the other periods did since the old clan times, more than the '98 men or Emmet, or the '48 men or the '67 men.' Elsewhere, the triangular dialogue of cultural politics involving Sorel, T.E. Hulme and T.S. Eliot, put Original Sin at the centre of matters. MacDonagh at that moment was less than enthralled to the Church, remarking in the same letter that 'Muriel [Gifford, his future wife] and I are of the same religion, which is neither Catholic or Protestant nor any other form of dogmatic creed.'[14] Faith in Original Sin features specifically in Hulme's presentation of Sorel to the English-reading public in 1916 though, as Ron Schuchard acutely observes of the British context, the doctrine has been cast free of its moorings in orthodox Christianity.[15] Behind both Sorel and Pearse one detects the enormous shadow of Max Nordau's popular *Degeneration* (1895) and, at a greater distance, lightning from Nietzsche's mandarin dismissal of modern culture.

While Pearse and Connolly worked to consolidate a nativist pedigree for their thought, Hone was more inclined to concentrate on a distinctive *inter*-national traffic in ideas. For example, the French Count Gobineau's racial theories were taken up in Germany, while the German 'doctrine of conquest' (predicted by de Tocqueville) was elaborated by Seillière, a Frenchman. Even Hone's approach to Mitchel was effected by translating an early French essay on that scourge of British imperialism, an essay which emphasised pan-Celtic dimensions in western European culture. Thus French Sorel as an inspiration for Italians was no embarrassment.

Two or three post-insurrection details are worth bringing together. When Yeats travelled to France, ostensibly to notify Maud Gonne MacBride of her husband's execution, he stayed on at the Gonne establishment in Normandy, in turn proposing marriage to Maud and her daughter. Both declined the offer. The mix of sex and violence was heady, analogous perhaps to the confusion of Left and Right each in its radical *déshabille*. Maud had divorced John MacBride on grounds of domestic violence, which is said to have extended into abuse of Iseult; now he was gloriously dead at the feet of British riflemen, his body a platform upon which the English widow was happy to stand, despite the pleadings of her literary suitor. He, in time, would immortalise MacBride as a former 'drunken vainglorious lout', but meantime sought admission to the legalised favours of the lout's either victim.

Iseult managed the situation by introducing Yeats to some contemporary French poets, or rather, to texts that they read together. The three names recalled by Yeats were Paul Claudel (1868–1955), Francis Jammes (1868–1938), and Charles Péguy (1873–1914), and through her father she also had some contact with Barrès' literary salon. As a playwright, Claudel was taken up in semi-professional Dublin theatre groups in the 1920s. Jammes became a long-serving figure on the French literature syllabus approved by the Irish Department of Education. For Intermediate Certificate students, he was well represented by two poems ('La Salle à manger', 'Village à midi'); François Coppée by one ('Un Baiser au Drapeau'); Casimir Delavigne by one ('La Mort de Jean d'Arc'); and Paul Deroulède (by 'Chanson').[16] In the Leaving Certificate anthology, the last poem included was Péguy's 'Sainte Geneviève'. Though these inclusions do not constitute any predominant ideological bias in anthologies of some length, one might note that Deroulède (1846–1914) was active in extreme right-wing politics and famed for his part in suppressing the Paris Commune. His best known work was *Chants du Soldat* (1872) — cf. Peadar Kearney's 'Soldier's Song'.

Of the three, Péguy was the most original writer and the most complex political figure. (*The Irish Times*, with more than its usual myopia, noted in September 1915 that 'no well known English writer comes anywhere near the record of M. Peguy and Dumas in the matter of long sentences.'[17]) A Dreyfusard and an ardent socialist in the 1890s, he returned to the Catholicism of his childhood and developed a highly personal style through which religious themes of grace, martyrdom, and redemption were articulated. *Le Mystère de la charité de Jeanne d'Arc* appeared in January 1910. Péguy combined fervent patriotism, idiosyncratic socialism ('class warfare is bourgeois'), and mystical Catholicism in ways that bothered admirer and hostile critic alike. He died in action before the end of 1914. Barrès and Péguy were not the only seekers after a French soldier-saint in these years. The elusive Major Stuart-Stephens (who was probably Irish) nominated Ferdinand Foch for the distinction though, in doing so, he associated the *maréchal* with Gordon of Khartoum rather than the *pucelle* whom the English had burned.[18]

It would be mistaken to assume that Miss Gonne/Millevoye had suddenly taken up Péguy on Yeats's hot-foot arrival from Dublin (or was it London?) in the summer of 1916. Ever since his death Péguy had been a 'cause' in Catholic France, even a sacred cause, much as Pearse would become one after his execution. An affinity, to say the least, between the underlying beliefs of Pearse and Plunkett (on the one hand) and Jammes and Péguy (on the other) was in place long before the call to arms of Easter 1916.[19] The rhetoric of blood sacrifice Pearse employed in verse and prose is far closer in every respect to Barrès, Péguy and Sorel than it is to Tone, Davis, Mitchel or Parnell. In the words of one historian, 'when we reach the height of the nationalist agitation at the end of the nineteenth century, the French literature of "sacrifice" is as rich and elaborated as perhaps any that could be named.'[20] In Ireland (and arguably, in France too) the New (international) Nationalism continued to thrive in the new century. A neglected counter-text of 1898 was Hubert and Mauss' durkheimian *Sacrifice: its Nature and Function* (see p. 25 above).

Though Yeats's encounter with the work of these French writers in the immediate aftermath of the Rising is generally taken as an exotic excursion into the *recherché*, a literary distraction undertaken at a moment of politico-sexual intensity, his reading matter was well-known in other quarters. In September 1916 the young T.S. Eliot was offering a course of public lectures on French literature which covered the writings of Barrès, Bergson, Claudel, Péguy, Sorel and others. A basic text for the working-men of Ilkley in Yorkshire (a staunchly non-conformist town), where the lectures were delivered, was *Reflections on Violence* in the translation by Hulme reviewed by Hone.[21] T. Stearns Eliot, as he then signed himself, was no incendiary; his interpretation of all this material was directed towards a commendation of royalist and authoritarian values in politics and culture. Catholicism was the spiritual goal, even if Eliot personally took years in reaching the Anglo-Catholic intermediary position. The Fenians' return to the fold was not a purely local phenomenon; it had exhilarating French precedents in the re-converts Bourget and Péguy, not to mention the mass appeal launched by the Catholic Church after the anti-clerical regimes; it was contemporary with a small but culturally significant British declaration in favour of (if not strictly for) Rome, authority and social hierarchy.

Shakespeare's Falstaff knew that discretion is the better part of valour, and modern commercial enterprises like M.H. Gill & Son have learned the lesson well. If *The Catholic Bulletin* promptly set about redeeming the Fenians with a sustained campaign of tribute and commemoration, the publisher's older journal, *The Irish Monthly*, largely ignored the Rising, perhaps with a view to holding its sales in those respectable households which backed Redmond. Though its tone was parochial and complacent, the *Monthly* was alert to events in the wider world, both intellectual and active. The May/June issue of the *Bulletin* opened with defiantly blank pages; its sister gave prominence to the work of an unnamed French priest, then recovering from wounds suffered on the field of battle.

Published in two instalments, 'What Makes a Fatherland?' addressed fundamental issues which concerned Tom Clarke and the older Fenians of 1916, but the *padre* adopted a more reflective position. Much French authority, and some German, was brought to bear on the question, including Barrès, Maurice Blondel (1861–1949), Numa-Denis Fustel de Coulanges (1830–1889), Gustave Le Bon (1841–1931) and Hone's favourite Emile Montégut (1825–1895). Barrès, as we have seen, had some links with Ireland through de Basterot and Duras House, reinforced through Maud Gonne's presence in Paris. Montégut had published a lengthy and early essay on Mitchel in the *Revue de Deux Mondes* (June 1855), which Maunsel and Co. re-published in English translation. The list of names predominantly represented a generation of French thinkers earlier than that of Barrès and Sorel, though Blondel (a neo-Catholic philosopher, author of a thesis on *L'Action: Essai d'une critique de la vie et d'une science de la practique*, 1893) has been hailed a theologian influencing the Second Vatican Council.[22]

Barrès arguably got closer to the Irish insurrectionists' outlook, albeit as a propagandist for the Allied cause. The early months of 1916 saw him much quoted in the Dublin press. A contributor signing himself H.R.B. provided *The Irish Times* with a translation of the novelist's recent contribution to the *Echo de Paris*, 'Once More the Suffrage of the Dead'. Much of the article was designed to compensate the widows and orphans of France for the loss of their menfolk-in-arms and to strengthen their resolve at a low moment in the nation's struggle. Barrès' central device was, however, political in a far more essential regard: quite literally, he proposed to enfranchise fallen soldiers, to give them the vote:

The dead must live on, his thought must not stop acting in this homeland which he has saved. I ask that the hero, fallen for France, shall be saved from the abyss by our grateful wish. He will not pass away, he will live in the civic register of his commune; he will speak in the great councils of the nation ... It is the suffrage of the dead.[23]

If Yeats noticed this extensive article, he may have remarked Barrès' rather vulgar appropriation of some ideas voiced by Edmund Burke more than a century earlier: 'The Heart of the Sublime', one sub-heading declared. On the other hand, Yeats may have worried over the uses of necromancy and the occult for military ends. 'The widow will vote for [i.e. on behalf of] her husband; the mother, if he was not married, for her son.' Perhaps H.R.B. had not polished his translation, but the fundamentals of Academician Barrès' revision of the franchise clearly empowered the dead, and hence 'the dead generations' (a phrase proclaimed a month later), even if this was to diminish the role of survivors, the rights of the living. And the assumption was that the spectral deputy in council somehow conveyed his political ideas to the general electorate. This was not Barrès' only contribution to the battle of words in Ireland. To counterbalance an acute concern with the French psyche, another article provided details of 'How Our Enemies Eat' — France is spiritual; Germany carnal, a nation of appetites.[24]

Irish history was well known to the German economic historian Moritz Bonn, who published *Irland und die irsche Frage* in 1918 as a thoughtful response to Easter 1916. Though his major study of Irish economics reached back to the earliest period of English (or, rather, Norman) colonisation, Bonn had also taken note of nineteenth-century developments, commencing with Fintan Lalor and culminating in the various Land Acts. Thus, in 1906 he observed that 'the fight for agrarian reform was coloured by aims going far beyond that object. Land reform was demanded not in order to obtain it but to get possession of an inexhaustible material for agitation against English government ... Agrarian reform for a large number of Irish politicians is not the ultimate aim; it is rather a means of keeping alive the claims of national independence.'[25]

Bonn, a cheery pessimist, was articulating in 1906 a suspicion about the relation between social objectives and 'larger' national issues consistent with the immediately contemporary Sorelian theory of political myth. According to the latter, the nation trumps class or economics or other factors in stimulating mass action. After the Easter Rising he returned to Irish affairs, concluding with a chapter which discussed Parnell, Douglas Hyde, and Padraic Colum; quoted Pearse's 'On the Fall of the Gael', and carefully noted Casement's landing in Kerry and his German support. Analysing the disparate activists of 1916, he lists three distinct groups — Republicans, Syndicalists, and Writers.[26] While a translator might worry about the possible substitution of 'trade unionists' for *Syndikaler*, Bonn's ungrateful protégé Carl Schmitt will shortly take up the topic, expressly linking Pearse and Connolly to Sorelian myth-as-motivator (see Chapter 7 below).

From a more discrete corner of the conservative worldview, A.J. Balfour had also detected a foreign influence at play. In May he wrote to Archbishop Bernard of Dublin: 'mixed up with the forces of disorder which indulge in purely Separatist ideas, there is a good deal of Syndicalism at work among the Dublin mob.'[27] Of course, it was quickly plain that nothing close to Sorel's 'absolute revolution' had been attempted, let alone achieved.[28] So quickly after 1913, a general strike was impossible, and Connolly had never sought to bring one about in 1916. Yet there was a Sorelian benefit: the official socialist doctrine that 'the ballot-box has replaced the gun' had been annulled in practice.[29]

We live, or die, under that annulment.

# Chapter 7
# Sovereignty and German Decisionism: Carl Schmitt and Friends in 1923

*Il y la deux salauds parmi nous, dit Mac Cormack.*

Raymond Queneau

In the two decades or so before the Great War, the international traffic in ideas was rapid and intense. Nietzsche's influence in 'Anglosaxony' came through France and reached Irish writers principally through London. Synge unquestionably had noted the *Übermensch* in Paris, while Shaw's encounter involved his great urge to interpret Wagner in somewhat Marxist terms. Meanwhile, at home, Nietzsche was being systematically distorted, most disgracefully by his own sister (who forged documents), but also by xenophobes and anti-Semites. *The Wagner Case: a Musician's Problem* (1888) deserves particular attention because Nietzsche therein scathingly dismisses German attitudes towards nationalism and race including German anti-Semitism. He is equally contemptuous of 'equal rights for all' in the democratic sense.

The Nietzschean cult is perverse, but that is in great part the fault of Elizabeth Förster-Nietzsche, at least until the Nazis take over. Nietzsche's influence on the jurist Carl Schmitt (1888–1985) is problematic, but can be brought into focus by concentration on the philosophical implications of technology, a topic not much aired in Anglosaxony (including Ireland).[1] Nevertheless, the primitivist-pastoral strand of Irish cultural thinking, in Yeats and later in Pearse, accords with the anti-technological animus.

An incident of early 1903 in a Parisian café will serve by way of prelude. An Irish medical student, just turned 21, is in heated debate amid a cosmopolitan group of young men. They begin a discussion in French about literature; they have recourse to Latin. One of the group is named Villona, who may have been Hungarian. Another is Theodor Däubler (1876–1934), a German or Austrian poet born in Trieste, and so on. Däubler takes offence at some remark of the Irishman, and threatens a duel. The Irishman responds the following year with Villona's name appearing in a short story, 'After the Race'. Däubler takes comfort in becoming the subject of Carl Schmitt's first publication (in 1916).[2] Later, Theodor Adorno sets three poems by Däubler to music (opus 8). Joyce, for it is he, spends Saint Patrick's Day in the company of an old Fenian. His generally preferred companion in Paris during these weeks is J.M. Synge. He remains sufficiently interested in Däubler to ask Philipp Jarnach in 1919 to lend him work by the mystical Triestan.[3]

The incident is memorable only in a Joycean context, yet it opens up highly diverse intellectual potentialities available to the generation of Frank Skeffington (born 1878), Pearse (born 1879) and Joyce (1882). In the *Bildungsroman* notably dated 'Dublin 1904 Trieste 1914', Joyce indicates through Stephen's inner monologue his views on the nativist alternative, 'the broken lights of Irish myth'. Davin, a character described as a young Fenian, 'stood towards this myth upon which no individual mind had ever drawn out a line of beauty and to its unwieldy tales that divided themselves as they moved down the cycles in the same attitude as towards the Roman catholic religion, the attitude of a dull-witted loyal serf.' Dedalus, we should insist, did not write *Finnegans Wake*.

These dissentions behind the ideological framework of Easter 1916 are not only international but historically mobile. With France, in the preceding pages, the undertaking was to explore political and cultural innovations in the late nineteenth and early twentieth centuries that prefigured the assumptions made by signatories to the Easter Proclamation. With Germany, the focus has moved forward in time and history, beyond 1916 and beyond the epochal changes of 1917 and 1918. We have to consider the IRB insurrection in a post-revolutionary and post-war context, in which issues of sovereignty featured prominently as new states emerged from the wreckage of empires, Austrian, German, Ottoman and (to a much lesser extent) the British and Russian also.

France and Germany are not hermetically sealed off from each other. Carl Schmitt made curious links between Sorel and the Irish nationalist renewal. These are reflected in two or three texts of 1923 — (i) a brief essay now available through French translation, (ii) the substantial and influential *Crisis of Parliamentary Democracy*, and (iii) the far slighter *Roman Catholicism and Political Form*. Each deserves attention in any assessment of Schmitt's view, or knowledge, of the rebellion of 1916.[4]

Towards the end of *The Crisis*, in a lengthy reflection on Sorel's theory of myth, Schmitt instanced the 'friendship' of Pearse and Connolly in 1916 as a demonstration of nationalism's superior ability to engage support than any Marxian programme. The wording deserves close attention:

> Sorel's other examples of myth also prove that when they occur in the modern period, the stronger myth is national. The revolutionary wars of the French nation and the Spanish and German wars of liberation against Napoleon are symptoms of a national energy. In national feeling, various

elements are at work in the most diverse ways, in very different peoples. The more naturalistic conceptions of race and descent, the apparently more typical *terrisme* of the celtic and romance peoples, the speech, tradition, and consciousness of a shared culture and education, the awareness of belonging to a community with a common fate or destiny, a sensibility of being different from other nations — all of that tends towards a national rather than a class consciousness today. Both can be combined — for example, in the friendship between Patrick Pearse, the martyr of the new Irish national consciousness and the Irish socialist Connolly, who both died victims of the Dublin rising of 1916.[5]

Like Sorel's reference to Parnell in the *Reflections*, this is an isolated show of interest in Irish affairs within *The Crisis of Parliamentary Democracy*, but without any documented source. The question of source will be important. But, first one should consider a parallel reference in another of Schmitt's 1923 writings. Here is the Pearse of *Roman Catholicism and Political Form*:

> It is not easily understandable that a rigorous philosopher of authoritarian dictatorship, like the Spanish diplomat Donoso Cortés, and a 'good Samaritan' of the poor with syndicalist connections, like the Irish rebel Padraic Pearse, were both staunch Catholics.[6]

It would certainly have amazed Connolly to find himself interchangeable with a mid-nineteenth-century absolutist, but Schmitt was ever capable of playing two games at once or, at least, during 1923. In the second text (just quoted) of that year, his objective was to demonstrate — he would insist, prove — the *complexio oppositorum* inherent in the universal church.[7] In the first, the Sorelian priority of myth before social analysis is a more thoroughly political objective, hence a public one. Schmitt's treatment of Pearse had its private dimension, quite apart from descendants of Cortés, the stout conquistador of Mexico.

In *Roman Catholicism and Political Form*, Schmitt also passingly alludes to an Irish Franciscan who had supported workers on strike. He probably had Fr Aloysius OFM in mind, who had concerned himself with the state of the poor in 1913 Dublin, remaining benignly neutral on the issue of trade union militancy. The opening sentences apparently refer back to the summer following the Lockout and the zeal of churchmen across Europe to encourage war:

> How often one sees the picture drawn by bourgeois socialists and anarchist pacifists: High Church dignitaries blessing the guns of all warring parties; or neo-Catholic literati, partly monarchist, partly communist; or finally, to cite another sort of sociological impression, the [French] abbé, favoured by court ladies, side by side with the Irish Franciscan encouraging striking workers to stand firm.[8]

Fr Aloysius plays two parts in the drama, as he heard James Connolly's last confession in May 1916.[9] But Schmitt's larger point was to demonstrate the odd alliances that could arise through the strength of myth or traditional authority. Whereas Sorel drew on an article by Bonnier, any public source for Schmitt's Irish instances of mythic politics remains unclear, though his benign and misguided mentor, Moritz Bonn, had published *Irland und die irische Frage* in 1918, and German newspapers carried some occasional accounts of events in Ireland. By 1923, however, the Easter Rising was itself already history, and the pre-war Lockout old history. The year of these publications was nonetheless difficult in both Ireland and Germany. The Civil War continued to smoulder in rural Ireland, as reported by the ageing parliamentarian John Dillon to his student son abroad; rationing and currency shortages plagued the German towns.

Schmitt's brief display of interest in Irish affairs formed a minor prelude to his sustained engagement with the triangulated problem of constitutionality, parliamentary rule, and dictatorship, during the Weimar period. The definitive statement on these issues came in March 1922, a year before Schmitt's published Irish allusions — 'Sovereign is he who decides on the exception.'[10] The concept of sovereignty is long familiar to political and legal scientists. Less exact usages may distress the professors of these disciplines and yet demonstrate the applied or modified condition of all terms. Thus when Nietzsche, paraphrasing Paul Bourget, complained that the word as such had become sovereign, displacing or downgrading life as a whole, he was pursuing his own professional zeal as a philologist. Schmitt's declaration, while it will be regarded in time as a prelude to fascist dictatorship, also confirms the power of the word (edict, law, proclamation) to change the world by commanding its enforcement.

Though Schmitt's theory of the exception arises from specifically German (or at least continental) conditions, it is not wholly unconnected to claims made in the Easter Proclamation. The occasions where the term 'sovereign' (noun or adjective) occurs in the 1916 text link it to a right, otherwise unchallenged and unexplained, 'We declare the right of the people of Ireland to the ownership of Ireland, and to the unfettered control of Irish destinies, to be sovereign and indefeasible.' In this paragraph, *right* occurs five times, always as precursor or precondition of the declared sovereignty; 'standing on that fundamental right ... we hereby proclaim the Irish Republic as a sovereign independent state ...' Schmitt declared that 'from a practical or a theoretical perspective, it really does not matter whether an abstract scheme advanced to define sovereignty (namely, that sovereignty is the highest power, not a derived power) is acceptable. About an abstract concept there will in general be no argument, least of all in the history of sovereignty. What is argued about is the concrete application, and that means who decides in a situation of conflict what constitutes the public interest or interest of the state, public safety and order, *le salut public*, and so on. The exception, which is not codified in the existing legal order, can at best be characterised as a case of extreme peril, a danger to the existence of the state, or the like.'[11]

Two qualifications are required in associating this pronouncement with the Easter Proclamation. First, it is not the state but the nation which is seen to be in peril according to the latter — 'destruction of the Irish people' — for the Irish state comes into notional existence only with the Proclamation. No other state is mentioned or implied, though there is a 'foreign people and government', and 'an alien government.' Second, and more positively, Schmitt's characterisation of the exception as 'a case of extreme peril' etc. clearly indicates urgency, conditions in which time is the dominant consideration in avoiding what he presents as catastrophe.

German intellectual or academic interest in Ireland owed much to Moritz Bonn. But others were active in the field. In 1927 Leo Kohn completed a Heidelberg PhD, published five years later in English as *The Constitution of the Irish Free State*, just in time for a future constitution maker, Eamon de Valera, to imbibe its contents.[12] Also in 1927 the cussedly independent Irish cultural critic, signing himself usually as 'Pat', chose *The English Review* for a scathing account of 'Democracy in the Free State'. Not content with lambasting the Dublin government, 'Pat' (i.e. Patrick Dermott Kenny, 1862–1944) assailed the Easter architects of that unfinished airless fabric, echoing (no doubt without intention), Carl Schmitt, 'Tiring of "Parliamentarianism", and always incapable of truth, they substituted the still more barren cult of looking backwards to save Ireland by "language and history", but after twenty-five years of expensive pretence they remain profoundly ignorant of both.'[13]

Schmitt is exceptional in that something other than, or additional to, academic concerns were at work. There is one further Irish allusion in his work which, once decoded, points one away from his political and constitutional studies into a more subjective area. 'An Irishman reflecting the embitterment of his Gaelic national consciousness, opined that Ireland was just "a pinch of snuff in the Roman snuffbox".' Unlike Pearse or the unnamed Franciscan, this Irishman turns out to be a fictional character, traceable to a short story by George Moore.[14] Curiously, 'The Wild Goose' mixes the violent death of a chicken, satire on the Irish priesthood, and the activities of French cattle-dealers in rural county Dublin at the end of the nineteenth century, as if picking up on Bourget and making a pre-emptive move against *The Catholic Bulletin*.

According to Reinhard Mehring, Schmitt's latest biographer, the future adviser (*Kronjurist*) to Hitler's regime fell in love with an Irish-Australian, Kathleen Murray (1895–1970?), and wished to marry her. Bonn has recorded his belief that the official Frau Schmitt (Serbian, of 'ferocious' nationalist opinions) had led the cold jurist astray;[15] Murray, it would appear, offered an Irish substitute or booster. Though the implications of their affair in 1921–2 for his comments on Ireland deserve further enquiry, the affair itself complicated Schmitt's relations with the Catholic Church which eventually resulted in excommunication. More intellectually intriguing is the issue of Schmitt's possible debt to the Proclamation of 1916, as relayed to him by Murray or through other sources.

Little notice appears to have been given to the decidedly and unambiguously non-parliamentary arrangements offered by the rebels in the (unlikely) event of their success. After a suitable lapse of time, during which we are to imagine the Irish republicans choosing the most suitable German prince as head of state, elections were to be held, in which men and women would participate on equal terms. However, these elections were intended to establish a government, not a parliament, not (as far as one can tell from the inevitably laconic Proclamation) a representative assembly of any kind. Perhaps the spirit which inscribed universal suffrage in the future arrangements would have devised some place for legitimate opposition, though Schmitt would not have urged any going to great lengths.

The Irish allusions in Schmitt's writings of 1923 are not in keeping with his usual style which eschewed romantic imagery in favour of professional decorum and pedantic irrationality delivered with some literary flair. As specifics they do not outlive the period of his involvement with Murray. She however was not the only Irish person around the city of Bonn. Registered students in philology or Celtic Studies included several people later eminent in their individual fields — Myles Dillon, Oliver Edwards, Kathleen Mulchrone, and John Ryan.[16] Edwards, who was a friend of Yeats in the 1930s, taught German in Magee University College, Derry. His literary interests might have prompted quotation from *The Untilled Field*, but Murray was undoubtedly closer to Schmitt. Ryan is of more than passing interest, though he was leaving Bonn just as Myles Dillon arrived. As an undergraduate he had attended some of Thomas MacDonagh's lectures at UCD. In 1930 he was appointed a lecturer in Early Irish History in the same college, succeeding Eoin MacNeill as professor in 1942.

Murray was no frail vessel passing in the night; in 1938 she proposed to Schmitt that they should marry (his second wife had just died, the first having been divorced) and even after the war the two remained in contact.[17] From these dates, it seems that she stayed in Germany throughout the Reich and beyond, having arrived as a student in happier days. In 1924 she published a short thesis on *Hippolyte Taine und die englische Romantik* as a requirement for her degree, apparently completed in Sydney, and dedicated 'To Professor Dr Carl Schmitt at Bonn am Rhein'.[18] While noting the existence of four significant Irish writers from the period in question — Edmund Burke, Maria Edgeworth, Thomas Moore ('a typical Irishman') and Lady Morgan —

Murray is ultimately focused on 'Die Typen des Englanders und des Bourgeois' in the romantic movement. She published nothing more, at least not at book length. Taine, it might be noted, has been long identified as a major influence on Sorel, releasing him from the 'mythe révolutionaire' of 1789[19] and thus facilitating a locum arrangement of non-historical myth-substitution. In the early 1920s Schmitt was much preoccupied with Sorel, as recently explored in a valuable French casebook.[20] Between Taine's heyday in the 1850s and Sorel's half a century later, concepts such as the former's 'race … milieu … moment' had undergone subtle and brutal changes. Kathleen Murray invokes the Tainian triad, but she and Schmitt would have understood something different than the scientifically inclined Frenchman.[21] Professor Mehring considers Schmitt to have been an undeclared part-author of Murray's book; its publisher, the firm of Duncker & Humblot, was already issuing Schmitt's work and would continue to do so for decades.

Murray's own political outlook was deeply conditioned by her Catholicism which merged into a reverse-genuflective hatred of Britain and all things British. These were not uncommon attitudes though, under the gaze of Schmitt's pitiless theory of the exception and of dictatorship, they left little room for social compromise. Writing explicitly about Sorel's approval of myth as a determination to act, Schmitt could approve Pearse and Connolly's compact as an example of *decisionism*, based on the substitution of national for social ideology. The signatories of the Proclamation, it would follow, were sovereign, despite any fancy invocations of Mother Ireland. Indeed, if Murray (or Bonn) had drawn Schmitt's attention to the Proclamation, it may have contributed a minim to the critique of parliamentarianism on which he was at that moment engaged. Pearse & Co., while promising an eventual election, intended it to produce a government, without an opposition that might have to be brooked. In practice, the signatories would remain sovereign.

Though at times indulgent of *Kulturpessimismus*, Schmitt was impatient with the martyrological dimension to Sorel's theory. Despite this scruple, *The Crisis of Parliamentary Democracy* cast Pearse and Connolly as 'victims [sic] of the Dublin rising.'[22] And despite the absence of any material evidence, one can with some confidence ascribe this inversion of the facts to Murray. Schmitt's translator, Ellen Kennedy, provides a broadly similar indulgence. Annotating the passage in the mid-1980s, she wrote that 'Connolly's death took on an almost mystical importance in Irish politics partly because he was already so badly wounded that British troops had to tie him to a chair for the execution. Connolly's Marxist analysis has had little impact ... Although the metaphors [sic] of their nationalism differed — Pearse's is a mystical Catholic nationalism, Connolly's is Marxism — they are both united by the definition of a mystique of death and national salvation that is still current in Irish politics today.'[23]

## Chapter 8

# Hans Franzen in University College Dublin 1937–1938

*The scene was a wax-work show. A guide was conducting a company of old and young visitors from figure to figure and commenting on them: 'This is the Duke of Wellington and his horse', he explained. Whereupon a young lady asked: 'Which is the Duke of Wellington and which is his horse?' 'Just as you like, my pretty child,' was the reply.*

Sigmund Freud (1905)

C arl Schmitt had no lasting interest in Easter 1916, not even through his involvement with Sorel as French ex-Marxist begetter of Italian Fascism. Schmitt's objective was the triumph of triumph. When that became possible after February 1933, he was happy to serve, notably by justifying Hitler's actions on the Night of the Long Knives as 'the highest form of administrative justice' (*höchste Form administrativer Justiz*). Shortly afterwards he was denounced as an opportunist in an ss journal, his anti-Semitism a mere sham.[1] Effectively neutralised in the Reich, Schmitt retained professional influence and some trace of an Irish perspective remained. In 1938 he advanced the career of Hans Franzen (1911–2007), whose *Habilitation* dealt with aspects of Irish constitutional law, and we may presume an earlier association between the two. Though the local newspapers treated

Franzen as an interesting academic tourist, more lay behind the volkisch blarney. Superficially, Dr Franzen was a German Exchange Student at University College Dublin during the academic year 1937–38 and (it seems) in receipt of Irish funding.[2] According to *The Irish Times* reporter of college news, Franzen was studying 'certain constitutional problems peculiar to this country' [i.e. Ireland] with a view to publication.[3] His status as a former student at the universities of Marburg, Munich and Berlin was noted, together with the doctorate from Bonn. The correspondent declared Franzen to be 'well-known in legal circles in Germany, and, indeed, on the Continent, for a number of published works, the chief of which being his *Gesetz und Richter* (1935)'. Its title more fully stated than the newspaper ventured, the doctoral dissertation treated the rule of law and judgement 'according to the principles of the National Socialist state' [nach den Grundsätzen des nationalsozialistischen Staates].

Something of these principles can be gauged from the Nazi invasion (if you prefer, annexation) of Austria while Franzen was in Dublin. Among those who had to flee was Sigmund Freud: as Jew and psycho-analyst, he was doubly hated — trebly, if one counted his work on anthropological topics. In *Totem and Taboo* (1913) he had drawn on details from the thirteenth-century *Book of Rights* [Lebor na gCeart] to illustrate the minute obligations imposed on kings in Gaelic Ireland.[4] Freud relates these restrictions to the eventual division of priestly kingship into distinct spiritual and temporal realms. By way of illustration, he takes an African case: 'among the natives of Sierra Leone the objection to accepting the honour of kingship became so great that most tribes were obliged to choose foreigners as their kings.'[5]

Freud did not concern himself with the *Fuhrerprinzip* of contemporary Europe. The work on taboo had noted that 'in Australia the regular penalty for sexual intercourse with a person from a forbidden [totem] clan is death.'[6] *Mitteleuropa* was in the process of introducing something along the same lines. In 1938 he was at work on *Moses and Monotheism*, in which he articulated a question almost impossible for fellow Jews, 'what if Moses was Egyptian?' The resulting book excavated patterns of leadership ancient and modern in which a figure of alien or foreign origin achieves charismatic status at the head of 'his' people. By the time Freud was escaping to England (under Roosevelt's protection), and Franzen was snuggling into Earlsfort Terrace, a steadily Gaelicising Irish administration looked to the only child of an elusive Juan Vivion de Valera who may have been born in the Basque Country. Franzen's central text was Dev's constitution by which, for the first time, Irish nationality was formally linked to a specific religious entity (through 'the special position of the Roman Catholic Church') claiming universal authority. The baptism of 1916 now achieved confirmation, having reached the age of twenty-one.

As Schmitt had become (in November 1933) a privy councillor and head of the *Vereinigung nationalsozialistischer Juristen* (Association of N-S Jurists), his role in Franzen's Irish research can be translated from mere examining approval to active support. Indeed *Gesetz und Richter* enunciated the principles upon which Schmitt effectively protected Hitler against any charges arising from the murder of Ernst Rohm and his Brown Shirts.[7] Sometime later, Schmitt experienced a limited fall from grace (or from disgrace) though he was allowed to continue his academic work in Berlin. One wonders to what extent Franzen worked as proxy for his examiner.

While active in the UCD undergraduate German Society, Franzen's principal contribution was a regular Monday morning lecture on 'general cultural topics'. Research for his Habilitation may have brought him to the attention of Fr John Ryan SJ, in the Department of Early Irish History, despite Franzen's dominant engagement with contemporary issues involving the successive constitutions effective in Ireland since 1921. It was a manifestly political enquiry by an undisguised, though locally unrecognised, apologist for the regime.

Franzen's research was published in the *Jahrbuch des Offentlichen Rechts* of 1938, available c. March 1939 — the next issue appeared in the early 1950s. Acting with Schmitt in this procedure was Viktor Bruns (1884–1943), a leading German authority on international law and a member of the *Vereinigung nationalsozialistischer Juristen* but not, it seems, of the Nazi Party. After the War began he published a paper on the position of neutral states (like Ireland) in relation to the belligerent Great Powers, paying attention to Britain's waging of maritime economic war.[8]

Although he was to play a very minor role in German diplomatic assessment of his host country during the War, Franzen in 'Irland und Grossbritannien seit 1919; ein Beitrag zur Verfassungslehre' [Ireland and Britain since 1919; a Contribution to Constitutional Learning] provided a framework of legal considerations, starting with a rapid summary of Irish history from 1171 onwards, and ending with the texts (in English) of the 1921 Treaty, the Statute of Westminster (1931) which so excited Yeats, and de Valera's Constitution of 1937.[9] Any discussion of it here depends more on Franzen's repeated references to Carl Schmitt, five of whose books are quoted or cited, than on its limited importance in the larger potential for Irish republican engagement with Nazi war aims, an engagement which (pathetically, one might say) involved a re-issue of the Easter Proclamation of independence.

To see this acknowledgment in its crude proportions, a list of Franzen's academic or similar book-length authorities is needed — Diarmid Coffey, *Douglas Hyde* (1917); Edmund Curtis, *A History of Ireland* (1937); Wilhelm Dibelius, *England* (1931); A.V. Dicey, *Introduction to the Study of the Law of the Constitution* (1915); Alice Stopford Green, *Irish Nationality* (1914), Arthur Griffith, *The Resurrection of Hungary* (1903); Denis Gwynn,

The Irish Free State 1922–1927 (1928); W.K. Hancock, Survey of British Commonwealth Affairs (1937); Thomas Hare, A Treatise on the Election of Representatives (1859); Henry Harrison, Ireland and the British Empire (1937); Mary Hayden and G.A. Moonan, A Short History of the Irish People (1935); [Hans] Kelsen [no title given]; [A.B.] Keith, The Anglo-Irish Dispute (1934); Keith, The Dominions as Sovereign States (1938); Leo Kohn, The Constitution of the Irish Free State (1932); R.T.E. Latham, The Law and the Commonwealth (1937); Louis N. Le Roux, La Ligue Gaelique, son Origine et sa Mission (1934); Dorothy Macardle, The Irish Republic (1937); Nicholas Mansergh, The Government of Northern Ireland (1937); Mansergh, The Irish Free State: its Government and Politics (1934); Friedrich Müller-Ross, 'Ulster zwischen Irland und Grossbritannien' (1938); Barra Ó Briain, The Irish Constitution (1929); George O'Brien, The Four Green Fields (1936); Nora Connolly O'Brien, Portrait of a Rebel Father (1935); Seán O'Faoláin, King of the Beggars: the Life and Times of Daniel O'Connell (1938), P.S. O'Hegarty, The Victory of Sinn Féin (1924); Alfred O'Rahilly, Thoughts on the Constitution (1937); Frank Pakenham, Peace by Ordeal (1935); G.E.H. Palmer, Consultation and Co-operation in the British Commonwealth (1934); Michael Rynne, Die völkerrechtliche Stellung Irlands (1930); Carl Schmitt, Verfassungslehre (1928); Schmitt, Legalität und Legitimität (1932); Schmitt, Über die drei Arten des rechtswissenschaftlichen Denkens (1934); Schmitt, Staat — Bewegung — Volk (1933); Schmitt, Der Leviathan in der Staatslehre des Thomas Hobbes (1938); Karl Spindler, The Mystery of the Casement Ship (1931); Wade and Phillips, Constitutional Law (1933); K.C. Wheare, The Statute of Westminster and Dominion Status (1938). Here one obtains a practical insight into how the lower echelons of the German legal/academic bureaucracy assessed the question of Ireland's constitutional existence. Specialists will no doubt smile at prominent exclusions.

Franzen does not grant any constitutional importance to the Easter Proclamation, though he concedes a Blutopfer (blood sacrifice) dimension and mentions Pearse on several occasions.[10] De Valera is the eternal recurrence, established as such by his successful introduction of a new constitution the year before Franzen submitted his findings for publication. On the question of authorities, Schmitt outnumbers all other Germans lumped together.[11] The focus, however, is shifting away from the Schmitt/Murray concern for Pearse and Connolly in a potentially Sorelian transvaluation of 1916, towards a somewhat later date to which Schmitt's *Dezisionismus* theory can be re-applied. Thus the second and longest Part of Franzen's thesis is devoted to tracing developments 'from the revolutionary republic to the British dominion', that is, from 1919 to 1932.

By implication, Easter 1916 does not come within the revolutionary period. Instead, the material for a constitutional theory arises with the commencement between 12.30 and 1.00pm of the guerrilla Anglo-Irish war at Soloheadbeg (21 January 1919) — two Catholic policemen killed — and the first meeting of Dáil Éireann at 3.30pm. In Paris the peace conference had just opened and, with it in mind, the Mansion House assembly heard the Irish Declaration of Independence read not only in Irish and English, but also (by George Gavan Duffy) in French. In late November 2010 as the International Monetary Fund began to examine the bankrupt Irish government's books, dissident republicans, the inheritors of Pearse's decisionism, erected a stall in front of the GPO. Their placard declared 21 January 1919 as the founding-date of Irish sovereignty.

Nevertheless, Franzen acknowledges 'the legal way' in which the Irish state has evolved from that decisive violence, citing both Schmitt's *Legitimität und Legalität* and his *Leviathan* in the process. One gets some sense of how violence and the legal way interconnect for him, when he proceeds in the next sentence to cite as a typical recent example of this phenomenon 'die Nationale Revolution des deutschen Volkes vom Jahre 1933'.[12] What is remarkable here is the breadth of the analogy, not any acuity in its formulation. The Irish 'dualismus' of politics and guerrilla warfare is related by him to the entire Nazi achievement of 1933 — the elections, the prompt establishment of concentration camps, the ferocious persecution of Jews and political opponents, and the emergency laws neutering the vestiges of German democracy. Just as National Socialism brought an end to the Weimar Constitution, so the Revolutionary [Irish] Republic broke the previous set-up, though not for long. The Revolutionary Republic was lost to Dominion status, and only de Valera's constitution (prefaced by gains under the Statute of Westminster) promised restitution.

These pages are the most overtly political in Franzen's thesis, and they provide a climax to his repeated citations of Schmitt, who gets at least eighteen footnotes to himself. The stark contrast is supplied by the internationally renowned but near-absent Hans Kelsen, an Austrian (Jewish) legal expert who had moved to Prague and soon would reach Harvard: he gets no footnotes, despite his having helped to draft the Austrian constitution in 1920. The thesis is printed by early spring 1939, not a moment too soon.

The *Jahrbuch des Offentlichen Rechts* was not avidly read in public houses off Grafton Street or in the cottages of south Connemara. But those venues had embraced the cult of Pearse, the commemorative programme of 1936; their denizens understood the relationship between Easter 1916 and the new constitution under which they lived. Had not de Valera been condemned to death? Had not important cabinet ministers — Sean Lemass, James Ryan and Sean MacEntee, to go no further — taken part in the struggle? Pearse's loyal pupil and chronicler, Desmond Ryan, had published a study of the future Taoiseach entitled *Unique Dictator* (1936), not consciously in tribute to Schmitt's *Dictattheorie* as mentioned in Franzen's despatches, but not unrelated to it either; a German translation promptly appeared in 1938. *Irland und Grossbritannien seit 1919* would serve a slow-burning purpose.

A topic upon which Franzen has remarkably little to say is sovereignty, a key claim of the 1916 Proclamation. Schmitt had not only declared that whoever creates the exception is sovereign but also, with less pith and pomp, 'it really does not matter whether an abstract scheme advanced to define sovereignty (namely, that sovereignty is the highest power, not a derived power) is acceptable.' Where, in the sequence of Irish constitutional texts, did or does sovereignty lie? The Proclamation spoke of God; de Valera went further in 1937 specifying the Lord and Trinitarian Christianity, before granting special recognition to the Roman Catholic Church. The source from which authority to govern derived was obvious, though with more safeguards of a democratic kind than the brief Proclamation had specified. Irish sovereignty had been bedevilled for more than a decade by the argument about dominion status, the role of the crown and the oath of allegiance. De Valera avoided the term 'republic' in his constitution, regarding that matter as depending on a future re-integration of the national territory.

Least juridical of the Habilitation's sub-themes is the Gaelic language. Having stressed the role of the Gaelic League in stimulating a new national consciousness, Franzen notes Douglas Hyde's selection as first President under the new Constitution. Rather touchingly, he lists Diarmid Coffey's short biography of 1917, though he also renders the author's surname into poor-printed Gaelic — O'Cobhthargh [sic].[13] Franzen can get things wrong, for example when he describes Seán O'Faoláin's *King of the Beggars* as a novel. But his lapses can also be indicative. Few commentators on the Gaelic League would choose Louis Le Roux's *La Ligue Gaelique, son Origine et sa Mission*, published in Rennes in 1934, as brand leader, unless a second objective impended. Le Roux, a fantasist variously said to have been secretary to Pearse, Ramsay MacDonald and Harold Macmillan, was in Dublin during the summer of 1938, denouncing minorities and calling for imposed national unity. In a brief introduction, Franzen thanked his many friends in Dublin; these must have included Helmut Clissmann who organised student exchanges; the archaeologist Adolf Mahr, director of the National Museum of Ireland and head centre of the local Nazi group; and perhaps Le Roux who had published a biography of Pearse in 1932. No doubt there were Irish friends also. In a brief comment on the Governor General's role in constitutional arrangements, Franzen notes James MacNeill (brother of Professor Eoin MacNeill) as holding this position from 1928. Later, in the 1930s when the Nazis got Eduard Hempel installed as head man at the Dublin legation, Mrs James MacNeill took the trouble to introduce Yeats in order for him to learn more about the new German order. Tea parties ensued.

A framework through which these social exchanges occurred had been in existence for years, its participants not to be lumped carelessly into the Nazi camp. There were professional shared interests also. Michael Rynne (1899–1981), author of a lengthy Munich doctoral dissertation which Franzen mentioned in passing, was at the Department of External Affairs, having come to terms with de Valera's accession to power: in due course he would be Irish ambassador to Francoist Spain.[14] Colm Ó Lochlainn did occasional business in Germany, closely linked to his work as a printer and designer. Nothing was impervious to attempted subversion from Berlin. The UCD German Society had been subject to indirect Nazi influence even before 1933. In December 1931 its pre-Christmas party featured a 'skit' on Goethe's *Faust*, in which a German exchange student — characterised as a 'Hitlerite' — arriving at UCD was welcomed and questioned by the local students. The wandering scholar was played by Colm Gavan Duffy, son of Casement's solicitor in 1916 who, in 1919, had read the French text of Ireland's declaration into the records of Dáil Éireann. Other parts were taken by a daughter of the Minister for Education (J.M. O'Sullivan) and by Mr Donal O'Sullivan, BA. The audience consisted largely of dignitaries on the College academic staff, but also included Mahr.[15]

Towards the end of the Habilitation, Franzen notes with volkisch approval the new Constitution's establishment of a *Nationalsprache*. In a final tribute, he salutes 'Ireland Gaelic — Ireland free!' a phrase shaped by Pearse the rhetorician, and perhaps the educator, but hardly the work of a political or juristic thinker.[16] Unlike the French influence upon 1916, the German response as traced in Schmitt and Franzen had little time for cultural mediations. He clearly had not read the one 'novel' he lists, nor does he mention Yeats who had been widely celebrated in Germany during 1934–5 and would be fondly recalled in German obituaries. Culture amounts to the language question, which in turn is reduced to a formula quoted out of context.

Franzen survived the war and quickly exchanged the leather of Nazi uniform for a love of fine book-bindings. Some time before his death he 'privately published' an autobiography addressed to his son. Less odiously self-serving than Schmitt's *Ex Captivitate Salus* (1950), Franzen's *Aus Meinem Leben und Mein Zeit* (c. 1971) nevertheless contributes to the post-war genre of self-exoneration. Two of its nineteen short chapters are devoted to Ireland and the dissertation on Irish constitutional questions. Hempel naturally is mentioned, being the official German representative in Dublin. So is Mahr. Schmitt is acknowledged in connection with the Habilitation. Several women's names appear also — Bride and Odile. Among these inevitable and passing references, a number of other individuals are mentioned, indicators of Franzen's adroitness in negotiating Irish channels of influence. These include D.A. Binchy, Gerald Fitzgerald, a Mr McLeod with his daughter Catriona, and 'the eighteen-year-old Desmond Williams'.[17] After the War, Williams (who was fluent in German) assisted in the translation of documents on foreign policy which fell into Allied hands, at the request of the British Foreign Office. Before it, he spoke at the college debating society (it is recalled by one UCD old-stager) in favour of a German victory. Binchy, an older man, had served from 1929 to 1932 as Ireland's first minister appointed to Berlin, advising his government on German policy and signalling the menace posed by Hitler; in 1941 he published *Church and State in Fascist Italy*. MacLeod, whom Franzen describes as de Valera's parliamentary secretary, is far more elusive than his daughter: in 1935 Catriona MacLeod contributed a short biography of Robert Emmet to a series of Noted Irish Lives in which J.M. Hone, Roger McHugh and Louis M. Walsh also published. The August 1937 number of *The Irish Monthly* carried an article by her on Charles Péguy, a central figure in the sacrificial politics of Francophone Irish Catholics. Franzen characterises her as a melancholic.[18] Fitzgerald was a 'hobby journalist' associated with *The Irish Times*.

Catriona MacLeod was, allegedly, not just melancholic but given to 'Selbstironie'. Perhaps so. Her mother, a Scottish widow, had married Patrick Joseph Little (1884–1963) who *was* parliamentary secretary to de Valera in 1938, and who later became the first Director of the Irish Arts Council. At least three members of the Little MacLeod family had attended the first dance organised by Dublin's self-styled German Colony in February 1935, including Catriona. The visiting student Franzen's social world took him very close to the political centre and, given his academic interest in the de Valeran constitution, this was professionally useful. By the early 1950s, Catriona MacLeod was in charge of the National Museum's textile collection.

Franzen hardly matters without his mentor. Yet that's as much as there is to be said on the topic of Carl Schmitt, Easter 1916 and its declension into Fianna Fáil. His name, however, unexpectedly appeared in two recent Irish discussions, one in the columns of the *Field Day Review*, the other at a conference on Edmund Burke in the Royal Irish Academy. Among his occasional essays are two focused on Shakespeare's Hamlet; first, in 1952, *Hamlet, Sohn der Maria Stuart*; then, four years later, *Hamlet oder Hecuba*. These are, to the best of my knowledge, his only published excursions into English literary culture. Because the former takes up the notion of Shakespeare being (in some important sense) a Catholic writer, while the second expounds a rather lame version of the 'Britain, Tyrant of the Seas' theme, one wonders if Kathleen Murray repaid the debt of 1924 by contributing a mite or two under Schmitt's name. Seamus Deane's unforced embrace of Schmitt relies heavily on the later Hamlet essay in translation, despite some elusive quotations.[19]

My curiosity about Schmitt's references to 1916 initially prompted questions as to whether he had encountered Irish nationalist emissaries to Germany — Casement, Plunkett, Frank Aiken, Charles Bewley, Bob Briscoe, Chatterton Hill and others — at any time between 1914 and 1923. It seems not. But in offering this negative report, Dr Mehring provided Kathleen Murray, daughter of an Irish-born Australian government official, instead. Deprived of Plunkett's charisma and George Gavan Duffy's legal sagacity, Schmitt absorbed something closer to the view of Easter 1916 propagated through *The Catholic Bulletin*. It was, however, conveyed to his German readers specifically in the context of Sorelian myth.

Après the 1938 *Jahrbuch*, the deluge of 1939–1945. In Ireland a small cadre of IRA veterans assumed the right to speak for 'the Republic' by transferring all powers to yet another Military Council. Though its members included Count Plunkett, one of his surviving sons was threatened with execution if he refused to maintain radio contact with wartime Nazi Germany. The IRA's bombing campaign in England followed Franzen's Dublin studies, not as effect follows cause, but within a coherent pattern of enquiries, consultations, collaborations, and shared objectives, notably the humiliation of Britain. The campaign itself is discussed below (pp 178–185).

By late 1940 official France and Germany had come to terms. As a very minor but symbolic by-product, an Ecole Nationale des Cadres was established near Grenoble with the approval of the collaborationist Vichy government. Like Saint Enda's (but with plenty of money and access to power), the ENC was devoted to training a young generation of future leaders. The study-plans emphasised Catholicity, traditional honour, physique, community (including 'the community of blood'), etc. Authors recommended to the initiates included Henri Bergson, Henri de Man, Charles Maurras, Charles Péguy, and others less renowned.[20] The ethnologist emeritus, Paul-Henri Chombart de Lauwe, 'struck a [Maurice] Barrèsian note as he waxed eloquent over the peasant communities of rural France, rooted as they were in the soil.'[21] The young Fr (later Cardinal) Henri de Lubac SJ lectured on the doctrine of the National Revolution. There was also a semblance of a new Catholic Left outlook but, as de Man's fate in Belgium indicated, this cut little ice with the occupying National Socialists. In the end Nazi demands exceeded the compliant Knight-Monks on the Jewish Question, and the ENC went into a timely form of resistance.

The Uriage experiment differed from Saint Enda's in important ways. For a start, its cadets were between twenty and twenty-five years old, and so ready to play out the martial quest for a New Middle Ages. In origins, the two had quite opposite relations to power, Saint Enda's defiant of a proud foreign establishment of long standing, Uriage dependent on the good will of Vichy's hollow and untested resources. No empiric link between them has been found except the instructor ('Morality and Honour') Bertrand D'Astorg who later became a promoter of Francis Stuart's fiction.[22]

An indirect link, at the most, yet it serves to introduce a qualification to the comparative method employed in the immediately preceding chapters. Uriage came into being when France was partly occupied, and the 'free' portion of its territory fell under collaborationist, racist if native control. These were times of appalling brutality, by which the ENC was moulded and to which it contributed the promise of doctrinal, culturist 'principles'. Nothing in Ireland approached these conditions of prolonged violence, starvation, and abrogated politics, not even during the comparatively brief Black-and-Tan campaign.

The decisionist 'junta executing a coup' aspect of the 1916 Rising was in the end moderated by the influence of representative political practice, notably through Dáil Éireann and county councils, but deriving in large part from a British (and then a UK) tradition of emergent democracy to which Ireland had contributed through the Chartists and through Daniel O'Connell. Irish conditions did not favour a Catholic literary and intellectual renaissance like the French one, nor did Irish conditions favour or call for a development of radical-right ideas along the lines traceable in Carl Schmitt's professional career as German jurist. The Conservative Revolution took on a nativist coloration in Ireland (as elsewhere), guided by a shrewd appreciation of advantage in maintaining workable relations with the old enemy. But these Irish initiatives emerged neither *ex nihilo* nor from Lebor na gCeart.

Resistance took appropriately unexpected forms. Among the multitudinous publications of the late 1930s, Joyce's *Finnegans Wake* brought no one to the barricades, yet it was declared by Philippe Sollers to have been 'the most formidably anti-fascist book' of the interwar years.[23] Recent scholarship has investigated how Joyce absorbed material from some work by Freud published in *Collected Papers* (vol. 3, 1925).[24] It may be possible to go further. Even some non-addicts will have come across the passage in Chapter 1, beginning

This is the way to the museyroom. Mind your hats goan in! Now yis are in the Willingdone Museyroom.

The petrification of history emerges through the re-present-ation of past heroes — 'Wallinstone ... Stonewall Willingdone ...' The focal point, in the blurry wars, is the Duke of Wellington as perpetually commemorated. 'This is the Willingdone on his same white harse ...'[25] The intricacies of this page, and the multitudinous echoes of other military leaders and battles in the following pages, need not detain us.[26] What deserves consideration is Freud's *Jokes and their Relation to the Unconscious* (1905) as a source for Wellington and his horse. It is not simply the emphasis on an equestrian representation of a man — or a wax representation of an iron duke — but rather the implicit inversion of power and service in the young visitor's question to the museum guide (see p. 133 above) — 'which is the Duke of Wellington and which is his horse?' In the *Wake*, leaders fall and thus in a Joycean perspective, the horse upstages the rider. The *Fuhrerprincip* is unseated, if only on the page.

Joyce read some of Freud's case studies, and he liked a joke. He may even have come across Freud's source, the art-historian Jakob von Falke's *Lebenserinnungen* (1897) with its account of the Dublin wax-works show.[27] Any Dubliner reading the wax-works episode would associate the young woman's question with the duke's well-known comment on nativity — 'to be born in a stable does not involve being a horse,' which *Finnegans Wake* (FW) may also echo: in the politics of modernism, we cling to the uncertainty principle, bolstered in this case with the fact that Frau Emma Falke (née Stevenson) was a Dubliner.[28] Roland McHugh proposes that, among the materials furnaced for the reader of FW8, a comment attributed to Eamon de Valera about Easter 1916 may be identifiable — 'if only you'd come out with knives and forks.' This may not be very profound but it prepares the reader for the 'closing' pages of *Finnegans Wake* where HCE's trials and tribulations are related to 'life's high carnage of semperidentity' (FW582.15). Though Latin 'identidem' (=repeatedly) has been disinterred here, the surface meaning is closer to 'always or perpetual' identity. (The military march *Semper fidelis* also lurks.) Joyce and Freud, in strikingly different ways, challenge this violent imposition of rigid identity, Joyced variously as 'monomyth' or 'porkego' (see FW581.24 and FW566.26). Franzen and Schmitt are right behind it.

Geographic factors certainly contributed, as a small island on the last periphery of western Europe stirred itself to ignore the worldwide convulsions of the twentieth century. In Seamus Heaney's words for a later crisis, it seems we must 'hug our little destiny again.'[29]

## Chapter 9
# Bloody Frivolity

*There will be time to murder and create.*
T. S. Eliot, 'The Love Song of J. Alfred Prufrock'
(1917)

### When was the Left Right?

Characterising the fourth paragraph of the document proclaimed on Easter Monday 1916, Liam de Paor added laconically the phrase 'Credo quia absurdam' [I believe it because it is incredible].[1] Thus had Tertullian (160–220 AD) declared his belief in Christianity, according to a mixture of tradition and text, ancestor perhaps to the shimmering philology complained of in earlier pages. Never accorded the status of being a Father of the Church, this pagan by birth nonetheless remains a major figure in the history of primitive Christianity, the author of very early theological works in Latin and the hammer of heretics, Jews and (yes) pagans. He fell out with the hierarchy, and may even have been prematurely (that is, accidentally) buried alive. Perhaps it was this last shimmering, frantic detail that led Yeats to invoke the Carthaginian in his play of 1938, 'Purgatory'. Debating in his mind the conflict of pleasure and remorse in the mind of one in Purgatory, the Old Man declares (absurdly):

Go fetch Tertullian; he and I
Will ravel all that problem out
Whilst those two lie upon the mattress
Begetting me.[2]

The play, written in 1938 and launched at the Abbey with a calculated approving nod towards Germany's eugenic programmes, is much concerned with biological generation, just as Pearse had been in his final months. Whereas the younger IRB man longed to overcome generational failure through blood sacrifice — *credo quia absurdam* — his elder if sedentary fellow-revolutionist dramatised the cancellation of blood lines in a father's murder of his son. Historicist interpretations of the play are not in short supply, ever since Donald Torchiana began to plot dates in 1966, the fiftieth anniversary of the Rising.[3] Most efforts in this direction propose delayed eighteenth-century or (as with 'Torch' himself) Parnellite contexts for the play's implied action. Closely examined in its thematic not chronological terms, the play is haunted by Pearsean impulses, the need to overcome, the need to cancel. Yeats died while correcting the proofs. 'The Death of Cuchulain', borrowing from Sheppard's bronze belatedly installed in the GPO, became Yeats's last play.

An IRB bulletin of January 1939 invoked events of twenty years earlier, of 21 January 1919, 'when the Proclamation of 1916, from being a heroic and historic document, passed into the history of our country as the basic code and constitution under which the Government of the Republic of Ireland elected to function.'[4] With this, a campaign of street-terrorism was launched in England, climaxing on 25 August when five civilians were killed and 72 injured by an early-afternoon time-bomb exploding in Coventry's Broadgate. Nothing further from the deluded courage of Connolly, Pearse, and Plunkett can be imaged, though George Noble Plunkett (father of the signatory) was god-father to the bombers and biological father to one of their radio experts.[5]

The event's grossness well matches the bulletin's crudity, a mismatch of alleged precedent and self-anointed respondent. In the latter, the public was invited to accept that a formerly *historic* document had only passed into the *history* of Ireland on a date when the elected assembly had made little or no reference to it. Of course 21 January 1919 had been a day of two separate parts — violence in Tipperary, followed in Dublin by solemn enunciation. The democratic process by which Dáil Éireann indirectly emerged — others duly elected (as Unionists, etc) chose not to assemble — was based on British electoral provisions, and indeed the opening proceedings echoed many parliamentary conventions familiar in Westminster. By contrast and by verbal befuddlement, the IRA of twenty years later insists that the first Dáil *elected* to function under the Proclamation, taking it as a basic code and constitution. ('Basic code' rings with a Germanic, not Irish republican, tonality though no evidence of Nazi involvement in the bulletin has been discovered.) The two distinct meanings of the verb to elect — (a) to choose (others); (b) to decide within one's own terms and conditions [e.g. 'he elected for trial by jury'] — mark off crucial differences between more obvious binaries.

Left and Right — these over-familiar terms of political classification derive from seating arrangements adopted in the French National Assembly of 1789 and in subsequent continental legislatures, deputies with liberal or democratic views ranged to the left of the chairman, president or speaker, and those with monarchist or anti-democratic views to the right. Between 1789 and 1939 France experienced a series of constitutional innovations and reversals; one could characterise the Bourbon Restoration of 1815 as a triumph of the Right, though its Napoleonic predecessor could scarcely be thought an exemplary Left regime. With Charles x came not just the monarchy, but the aristocracy and a Catholic Revival, 'throne and altar'. The Right is thus often associated with hierarchy and established religion, property and class-division.

In a valuable essay concluding *On History*, Eric Hobsbaum strongly argued that 'Identity History is not Enough', drawing specifically on issues arising from conditions in post-war Italy. The message has not been fully absorbed in Ireland, where identity is invoked as a form of conscription, subtly coercive, at times cuddly. However, some pages earlier he had been addressing a different question, 'Can We Write the History of the Russian Revolution?' Different issues arise, especially if one were to substitute 'Irish' for 'Russian'. Pressing the difficulty further, let us ask if the only substitutions to be tried are national/territorial ones — American Revolution, Cuban Revolution, French Revolution, etc. There are, if you like, applied usages, as in Copernican Revolution, Industrial Revolution and so forth. It is worth remembering that, for Edmund Burke, revolution did not denote an irreversible, total and 'forward' change, but rather a movement which involved (or revolved) some aspect of the past — past liberties or practices, for example. The Leninist usage, like that employing Copernicus' name, denotes that totalising shift in everything — metaphysics, science, economic relations, 'identity'. The twentieth-century movement of thought and passions, known loosely (perhaps) as the Conservative Revolution, was in essence a return to the earlier sense of revolution, whatever the cost.

Hobsbaum ventures a challenging comparison. 'I am inclined to think', he writes, 'that Lenin would have wanted to storm the Winter Palace even if he had been certain the Bolsheviks would be defeated, on what might be called by the Irish the "Easter Rising" principle: to provide inspiration for the future, even as the defeated Paris Commune had done.'[6] Unfortunately Ulyanov Senior was dead by October 1917 and could not have been despatched to the Vatican as G.N. Plunkett had been nineteen months earlier, in search of divinely sanctioned approval. Thought of this virtual consultation makes one realise that some comparisons are no more than spectral. Hobsbaum is able to find an alternative exit from the impasse: 'taking power and declaring a socialist programme made sense only if the Bolsheviks looked to a European revolution.' No such European take-up was to follow the example of Easter 1916 though, more slowly, Indian, Israeli and African independence movements absorbed some of the theory but not the practice. It would be more honest to phrase a much advertised association with the Third World in terms of its *following* Irish examples in a few respects rather than in terms of Ireland *leading* the way: independent Ireland sent no Che Guevaras to India, Algiers, or the Central African uplands, though it did lose the Plant brothers to the US where they worked for the Mob (not the mob), and it expelled hundreds of thousands to work on English building sites for oppressors with imperialist names like Murphy.[7] Irish anti-colonialists have yet to address the Niemba ambush.

These are the less than heroic legacies of 1916, so often cited that they no longer convey anything. In mid-1919, before the full impact of disillusion had set in, the Wagnerian T.W. Rolleston issued a pamphlet with the warning title *Ireland's Vanishing Opportunity*. He naturally had a solution, and it consisted largely in the Parnellian strategy of forcing England 'out of our light' by exploiting the Imperial Parliament — that, and some major investments in a tunnel 'say, from Antrim to the Scottish coast.' As if to acknowledge the futility of useful ideas, he also resorted to allegory. He presents Ireland 'with its bitter and barren politics, its incomprehensible administration, its seeming hopeless isolation from the tide of the world's life' as occupying that waste land in which a hero arrives innocently to lead the quest. (T.S. Eliot's poem on the same theme was still in progress.) As *The Irish Times* reviewer asked with forgivable bathos, 'will an "Irish Parsifal" appear to find the Holy Grail?'[8] The ambiguity of 'appear to find' is apt.

Though Rolleston was not one of these, it is worth noting that intellectuals of decidedly Left-ist affiliation have often found sustenance in seemingly alien territory. Philosophical and even theological writings conventionally taken to celebrate a transcendence incompatible with the secularist and democratic values claimed by the Left have rewarded close study. Lucien Goldmann's *Le Dieu Caché* (1959) explored Pascal's *Pensées* to elucidate the practice of dialectics.[9] This acknowledgement of a cultural sphere wider than any implicit in a metaphor drawn from proximity to the President's chair in 1789 is simultaneously historical, intellectual, and political. It should not be confused with the tendency of some commentators from the beginning of the twentieth century onwards to argue that Left and Right are extremes which meet and even merge.

## Populist Authoritarianism

That tendency has its own specific trajectory, with important modifications carried out in recent years to explain 'the end of history' or the end of the Cold War. In relation to the Second World War and its historiography, the supposed equality in evil of Hitler and Stalin required another statement of this kind. But the practical origins of the tendency may be traced back to the 1880s in France when, after the stabilisation of the Third Republic, General Boulanger embarked on a spectacular political campaign ending in personal disgrace and suicide. His, at times secretive, backers were principally royalists, and his preferred modus operandi was the *coup d'état*. Among public supporters was Count Arthur Dillon (1824–1922), retired cavalry officer and scion of a 'Wild Geese' family, who won a seat (Lorient) for the Boulangist faction in 1889 and was for a time second-in-command to the General.[10] Lesser supporters included Lucien Millevoye, lover of Maud and father of Iseult Gonne, Yeats's younger muse in the summer of 1916 and his avenue to Claudel, Jammes, and Péguy. Characteristically, we lack a biography of Maud Gonne which takes her French political *milieu* seriously, an omission based on the lazy confusion of Left and Right.

In the words of a police informant, 'Peasants, tenant farmers, and all those who are tied in some way to rich conservatives are today perfectly won over' to Boulanger and his followers. Engels noticed this phenomenon of the *petit bourgeoisie* and even sections of the proletariat, worrying for the great theorist of the Marxist Left.[11] Boulangism, though routed as a personal crusade, re-emerged at the time of the Dreyfus Affair when Maud Gonne's anti-Semitic passions coincided with Millevoye's political instincts. French Right-wing politics chimed with some Irish nationalist positions as early as the mid-1890s. Barrès, the deputy, played the same populist card at the time of Dreyfus' rehabilitation.

The 'baptism' of Fenians in 1916 occurred not simply as the resolution of an internal Irish dispute but as part of a broader Catholic endeavour, including notably (in this case) the Literary Revival in France. This latter kept an eye on England; Louis Cazamian's *Le Roman social en Angleterre* (1903) emphasises Charles Dickens's 'philosophy of Christmas' and, while its remit did not allow for analysis of *A Tale of Two Cities* (1859), the general argument proposed the moral interventionism of writers as a preferable approach to social injustice than revolutionary politics. While pointing in a different direction, Cazamian (like Sorel in only this one regard) opposed orthodox Marxism and the Socialist Party, that is to say, he contributed to that revaluation of Left/Right which issues into Sackville Street and Boland's Mill on Easter Monday 1916. Maurice Bourgeois, who regarded the insurrection as a 'stab in the back', had dedicated his biography of J.M. Synge (1913) to Cazamian and his wife Madeleine — she shared Bourgeois' admiration of the Irish dramatist.[12]

If *The Catholic Bulletin* had concentrated on naming the dead and reproducing their images along with those of the widows and orphans of Dublin, *The Irish Monthly* and *Studies* indicated clearly where cultural sustenance was to be drawn in this crisis. Certainly not from the internationally renowned leaders of the Abbey Theatre (Gregory, Synge and Yeats) nor even from the legacy of Canon Patrick Sheehan (died 1913) whose novel of 1899, *The Triumph of Failure*, eventually provided — via Desmond Ryan — Ruth Dudley Edwards with an apt title.

Ryan, a former pupil at Saint Enda's, played a major role in reconciling messianic nationalism with the international socialism recorded in Connolly's writings, if not in his decisions of 1916. By February 1916 the commander of the Irish Citizen Army had taken over part of the blood-sacrifice 'theology': 'without the slightest trace of irreverence, but in all due humility; that of us as of mankind before Calvary, it may be truly said, "Without the shedding of blood there is no redemption".'[13] Wherever Catholicism enjoyed popular allegiance, socialism found it advisable to construct a dialogue, or at least share a vocabulary. Connolly's son Roddy who, as Ryan noted with more sympathy than caution, was 'associated with the small Communist group in Dublin', learned this lesson at some political and personal cost. In one version of Louis Le Roux's biography of Pearse (translated by Ryan, if indeed he did not contribute to the original), a call is made for Pearse's canonisation. Between the utter marginalisation of Roddy Connolly and the quasi-veneration of Pearse, the lesser figures of 1916 were assumed into a Catholic-nationalist sub-pantheon. In 1932 the latest claimants to Fenian identity, de Valera's Fianna Fáil, came to power by election.

The commemoration of Armistice (11 November 1918) became a flash point in the Irish Free State's internal relations. A pro-British minority wore the red Flanders poppy and paraded to Saint Patrick's Cathedral in Dublin. Among republicans who occasionally attacked the marchers was that paragon of the Left, Frank Ryan, later a victim of Franco's prisons and later still a reluctant guest of the Third Reich.[14] The left hand did not wish to know what the right was doing. The Anglo-Irish minority also had its contradictions. Sean O'Casey, no Anglo-Irishman but a Dublin working-class protestant by origin, offended many admirers of the republican cause with 'The Plough and the Stars'

(1926). Suspicious of popular Catholicism and insecure in confronting Britain, Yeats and others took up Paul Claudel through the Dublin Drama League. In February 1924 the League (borrowing actors from the Abbey) staged 'The Hostage' in a translation by Major Bryan Cooper, shortly to be associated with Yeats in a projected National Unionist Party. In the same week Yeats told an *Irish Times* interviewer that Europe was moving 'from democracy to authority', and that Claudel (with Mussolini) led a 'new school of thought'. Péguy, Charles Maurras, and even Edmund Burke were recruited by Yeats to the cause.[15] In September 1924 *The Irish Times* — no mouthpiece of intellectual Catholicism — quietly if tardily noted publication of a fifteenth-century French saint's life, adding for good measure that a poem by Claudel formed the preface.[16]

Remembrance events were not solely a British concern. The French minister in Dublin reported to Quai d'Orsay on the scene in 1924: 'there was much animation throughout the day. A foreigner to whom the new Ireland is represented as being against the English and the Allies, and pro-German, would have sworn that these were lies. He would have been right, and those who live in this extraordinary land, and believe they know it, are astounded by how Dublin looked yesterday [stupéfaits de la physionomie qu'a présentée hier Dublin].' Others in French officialdom continued to see 1916 as the point in which an Enlightenment influence on 1798 and 1848 was suddenly replaced by *Kulturnationalismus*, resulting in 'sympathies germano-irlandaises'.[17] It is ironic but true, and irony can be the only available truth in desperate circumstances, that the particular culture shaping and informing this replacement was not German but French. These tensions and anxieties endured throughout the 1920s in Ireland, as the Free State government cautiously assembled a portfolio of attitudes and reactions — the establishment in 1922 of the Dublin French Society, German trade relations culminating with the great Siemens investment in rural electrification (commenced 1925), and the engagement of emergent independent Ireland with the League of Nations. Amidst these external developments, the matter of defining the origins of the Free State itself, historically and ideologically, repeatedly involved citation of 1916 as the empty (or, at best, echoing) omphalos.

By the late 1930s the events and personalities of Easter Week had been re-inscribed on the Irish public mind in a dozen ways, through the naming of streets in honour of some leaders, through the publication of biographies, annual commemorative features in newspapers and journals, the issuing of stamps, and through 'high culture' (notably literature). Civic and national bodies contributed, as did the Labour movement, private individuals, and the illegal IRA. The presence of de Valera at the head of an Irish government served to demonstrate a visible connection between the 1916 rising and the 26-county state. The constitution of 1937 went further, in aspiration at least, by reference to reintegration of 'the national territory' some time in the future. Hans Franzen's dissertation should be read in this accelerating context. But one also needs to remember forward, that is to say, to hold in mind Remembrance Sunday 1987, when eleven civilians laying wreaths were killed by an IRA bomb in Enniskillen. The dissidents, you know, have not gone away.[18]

## Dreaming of Bones, Singing of Blood

The high cultural register was not entirely respectful of the official cult. Though the literary works of MacDonagh, Pearse, and Plunkett enjoyed a selective circulation (aided, in Pearse's case, by the intensified use of Gaelic in the civil service, including the educational system, after 1933) the names of Yeats and O'Casey easily trumped the celebrated dead of 1916. Other lesser writers added to the literature, notably Pádraic Ó Conaire, Eimar O'Duffy, Liam O'Flaherty, James Stephens and Francis Stuart. But Yeats, whose seventieth birthday was celebrated in 1935, remained king of the cats. His considered response to the Rising had emerged in two major texts, the poem 'Easter 1916', and the play 'The Dreaming of the Bones'. The first of these was collected in *Michael Robartes and the Dancer*, a volume published in the year of the Anglo-Irish treaty negotiations. The same also included 'Sixteen Dead Men', 'The Rose Tree', and 'On a Political Prisoner' (i.e. Constance Markievicz). The play, which drew (lightly) on the experiences of Liam Mellowes (1892–1922) in the days following the surrender by Pearse, employed so complex a style of formalised speech, music, action, and stage properties as to keep it out of the public eye for many decades. Crudely summarised, it advanced a deeply pessimistic assessment of any possible insurrectionary success.

With Yeats's drama now winning a more sympathetic and scholarly examination, it is easier to consider the degree to which he absorbed the external details of the Rising into his arcane system, later systematised in *A Vision* (first edition 1925; second and revised, 1937). 'The Dreaming of the Bones' is among the best of his Noh-style plays, bringing the remote dead and the anxious living into a single visionary scene, albeit one in which the contrasting parties cannot appreciate each other's presence.[19] The tragic dimension of this ghostly encounter makes for gripping drama, and the very specific location in North Clare adds poignancy to the effect. In the shadow of Corcomroe Abbey, just before dawn, the action is worked out on a hillside overlooking the little villages which served Lady Gregory's summer house at Mount Vernon and what had been Florimond de Basterot's retreat at Parkmore. (The latter lay some six kilometres from Corcomroe, a Cistercian foundation of *c.* 1180 AD.)

The dead of the play are Dermot MacMurrough (died 1171) and his illicit lover Dergorvilla, the couple who (according to a late traditional historiography) brought the Normans into Ireland, and so initiated the foreign presence which Pearse and his colleagues were gallantly striving to end. The play emphasises racial difference and the impossibility of forgiveness, themes familiar to anthropologists of conquered worlds in the Americas and elsewhere. But it is not de Basterot's casual writings which come to mind as part of Yeats's mental framework in shaping the drama, even if he recalled the impact of Duras House conversations on 'the national theatre'. Rather, it is likely to have been Bonn's massive study of English colonisation in Ireland from the twelfth century onwards.[20] A friend of many in Ireland, including Padraic Colum, Constance Gore-Booth, Lady Gregory, Edward Martyn, Horace Plunkett, T.W. Rolleston and Yeats himself, a sometime guest in Coole Park and Lisadell, Moritz Bonn strangely related the economics of Norman mediaeval Ireland and the cultural circle in which Pearse and Plunkett awkwardly fitted. (The Plunketts, of course, were Normans by origin, and the thoroughly obscure Michael Rynne, ambassador to Franco, was said to be descended from Edward I of England.) As an economic historian, Bonn's professional assessment of colonisation powerfully suggested that colonisation over such a span of centuries was irreversible. Yeats dramatises this intellectual crux by juxtaposing the treasonable lovers (who need forgiveness by one of their own race) and a Volunteer who has fled the GPO in Dublin. Listening for cock-crow and dawn, the former Volunteer awaits a boat to take him to the Aran Islands and safety. (Mellowes got away to the United States, a place lacking the primitivist attraction that Yeats appealed to.)

Though little of the Easter Rising gets into the play, 'The Dreaming of the Bones' constitutes a daring exercise in contemporary historiographical debate, less Irish than continental. Within a few years Yeats will have encountered Oswald Spengler's *Decline of the West*, originally published in German just a year after 'The Dreaming of the Bones'. The play might be read as a *pause en route* to the cyclical theories which Yeats (acknowledging Spengler) constructed in *A Vision*. The pre-Einsteinian categories of time and space are held apart, as a

pathologist might hold two fragments one in each hand for
sharper examination; as a consequence, figures across time (let us
call them Dergorvilla and Mellowes) co-exist, though not for each
other. It is a species of profane eternity, anticipating Yeats's oddly
godless 'Purgatory' (1938).[21] The tableau thus achieved, though
static and highly formalised, constitutes a tragic equivalent to the
decisionist or actionist drama worked out in the GPO. In 'The
Statues' (also 1938) Yeats uses more resonant names but raises a
question about the relationship of thought to action:

> When Pearse summoned Cuchulain to his side,
> What stalked through the Post Office? What intellect,
> What calculation, number, measurement, replied?[22]

A double problem haunts Yeats's spiritualist philosophy — what
W.H. Auden called his 'southern Californian' aspect — the problem
of defining or even acknowledging death, a problem also stateable
in terms of defining or acknowledging the human body. Pearse's
vertiginous notions of blood sacrifice embraced the first part by
ignoring the second. The sophisticated theory of art — sculpture,
to be specific — which Yeats explores and expounds in 'The Statues'
can be attached to Pearse in 1938, because a statue of Cuchulain
had been installed in the Post Office three years earlier. The tribute
is excessive, being unearned. In a somewhat earlier poem, Yeats
treats another of the 1916 leaders, who, though opposed to the
launching of an Easter insurrection, joined the GPO garrison from
a sense of duty. He died of his wounds in a nearby street.

   'The O'Rahilly' (written 1937) compacts the double-problem
in a manner disclosing the ultimate logic of a sacrificial politics.
It also compacts the Kerry-born Michael Joseph Rahilly (1875–
1916) into a quasi-Gaelic chieftainesque name prompting a rash
identification of poem and man, the body of the text and of the
hero.[23] This process also features thematically throughout a
highly self-conscious meta-textual poem:

Sing of the O'Rahilly,
Do not deny his right;
Sing a 'the' before his name;
Allow that he, despite
All those learned historians,
Established it for good;
He wrote out that word himself,
He christened himself with blood.
*How goes the weather?*[24]

The imperative verb demands a response which is to be vocal inscription, or repetition, of the subject's name. Before leaping to follow the repetitive trail, let us note theological infelicity in christening oneself, an office reserved for a man [sic] already ordained, confirmed, and baptised. This offence against Christian good taste is compounded by confusion of the 'water into wine' miracle of the Cana marriage (a dubious textual interpolation, found only in John's gospel) with the sacramental 'wine into blood' of the sacrament (retained in much of the Reformed tradition.) A Denis Wheatley body-side to Yeats in old age should not be discounted, any more than the Californian mental exoticism.

Repetition mimetically recurs throughout Yeats's text. Stanza 2 begins with the same opening line, but moves rapidly to conflate details of the historic [O']Rahilly into a more audacious image. Back in 1914 M.J. Rahilly had guaranteed funds for German guns landed at Howth to arm the Volunteers; in Holy Week 1916, he supported and distributed Eoin MacNeill's countermand of Pearse's mobilisation order. But Yeats abolishes the intervening years, perhaps unconsciously confusing the *Asgard* and the *Aud*. 'He'd gone to great expense / Keeping all the Kerry men / Out of that crazy fight; / That he might be there himself …'[25]

The third stanza is spoken by the hero, in which 'the word' is not just the honorific 'the' of Stanza 1 but the complex notification of countermand and mobilisation, in part supplied

(it appears) by a travelling man who 'Had heard I had not heard'.
The doubled word, doubled traveller, doubled hearing / not
hearing the word all lead into a phrase (Yeats's, not [O']Rahilly's)
which has entered popular discourse about the incident: 'Because
I helped to wind the clock / I come to hear it strike.'

It is a striking expression, about striking a blow (or more) for
Ireland. It also introduces the compaction of time which has been
noted above on several occasions in relation to Pearse's notion of
history, a notion which in turn may be related to early Bergsonian
discussions of the past and action. Winding the clock and the
clock's striking are to be brought together in the person, or body,
of the winder. The final stanza coolly announces that, in this light,
there is now nothing more to sing of 'But of the death he met'.
The scene is presented swiftly with a verbal repetition and a
darkened echo of the opening lines:

> They that found him found upon
> The door above his head
> 'Here died the O'Rahilly
> R. I. P.' writ in blood.
> *How goes the weather?*

Ignoring the refrain, we have the first and final stanzas achieving a
perfect rhyme in 'blood'. This deserves nomination as Yeats's
soundest entry for the Disgregation Prize of 1937, by virtue of its
poetic establishment of blood as sovereign word (see p. 127 above).
Christening and tombstone inscription circle in this spilt element
or split physics. The hand that wound the clock writes its own
epitaph within the same time. Writing the hero's name in his own
blood converts the poem of the same name into a micro-
physiological item, a glum enough term but one which may throw
light on the blunt oft-repeated refrain. For, whatever of coming
storms in the European late 1930s, is it not also an expression of
indifference, heroic perhaps in the subject, but close also to being

a mere cynical aside from the writer? All sacrifice is the sacrificing of others, despite the energetically worked-up tale of 'The O'Rahilly'. In Albright's editorial summary, the poem is an incitement to war.

*The Capuchin Annual* of 1936 and Yeats's poems about Casement and The O'Rahilly constitute high points of commemoration in what W.H. Auden would call — in an English context — 'a low dishonest decade'. The Second World War, or what de Valera termed the Emergency, cast the local events of 1916 into a temporary eclipse. It would be pointless to plod with the story through to 1966 and the fiftieth anniversary celebrations. Indeed the point of treating 'The O'Rahilly' in such detail is less to maintain a continuity of texts than to bring out an underlying philosophical theme. Yeats and the poets of 1916 have never been comfortably accommodated together. Academic scholarship has tended to discount MacDonagh, Pearse, and Plunkett's literary achievements, doubtless in part because they fail to measure up against 'Easter 1916'. Much historical research devoted to the Rising, especially in recent years, has been produced by scholars who feel more ideologically at home with Pearse than with Yeats, the latter being regarded as less than fully Irish, odd in his religious beliefs (if he had any), and insufficiently respectful of the common man.

It may be timely, therefore, to reconsider Yeats with 1916, who was in London when the action began. He had been, it might be remembered, an IRB member of many years' sitting, a member in comfortable arrears. The Rising disturbed him profoundly. His concern for the fate of the leaders was registered through an unexpected selectivity. The men for whom he expressed real anxiety were Connolly and MacDonagh. Apart from personal considerations, and an astute sense of relative merits in the literary domain, he had specific points of contact with both. Connolly, though unmistakably 'hard Left' and not of Yeats's persuasion at all, had been prominent during the 1913 Lockout when the poet (with AE, James Stephens and others) had denounced the employers' harshness. MacDonagh had distinguished himself as early as 1909 by attending J.M. Synge's funeral, a significant gesture for a Catholic at the time, even if he had links to the Abbey Theatre. Pearse too had softened in his attitude towards 'The Playboy of the Western World'. Inescapably, the younger poets wrote under the influence of Yeats, even if in some respects he was resented. In 1930 Ezra Pound, whose Irish authority was Yeats, noted Pearse and MacDonagh in his epic treatment of the Great War's literary casualties.[26]

What holds the greater figure apart from the lesser ones, in most assessments, is the view that literature had been subordinated to politics by them — perhaps to violent politics, in some unapproved fashion. The trio had inverted the priorities, had elevated practical and mundane affairs over the imagination and the spirit. When Yeats complained that Maud Gonne 'hurled the little streets upon the great', he added class accent to injury. There could be no second Troy unless, like the first one, it came to us through great poetry. Greatness, in the modern world, was difficult, perhaps impossible, not to be found in Liberty Hall except in so far as Connolly opposed the philistinism of William Martin Murphy and of Irish capital generally. Yeats's view of the Lockout was more aesthetic than political, though that in itself is a political option taken or not. The Union's headquarters may have found its name in Goldsmith's play of 1773, 'She Stoops to Conquer'. Connolly had his aesthetic side too.

The juxtaposition of poetry and politics, in this context, is largely based on a practical estimate of the rebels' objective. When Yeats came to write sympathetically about them, he did not waste much time on objectives; he was concerned with style, attitude, personality (in a suitably lofty form) and commitment. As they resigned their parts in the casual comedy, so they won a degree of approval, certainly of admiration, even envy. The objectives of course had always been couched in local terms for local consumption, being almost exclusively nationalist objectives.

(Connolly's internationalism had been shelved in his quest for action.) Nationalism, however, was never exclusively an Irish matter, and the New Nationalism of early twentieth-century Ireland had many sources beyond 'Fenian' tradition. In that wider context, Yeats and the 1916 poets occupied more common ground than has been usually appreciated.

## Bloody Frivolity

One could almost name the ground — France. It is not proposed here that the French Radical Right should take the credit for Easter 1916, thus banishing Irish nationalist history from Tone onwards to oblivion. It should, however, now seem acceptable that contemporary influences were at work and not just native ones. Likewise, the tracing of German responses to Easter 1916, notably (in the present book) through the writings and influence of Carl Schmitt, is no proof or demonstration of a proto-fascism active in the GPO. It should, however, now seem advisable to recall two subsequent developments. First, the kind of syndicalist myth, propagated by Sorel and part-implemented by Connolly in his final weeks was taken up successfully and openly by Benito Mussolini a few years later, with Yeats's approval. Second, Nazi propaganda in the 1930s made much of Casement, something of Yeats, very little of Pearse, and nothing of Connolly.

Before moving into any concluding repetition of matters discussed in earlier pages, we should note what seems a dull managerial instrument Yeats and his younger fellow poets alike employed — the secret society. The fact that MacDonagh, Pearse, Plunkett and his father, (and Yeats) were all members of the Irish Republican Brotherhood is the least salient detail. For the 1916 leaders, initiation into the IRB came late — MacDonagh (March 1915), Pearse (December 1913), Plunkett (post September 1914), G.N. Plunkett (April 1916). Of course the executions underscore the brevity of their membership (Count Plunkett excepted.) What is at stake is the issue of their only being admitted at a point where the die has already been cast by more traditional IRB-men, Clarke and MacDermott. The new recruits are not empowered by membership but controlled and limited by it.

An acute investigation of the political bent of Yeats's pre-war thought culminates in an Epilogue, 'The Secret Society of Modernism'.[27] Yet by 1916 Yeats had lost contact with his old Fenian associates, of whom John O'Leary (died 1907) had been the most influential on him. However, he resumed interest in the 1930s through the ministrations of Patrick McCartan, that is, at the time of the Casement and O'Rahilly poems.[28] Other pieces of that period, for example 'Three Marching Songs' (final version, December 1938), echo Pearse commending to his pupils the 'laughing gesture of a young man ... climbing to a gibbet.'[29] Although Yeats's renewed enthusiasm was in part stoked by the prospect of a large cash donation from American admirers, it fitted into the mood of calculated irresponsibility which he presented through verse and prose, high and low pronouncements from the mid 1930s till his death in January 1939. Most disgraceful of these was his August 1938 endorsement of Nazi legislation in matters of inheritance and eugenics. Before the end of the year, G.N. Plunkett demonstrated a further logic of conspiratorial politics; with six other absentionist members of the 2nd Dáil Éireann, the Count transferred the republican sovereignty he believed that body possessed to the IRA army council. 'Sovereign is he who decides on the exception' (Carl Schmitt, 1922). The council approved a bombing campaign in England and, by late 1940, the Chief of Staff was talking to Joachim von Ribbentrop in Berlin. One of Count Plunkett's surviving sons who had remained with the IRA was threatened with summary execution if he failed to maintain radio contact with the New World Order.[30]

James Longenbach, who set up 'the secret society of modernism' for our scrutiny, would doubtless argue the good teacher's tactic of provocation in defence of the phrase. A hard kernel of truth will remain even after sophomores have bathed it dry. Longenbach quotes a more intractable phrase from a letter Yeats wrote to Henry James in August 1915. Supplying a poem in answer to an invitation declined, Yeats refers to the Great War as 'bloody frivolity' — not to be his final dismissing of a multi-million violent death toll.[31] Twelve months later, the Easter Rising gave him a chance to revise his evaluation. Inversely proportionate to the events related, 'terrible beauty' will prove a tougher, sparkier nut. The processional narrow path opens into a wider, unearthly vista, accessible by a non-winding stair:

> Today while the great battle in Northern France is still undecided, should I climb to the top of that old house in Soho where a medium is sitting among servant girls, some one would, it may be, ask for news of Gordon Highlander or Munster Fusilier, and the fat old woman would tell in Cockney language how the dead do not yet know they are dead, but stumble on amid visionary smoke and noise, and how angelic spirits seem to awaken them but still in vain.[32]

Though Easter 1916 still lies ahead, a few local observations are in order. Lapsed Fenian or not, Yeats adroitly nominates a Scottish and Irish regiment for limited commiseration, not any English one. Though he might climb to see the medium, some one [else] — 'it might be' — might seek news of life and death. The enquirers, Yeats or another, are not described in physical detail, though the medium is fat and old, her voice specified as to local accent. All this fluffery or flummery paves the route to a radical distinction, between the material bodies of fighting men and those spectres 'who do not yet know they are dead'.

Just as 'bloody frivolity' anticipates the 'casual comedy' from which John MacBride and others have resigned, so the fantasy of climbing a Soho staircase for psychic palaver anticipates the sublimer 'Dreaming of the Bones'. The fugitive soldier from the GPO is assured by 'A Stranger (wearing a mask)' that many a man can see the dead plainly, and 'will pass them on the high-road / Or in the crowded market-place of the town, /And never know that they have passed.' Grammar in Yeats is always instructive. The verb 'to pass' first has many a man as its nominative, then the dead, as if lightly to underscore the constant unconscious traffic between them. A Musician records the journey Young Man and Stranger make: 'And now they have climbed through the long grassy field / And passed the ragged thorn-trees and the gap / In the ancient hedge …' In this passage [sic], those who are subject to the verb are the living fugitive and the dead Stranger, bring the action into a meta-dramatic statement.[33]

I am concerned, however, to focus on Easter 1916 which, in the world of telegrams and anger, lies between the Soho and Corcomroe scenes. The play vividly and seductively advances a notion of history as unalterable fate; the offence of Dermot and Dergorvilla is nothing less than a nationalist Original Sin to be expiated only by forgiveness proffered by 'somebody of their race'. They are presented in what might be hyperbolic terms — 'most miserable, most accursed pair' — but in terms not inappropriate to our primal parents, Adam and Eve. Those 'who sold their country into slavery' are by implication guilty of primal sin. Pearse's 'bordering on blasphemy' in his elevation of Emmet here finds an arcane, oblique, greater offence in which the retro-nation features as Paradisal Garden.

What these instructive observations of grammar and lexis point to is, bluntly, a mystical materialism. Yes, it is an apparent contradiction but so is the dramatist of 'The Dreaming of the Bones' whose racio-metaphysical maxim — forgiveness by blood kindred — rules out Pearse, MacDonagh, Roddy Connolly, all the (Norman) Plunketts and Dillons, all the Yeatses later, not to mention Swift, Goldsmith, Grattan, Burke, Davis, Mitchel, Parnell, Rolleston, Uncle Tom Casement and all etc. etc.[34] The play is decisively non-Hegelian. History cannot repeat itself; instead it is tragic *ad infinitum*, republican tragic with some resemblance to

'Coriolanus' and a fondness for lavish bodily exposure. Here the mystical materialism unfolds as a perverse sacrament, which J.J. Horgan and Fr Shaw sj detected in their time. Something of the kind has been detected in de Maistre, practised by Yves Klein whose portraits were achieved by applying paint to human bodies and wrapping or wiping these with canvas. Less might be more. In 1936, as the Free State came to celebrate the twentieth anniversary of the Easter Rising, Maurice Bourgeois completed a French version of Synge's 'Well of the Saints' for wireless broadcast. His invisible blind characters escape the impasse of Yeats's mediaeval and modern figures, escape from history into art.

Chapter 10

# Spectres and Materialisations; or, The Proclamation Re-proclaimed (1939)

*Habit is a violent and treacherous schoolteacher.*
*Gradually and stealthily, she slides her*
*authoritative foot into us; then, having by this*
*gentle and humble beginning planted it firmly*
*within us, helped by time she later discloses an*
*angry tyrannous countenance, against which we*
*are no longer allowed even to lift up our eyes.*

Michel de Montaigne

## A Dissident's Higher Affiliation; or, *Ireland To-day*

But nothing rests. The publishers of commemorative portrait postcards in 1916 thought it advisable to caption the images of executed leaders 'Irish Rebellion May 1916', that is, to incorporate the month of execution into the insurrection event itself. By a comparable adjustment, the image of four uniformed members of the Citizen Army on the roof of Liberty Hall is captioned 'Sinn Feiners'.[1] From the outset commemoration involved misrepresentation.

The habit persisted. *The Catholic Bulletin* prepared for the twentieth anniversary of the Easter Rising by commencing in January 1936 a series of articles dealing with the Great War, the rise of the Volunteers and other ancillary events. In addition, each successive number of the *Bulletin* carried a supplement, supposedly a reprint of the January, February, March, etc numbers for 1916. This probably involved the circulation of old unsold stock rather than active re-printing. The September 1936 issue bore a note stating that 'The Reprint of *The Catholic Bulletin* May 1916 which follows was actually never published,' due to censorship. Slowly, the magazine's archive was re-activated by way of a commemoration which only ceased with the death of the editor and closure of publication in 1939.[2] A broader contemporary perspective could be deduced from the editorial of October 1936. The opening paragraphs reported a papal address to Catholic refugees from the Spanish Civil War, unremarkable but for its strong preference of Just War theology over the Beatitudes. Less urgent but no less committed was the section headed 'Dealing with Poisonous Vermin' (that is, the literary figures who had briefly sustained the magazine *To-morrow* in 1924 — notably Lennox Robinson, Cecil Salkeld, and Yeats). 'Proclamation of the German Economic State' left readers in no doubt of the transcendent virtue of Hitler and his team.[3]

While Yeats was waiting for death in the South of France, other affiliates of the IRB were preparing to implement an S- (or Sabotage) Plan. Its principal supporters were Seán Russell (a veteran of Easter 1916) and Jim O'Donovan who learned his explosive skills from Tom Dillon, a brother-in-law of Plunkett. As Chief of Staff of the IRA, the former had the distinction of dying aboard a Nazi U-Boat, which was transporting him back to Ireland from the occupied port of Lorient. Russell was an out-and-out 'physical force' republican with no political frills attached; his companion and fellow-guest of the Reich, however, was Frank Ryan, a republican beyond doubt but one who had fought against Franco in Spain and who had sympathised with the left-wing Republican Congress at home.

Educated by the Jesuits in Glasgow, O'Donovan had 'bitterly disapproved' of the Easter Rising, but subsequently fell under the influence of Dillon as the emergent IRA's explosives don.[4] As an anti-treatyite, he had been interned, but later made a career in the Electricity Supply Board. The unlikely editor of *Ireland To-day* (1936–1938), he assembled a lively group of young literary contributors, while displaying little interest in any of Ireland's larger talents — Joyce, O'Casey, Shaw or Yeats. On a key political issue, he leaned towards supporting the Madrid government and retained Owen Sheehy Skeffington (a decided leftist and anti-clerical) as a columnist.[5] 'A Foreign Commentary' quickly drew down the wrath of a reactionary Church. *Ireland To-day* brought together a remarkable variety of contributors, with Michael Tierney (a notable supporter of the fascoid Blue Shirts) and Liam Ó Laoghaire (a film enthusiast) appearing alongside the earnest young Skeffington. Yet O'Donovan's magazine contained delicate indicators of its reverence for Easter 1916 — in the first issue (June 1936) a poem by Donagh MacDonagh (son of Thomas MacDonagh), and an advertisement for a lithographic portrait of Roger Casement (by Leonhard Fanto 1874–1958, art director of the state theatre in Saxony under the Nazis). Fanto had been consulted in the early years of the century by Hugo von Hoffmanstal about designs for a ballet, 'Die Triumph der Zeit', which paved the way for a strand of Conservative Revolution aesthetics. In 1909 he designed costumes for the premiere of Richard Strauss' *Electra*. Sean O'Sullivan's cover for *Ireland To-day* showed a dark phoenix rising from a triangle of flame. Nothing rests, and the very name of O'Donovan's magazine indicates its limited appetite for the past.

Perhaps because of its very diversity, *Ireland To-day* is less neatly schematisable than Plunkett's *Irish Review*. The French influence, so pervasive in the earlier magazine, is represented all but exclusively in the latter by Sheehy Skeffington, a supporter of the Popular Front government of Leon Blum. Niall Montgomery contributed some Gaelic translations of Baudelaire, and Denis Devlin reviewed St John Perse's *Anabasis* in Eliot's translation. Jim O'Donovan remained invisible, partly because he was employed by the semi-state ESB, and partly because he was a militant republican bent on destroying the state which paid his salary. His biographer emphasises, with some justice, the breadth of political opinion accommodated in the magazine until its demise in the spring of 1938.[6] But indicators are there to be unearthed. An early regular advertiser was the shipping line North German Lloyd, offering seven conducted tours to Germany, including visits to the Olympic Games. In December 1936 W.J. Maloney's fervently speculative book *The Forged Casement Diaries* was reviewed by Catriona MacLeod who danced with the German colonists in Dublin and was cultivated by Hans Franzen. Not surprisingly, Sheehy Skeffington was 'let go', and even his note of resignation was spiked by the nameless editor. His successor, signing as Michael O'Neill-King (but probably to be identified as Capt. John Lucy of Glenageary), calmly described non-intervention in the Spanish war as 'a case of closing the meadow gate after the horse has got in' (April 1937).[7] Skeffington promptly shifted his column to the Belfast-based *Irish Democrat* (edited for a time by Frank Ryan), an avowedly anti-fascist paper (and at times Stalinist), run by left-republicans and members of the Communist Party of Ireland. The poet John Hewitt was a contributor.

More locally the twentieth-first anniversary of 1916 required attention, despite the magazine's parlous financial condition, the twentieth having passed before *Ireland To-day* commenced publication. The January 1937 issue including two successive articles which referred specifically to the Republic of 1916–1923, a constitutional nicety of anti-treaty-ites to which Franzen responded.[8] J.B. Desmond presented the IRA as the organic *resurgence* of the Irish army defeated in 1690. Related terms proliferate — 'regrowth from our ancient territorial divisions', 'resumed armed and other growth from 1917 onwards', 'resurgence from native lands', 'natural upgrowth from the people', etc. The writer, said to be the author of two (unidentified) books on economics, opens and closes with invocations of James Connolly, though the argument is similar to that advanced in general terms by Carl Schmitt as a '*nomos* of the earth'. To quote one mobiliser of Hitler's pet jurist, the concept 'formulated the origins of law and claims to sovereignty'; and, in the words of another, 'land appropriation [is] the originary event of all human history.'[9] J.B. Desmond's argument seeks to unify historic legitimation of the latter-day IRA (declared illegal by de Valera in June 1936) with a theory of land which at once invokes 'ancient territorial' units and the actually existing network of parishes, owner-occupier small farms and their urban equivalents.

The succeeding article, by John Dowling (evidently a dentist by profession), wittily assaults the Abbey Theatre tradition by blaming it for what he calls 'the Immolation Idea', that is, the doctrine of blood sacrifice propounded by Pearse, Plunkett and (as we have noticed) Connolly also. Dowling cites Terence MacSweeney's declaration that 'Not those who can inflict most, but those to can suffer most will have the ultimate victory.' Here was an early exercise, courageous but toxic, in the masocho-nationalism of the man who whips his shadow, a tendency developed by Francis Stuart in his tribute to MacSweeney. Dowling recalls a production in Gaelic of MacSweeney's play 'Insurrection' for an audience of school children whom he wryly characterises as 'drinking the poison with widening eyes and storing up in their minds the Abbey sermon of defeat and doom. The players themselves, of course, would be quite unconscious of this effect, being fortified against it by a vivid memory of what conditions really were like between 1916 and 1923.' Here a later republican 'front-of-house' journal is carefully marking off the conditions of 1936 from those of twenty years earlier. Sure enough, the distinction between the nation and its children re-emerges, for the adult players 'who probably prided themselves on their activity in the cause of nationality' could draw on heroic memories unavailable to their juniors.[10] The task in hand is to overcome this generational dis-connect and, with it, overcome the allegedly Abbey-propagated notions of nobility, self-sacrifice and defeat. A Pearsian anxiety, largely biographic in origin, had become the problematic of internal partisans within the democratic Irish state.

In March 1937 Brian McCrudden's poem 'Easter Week' spoke oddly of 'our hot traditions / tactics and cold organisation'. The next issue opened with an editorial which skirted awkwardly around the topic of Easter 1916, taking greater pleasure in noting a compliment paid by a Presbyterian minister to the memory of Erskine Childers (1870–1922), a republican victim of Free State reprisals. *Ireland To-day* fascinates precisely for the uneasiness of its attempts to grapple with Easter 1916, while reluctantly acknowledging the success of de Valera in stabilising his elected regime and in preparing a constitution close enough to the republican heart-beat as to cause palpitations. The editor had other approaches in mind, whenever his magazine should eventually fail, as it eventually did in accordance with shifts of policy in the IRA.[11]

The office of Chief of Staff changed hands repeatedly, following the retirement of Maurice Twomey in 1936. His immediate successors were Tom Barry (for 1936–37), Seán MacBride (in 1936/7), and Sean Russell (for 1938–1939). Jim O'Donovan was close to Russell and is generally regarded as devising his S-Plan in answer to a request from the new Chief of Staff. A subordinate theory attributes some contribution to a low-level German agent named Gustav Simon based in England.[12] Pro-Germanism was a shared position among the IRA leaders, most of whom visited Berlin or other centres at one time or another — Tom Barry in 1937, Andy Cooney in 1936, Stephen Held in 1940, Seán MacBride in 1929, Jim O'Donovan four times in 1939, and Sean Russell in 1940. MacBride, who opted for a somewhat constitutional politics after 1937, may from this list appear to be untouched by the Nazi contagion. However, at the anti-imperialist congress in Frankfurt he met Helmut Clissmann and Jupp Hoven, both of whom became crucial intermediaries between Hitler's Reich, the IRA, and Irish cultural figures including Peadar O'Donnell and Francis Stuart. O'Donovan knew Clissmann well.[13]

The S-Plan, a lengthy document composed by Jim O'Donovan, sought to terrorise the British into withdrawing from Northern Ireland through bombing cinemas, public streets and utilities in England. It deliberately abandoned the traditional Fenian belief that Ireland's opportunity arose when Britain was engaged in war elsewhere, its first paragraph declaring that 'in order to exercise maximum world effect, the diversion [sic] must be carried out at a time when no major war or world crisis is on.' In its second section it called for the distribution of 1,000 facsimile copies of the 1916 Proclamation.[14] Though our 'gallant allies in Europe' were still German, the drastic ideological changes introduced there in 1933 indicated a need for discretion in admitting the high level of financial, paramilitary and propagandistic support provided to the IRA by the Third Reich. While the Capuchins revelled in commemoration of Easter 1916, the directors of *Ireland To-day* recognised an inheritance at least as awkward as it was sacred.

Despite his generous admission of a broad literary spectrum to the columns of *Ireland To-day*, O'Donovan was no adequate successor to MacDonagh or Plunkett as cultural mediators between native and foreign influences, traditional and innovative modes of writing. Relics of old decency can be found in his magazine; in a compact news summary for 16 November to 15 December 1936, the election of 'Dr Isaac Herzog, Chief Rabbi of Saorstát' to be Chief Rabbi of Palestine is welcomed, together with a Dáil Deputy's protest as the exempting of Kosher butchers from certain legal requirements. But the political drift is not so much leftwards (despite the magazine's evident preference for the Spanish Republic over Franco's rebels) as towards that merging of left and right exemplified in O'Donovan's circle by the nimble manoeuvres of his adviser, Helmut Clissmann. Nothing like the extensive Francophile interests of *The Irish Review* are evident, not even in a treatment of German (in place of French) culture, historical or contemporary. All one gets of substance here is a review by Seán Ó'Faoláin of Thomas Mann's *Stories of Three Decades*. One could repeat Marx's unsubstantiated claim that Hegel saw history as occurring twice, first as tragedy, then as farce — except that, with the S-Plan and later events of 1939, the farce turned out more violent than the tragedy.

Yet the architects of the new campaign unconsciously followed Yeats whose poetry from 1936 until his death on 29 January 1939 evidenced greater recklessness and unqualified violence than anything composed between 1916 and 1923. The bombing of English public places began earlier in the month of his death, and the patrons of it met 'round 3 February' in Dublin to review progress.[15] In his elegy for Yeats, W.H. Auden wisely insisted that 'poetry makes nothing happen', even in the case of one who asked 'Did that play of mine send out / Certain men the English shot?' By March 1940 Jack Plunkett was providing O'Donovan with specifications for premises in which a wireless transmitter could be installed, and lists of tools, including a 'power-pack', etc required for ciphered communications with Berlin.[16] De Valera's government moved against the IRA, interning George Plunkett (August 1939), Jack Plunkett (December 1939), and O'Donovan (September 1941) with a large motley of others in the Curragh Camp.

While interned O'Donovan wrote an essay on 'Germany and Small Racial Groups'. Dublin's new archbishop, John Charles McQuaid, came to the rescue, not so much of O'Donovan himself as of Catholic family honour. His two sons were enrolled in Blackrock College as boarders, with no requirement of fees; a Loreto convent took the daughters on similar terms.[17] French religious orders might be relied upon to counter the influence of a tear-away parent.

The younger George Plunkett died in January 1944 from injuries sustained in an accident near the family's new home at Ballymascanlon, County Louth. His brother lived till 1960, much damaged by a hunger-strike embarked upon at Mountjoy Jail in 1940. In a short undated letter from Ballymascanlon, Jack Plunkett wrote on two themes which pathetically or whimsically reflected his own altered mental world. First 'I have not learned any more about the atomic bomb … [then] I don't see any opportunity at the moment to make copies of those papers of Joe's [i.e. of Plunkett, the signatory].'[18] The conjuncture of literature and violence which indelibly marked the Easter Rising of 1916 here fractures into irreconcilable impossibilities — an Irish nationalist perspective on weapons of truly mass destruction, and the mobilisation of a personal archive.

Among O'Donovan's papers in the National Library of Ireland is a typed undated 5-page document relating to the S-Plan campaign and its consequences. A paragraph entitled ISSUE reads, 'The Issue is complete National Independence. This is the issue which must be fought out between the IRA, representing the Irish Nation, and the British.' Despite the repetition, the passage wholly fails to indicate how the Irish Nation came to be *represented* by the IRA in 1939 or at any other date. Adherents of the organisation have frequently invoked decisions made by some surviving members of the Second Dáil to invest the Army Council with legitimacy as the republican government of Ireland, but even this sublime manoeuvre fails to elaborate on any clear sense of representation as such. One should not exaggerate the extent to which Carl Schmitt's constitutional theories were taken up in Ireland. Yet there is still an opportunity to enquire at what discount the IRA's thoroughly formulated practices were consistent with the Schmittian paradigm. Something of this has already been suggested in relation to the article in *Ireland To-day* signed 'J.B. Desmond' and, during his more loyally Catholic phase, Schmitt had distinguished between a representation dependent merely on low political (that is, democratic) authority and that which stemmed from an utterly transcendent one (as in the Catholic case of God's representatives on earth or, in the Calvinist schema, 'the elect'). In this precise connection one can venture a precise indication of Schmitt's reception in Ireland. My own copy of *The Necessity of Politics*, published in November 1931, had two identifiable former owners — a person signing himself 'D Ó Brosnacháin' and Kerry Diocesan Library. Chapters 4 and 5 adopt contrasting views of the central topic — 'The Church and the Idea of Representation' and 'The Representative Idea in Contemporary Industrialism'.[19] It might seem odd that a republican movement should rely on the former sense, but the rebels of Easter 1916 were by no means perennial republicans. Pearse had earlier dreamed of turning Connemara into 'a little Gaelic kingdom of our own'. During the Rising some of its leaders had earnestly debated the wisdom of having a German prince as head of state, and their successors had on more than one occasion practised a form of apostolic succession in preference to vote-taking among the disciples. Schmitt indirectly acknowledges this in *The Necessity of Politics* when he remarks on the shared Catholicism of Donoso Cortes and Padraic [sic] Pearse, though he does so by invoking the Church's '"hermaphroditic" attitude (to use Byron's expression)': 'In accordance with the tactics of political warfare, any party which possesses a consistent philosophy is at liberty to form alliances with the most diverse groups.'[20]

The fourth section of the IRA document deserves quotation at greater length for it exemplifies more than a Schmittian tactic, and constitutes a merger of Left and Right in the Irish nationalist-republican project:

Our Revolution is divided into two parts: (1) The fight for complete National Independence, (2) Reform of the whole Social System. The first is incomplete without the second, and the second, which is the most [sic] important, is impossible without the accomplishment of the first. It is impossible to put our house in order while the wrecker occupies it. It is clearly our duty as volunteers to make it possible for the Social Reformers to take care of the second part of the Revolution and give practical expression to their ideas. Jim Larkin and James Connolly in 1913, as Social Reformers tried to uplift the people, whilst the enemy of occupation, whose duty it was to restrain any attempt to interfere with the System, still controlled the country. Connolly and Pearse, who were both Social Reformers, had to abandon the second part of the Revolution because they realised how impractical it was without first having possession of the country. They put on the uniform of the Citizens' Army and Volunteers, realising Tone's considered decision that our first duty was to 'Break the connection with England'.[21]

Then the longest paragraph of the document lapses into republican commonplace. But not before disclosing some remarkable distinctions. If the Revolution has two parts, there are two categories of participant — volunteers (that is, armed IRA members, including the bombers of civilian targets) and Social Reformers. Despite the impressive names of dead Social Reformers (and neglecting Larkin's robust pursuit of local housing improvements in 1939–40 as an elected member of Dublin Corporation), it is clear that their ideas will only follow from whatever conditions the volunteers establish and follow only with the approval of the latter. These conditions, however, are to be achieved primarily through a campaign conducted outside Ireland — viz, by means of the S-Plan.

Primarily, but not exclusively. A subsequent paragraph declares 'In the Six-County or Twenty-Six County areas, a Coup d'Etat will obviously mean putting up a front from which we must advance or retreat. Once we start, we must go ahead. That means immediate success or failure. Assuming victory in both territories, we will have, with a weakened people, to face the British, if our objective is to be obtained, as the establishment of our Republic does not end with our local successes.'[22] Again, there are striking internal contrasts of tone and presumption — for example, victory *and* a weakened people. The document clearly pre-dates implementation of the S-Plan in January 1939, yet this paragraph looks towards a *coup d'état*, a strategy in which Dr Edmund Veesenmayer (1904–1977) of Ribbentrop's Foreign Ministry was the Nazi expert. (Liam de Paor detected the language of a *junta* planning a *coup d'état* in the 1916 Proclamation.[23]) Russell apparently met Veesenmayer for the first time on 4 August 1940, though other IRA emissaries including Ruairi Brugha and Joe McGarrity had been in Germany just before the outbreak of war. Foreign dimensions to the s-Plan and its domestic Irish penumbra may also be indicated by the cryptic remark that 'the establishment of our Republic does not end with our local successes.' Russell had, of course, been in touch with the Germans during his extended visit to New York in 1936, and also with McGarrity. Veesenmeyer, an ss-man (ultimately a Brigadeführer) as well as diplomat, assisted the Holocaust in Croatia, and was jailed for 20 years in 1949 as a war criminal.

In terms of the longer perspective of *Dublin 1916: The French Connection*, no further pursuit of a micro-timetable is needed. Two broad conclusions may be ventured. For all its invocation of Wolfe Tone, the dead generations, and the Fenian tradition, Irish nationalist republicanism at the crucial points of its actionism was not simply a home-grown movement. It displayed significant affinities with political and cultural movements in other countries. This was not just a matter of picking up support on the basis of 'England's difficulty is Ireland's opportunity', nor was the relationship one of affinity without contact. The rich evidence of contemporary French thought found in *The Irish Review* and other magazines (especially religious ones) does not easily translate into a causative explanation of Easter 1916 unless the latter is interpreted in a wider context of military innovation, and understood anew as an event irreducible to being the climax of a long native endeavour. Second, pursuit of the Easter Proclamation's fate after 1916, together with the commemorative exercises, reveals the further entrenchment of a Right-Radical ideology which at times deploys a populist rhetoric and which, with time, aligns itself with German fascist power to the neglect of French influences and affinities.

O'Donovan died in 1979 after a prolonged illness. Though he did not openly support the Provisional IRA's campaign of violence, in many ways the Provos modelled their more sustained challenge to Northern Ireland's constitutional position on the sporadic efforts of 1939–1941, revived on home soil between 1956 and 1961. Provisional veneration of Easter 1916 has been sustained even after the Good Friday [sic] agreement of 1998. The various dissident IRAs (Real, Continuity and, no doubt, Other) are no less attentive to Easter 1916 as a rallying point, though they too follow the O'Donovan model rather than that adopted by Pearse. Like Enniskillen (1987), Omagh (1998) was Coventry writ large and not writ with the left hand. In fairness to these latter-day dissidents, Pearse and his associates were the dissidents of their day, ignoring the defensive strategies agreed by the Volunteer leadership, establishing a secret inner circle, betraying the trust of MacNeill, kidnapping Bulmer Hobson, and opting for aggressive minority action under the aegis of Blood Sacrifice. It is only fair to the democratic majority that the ideological basis of this tradition should be excavated, the French and German strata laid bare in their historical contexts. The Right-Radical fusion of nationalism and religious ecstasy, the collaboration with fascist regimes, and the practice of street-terrorism at home and abroad, are not automatically elided by invocations of post-coloniality or complaints about state-terrorism.

## A Democratic Programme of Commemoration?

As the centenary of Easter 1916 approaches, we should reckon the extent to which Sorel and Schmitt remain our contemporaries, not least through the influence of sedentary radicals in well-funded American universities. A long history of 'splits' and dissident atrocities — going back to the Invincibles — requires examination as a motive force in itself. The sequence is discontinuous and politically unstable. Saor Éire came into being in 1931, and the name recurred periodically. Republican Congress broke away from the IRA in 1934; the later 'Provisionals' split off from a movement influenced by the Congress's left-wing example. Since the Good Friday Agreement, we have felt the impact of secessions from the new orthodoxy — the Real IRA and its brighter shadow, the 32 County Sovereignty Movement; the Continuity IRA; Republican Sinn Féin, and (most recently) Éirigí (i.e. Rise Up!). Violence has resumed in Northern Ireland and, at the moment of writing, some four or five armed groups claim ownership of Irish sovereignty, by way of Count Plunkett's surrender of it in 1939. In less than four years the centenary of the most spectacular dissident event in Irish history will claim the attention of all and (perhaps) sundry.

It behoves those who rest content among the Sundry, without any desire to submerge into a monolithic All, to explore the highly diverse forces and influences at work on Easter 1916, shaping it, articulating it, financing it, arming it, reconciling it with authoritarian traditions (religious or other) and radical innovations of the Right. These various contributions — the shaping, arming, reconciling, etc — did not all follow the same path or lead in the same direction. Contradictions abounded. Stephen Dedalus is much quoted on the topic of serving two masters and — after some commonplace exchanges about empire and church — he mentioned 'a third ... who wants me for odd jobs.'[24] The oddness of the jobs which Irish nationalism required was not their strangeness but their multiple and unclassifiable character. Joyce is now a serviam industry, lucrative, no questions asked. His third master, a muscular revenant of uncertain temper, bids fair to cast Easter 2016 in unalloyed All-ness to which idol the Elimite and the Unitarian (and the Muslim, the agnostic, the Chinese and other 'children of the nation') must pay silent tribute.

Among events or documents in twentieth-century Irish history which have not prompted lavish commemoration, the Democratic Programme of 1919 is the most deserving of attention in this regard, its ninetieth anniversary having passed without incident. Scarcely radical in the Europe of its day, it deserves recognition for wholly avoiding the language of sacrifice, preferring 'willing service'. So far, not bad. However, as if by way of compensation to the promoters of martyrdom, the Democratic Programme attributed the Easter Proclamation *tout en court* to 'our first President, Pádraíg Mac Piarais' while systematically misquoting that multi-authored document.[25] Some of the re-writings could be read as left-leaning, for example 'all right to private property must be subordinated to the public right and welfare', and the Programme was adopted by a popularly elected assembly. Then it was rapidly forgotten by successive regimes bent on exacting gratitude and delivering oppression in equal measure.[26] The sins of Haughey and his cohorts were not original.

Easter 1916 remains an inescapable historical datum. It cannot be forgotten. But it does not logically follow that celebrations will be the proper centennial response. Certainly the occasion of the centenary should be marked, and the commemorative element focused on recollection of the event. Memory cannot officially be treated as a selective faculty — the unconscious has already done adequate work in that area. Acts of recollection need to be inclusive, even-handed, critical. Those who delight in the merger of left and right in the GPO could ask themselves if Connolly had not abandoned the possibility of a much wider alliance with the British working-class. Those who set the nation at the heart of their politics might reflect on the nation-state that we got. One unexpected, welcome but problematic engagement with the problem is John Marsden's *Redemption in Irish History* (2005) in which an unquestioning acceptance of Yeats's 'Countess Cathleen' as a model of self-sacrifice casts a shadow over much original thinking.

We have acquired an habitual mode of celebration, and habit is not a mentally acute or critical instructor. Some efforts were made in 1966 but largely went unnoticed. The painter Sean Keating's sketches for a commemorative tableau include a cockerel under a raised gun, as if to gesture sardonically towards the betrayal of Christ before Easter as well as a Chaunicleer in the neo-Fenian dawn. The Rising is annually celebrated at Easter, a moveable feast, not on the precise anniversary (24 April) of the event. By this misprision, the sacramental ambitions of Pearse were inscribed into the independent state's calendar, inhibiting any profane questioning of the consequences. Ironically, Pearse's role as a humane educationalist was for this reason underplayed in Irish schools where the Christian Brothers' version of history became the benchmark (or weal) for all. Thus, Montaigne's observation on custom (or habit) in the late sixteenth century acquires a striking contemporary aptness. It is, he averred, 'a violent and treacherous schoolteacher' who, once internalised, 'discloses an angry and tyrannous countenance against which we are no longer allowed even to lift up our eyes.'[27]

# Notes

## A Letter of Introduction

1. The words of Kearney's poem reflect some of the circumstances defining the Fenian rebellion of 1867. The title, however, echoes Paul Deroulède's *Chants du Soldat* (1872) which responded to the bitter experiences of the Franco-Prussian War and the Commune with high-flown patriotic bombast. Ivan Strenski has compared the rhetoric of Patrick Pearse to lines by Deroulède (1846–1914) translated as 'Death, it is naught. Long live the grave / when the country comes out of it alive.' Strenski, *Contesting Sacrifice: Religion, Nationalism and Social Thought in France.* Chicago: University of Chicago Press, 2002, pp 72–3. Deroulède's reputation was not exclusively based on his verse; a supporter of General Boulanger and later an anti-Dreyfusard, he was several times involved in *coup d'état* conspiracies. Thoroughly right-wing, though only a moderate anti-Semite, he opposed any extension of France's colonial territories on the grounds that it would distract from the more important business of squaring up to Germany. For a literary context, see Aaron Schaffer, 'Parnassian Poetry on the Franco-Prussian War', *PMLA* vol. 47 no. 4 (December 1932) pp 1167–92, especially (for Deroulède) pp 1167–70.

2. Joost Augusteijn, *Patrick Pearse: the Making of a Revolution*, Basingstoke: Palgrave Macmillan, 2010, p. 3. The autumn of 2010 brought publication of Augusteijn's book which draws on a great deal of material previously unavailable to researchers, and I am pleased to be able to confirm and extend some details of my argument about Pearse's family background. While he begins by situating Easter 1916 in a European context, the surrounding characterisations suggest a narrowing perspective — 'in many of these movements the Catholic clergy played a central role from Poland, Slovakia, Croatia, Ukraine, Brittany and Basque to Ireland' (p. 3). Separatist movements in which Catholicism played a much slighter role (or none) — for example Bohemia, Hungary and Norway — are simply ignored, as is the disturbing subsequent behaviour of some nationalities (and some religious orders) in their dealings with Nazism. Franciscan participation in German-Croatian atrocities was carefully publicised by the Irish writer Hubert Butler; see 'The Sub-Prefect

Should Have Held his Tongue' and 'The Arturkovitch File' in Butler, *Escape from the Anthill*, Mullingar: Lilliput, 1985, pp 270–305.

3.   Christopher E. Forth, *The Dreyfus Affair and the Crisis of French Manhood*, Baltimore: Johns Hopkins University Press, 2006, p. 15.

4.   Peadar O'Donnell, *Monkeys in the Superstructure*, Galway: Salmon, 1986, p. 28. O'Donnell was no nationalist, and declared that 'the world is not composed of nations, it's not a complex of nations. It's full of people! And they have one thing in common, they want to live.' Ibid, p. 29.

5.   Denis Donoghue, 'Beckett in Foxrock', *Irish Essays*, Cambridge: Cambridge University Press, 2011, p. 201.

6.   Samuel Beckett, *Murphy*, London: Calder, 1963, pp 33–4.

7.   A relevant instance, more recent than 1916, is investigated with courage in Shlomo Sand, *The Words and the Land: Israeli Intellectuals and the Nationalist Myth* (trans. Ames Hodges), Los Angeles: Semiotext(e), 2011. Sand notes that the founder of Zionism, Theodor Herzl, was not only present at the degradation of Captain Alfred Dreyfus, his fellow-Jew, but had attended frequently at monthly meetings organised by such violent anti-Semites as Alphonse Daudet and Édouard Drumont. 'During these encounters, Herzl became aware of something that optimistic liberals and socialists had a hard time admitting: scientific, aesthetic and spiritual progress does not necessarily come with moral progress.' He goes on to observe that Herzl, unlike others, did not underestimate the ability of Drumont, Daudet and their associates 'to read the mindset of the modern masses' (p. 35). Sand, however, nurtures a curious affection for Georges Sorel.

8.   See F.X. Martin (ed.), *1916 and University College Dublin*, Dublin: Browne and Nolan, 1966. There is no reference in any of the essays collected by Fr Martin to the novelist James Joyce, though a namesake member of the Irish Citizen Army is noted (p. 42). While the role of poets in the Rising is taken as emblematic, UCD students who took part were drawn from a variety of science departments (biology, engineering, medicine, etc.)

9.   Ernest Renan, 'What is a Nation?' in Renan, *The Poetry of the Celtic Races and Other Studies*, London: Walter A. Scott [1896], p. 66. Cf. 'l'oubli, et je dirai meme l'erreur historique, sont un facteur essentiel de la formation d'une nation, et c'est ainsi que le progès des etudes historiques est souvent pour la nationalité un danger.' Renan, *'Qu'est-ce qu'une nation? Conference faite en Sorbonne, le 11 mars 1882*, Paris: Lévy, 1882, pp 7–8.

10.  A revised and extended version of the Frazer Lecture delivered in the University of Glasgow, published in Dodds, *The Ancient Concept of*

*Progress and Other Essays on Greek Literature and Belief*, Oxford: Clarendon Press, 1973, p. 6.

11. Loc. cit., p. 21.

12. The founder of Positivism corresponded with at least one other Irish follower; see *Lettres d'Auguste Comte à Henry Dix Hutton*, Dublin [no publisher], 1890. Hutton (1824–1907) wrote on a variety of topics from European politics to the legal implications of a peasant proprietorship in Ireland.

13. Thomas Kettle, *The Open Secret of Ireland* (ed. Senia Pašeta), Dublin: UCD Press, 2007. It is some indication of Kettle's faulty assessment of contemporary French thought that he finds Fouillée 'universally regarded as the leader of philosophy in France, a position not in the least shaken by Bergson's brief authority' (p. 17). He also ignores the force of literature as such; no mention of Barrès or Bourget.

14. See Liam de Paor, *On the Easter Proclamation and Other Declarations*, pp 34–5.

15. John P. McCormick, 'Political Theory and Political Theology; the Second Wave of Carl Schmitt in English', *Political Theory*, vol. 26 no. 6 (December 1998), pp 830–54; see p. 831.

16. On Schmitt's debt to Nietzsche as critics of modern technology, see John P. McCormick, *Carl Schmitt's Critique of Liberalism: Against Technology as Politics*, Cambridge: Cambridge University Press, 1997, pp 82–93, etc.

17. A point of departure might be Maisie Ward, *Insurrection Versus Resurrection*, London: Sheed and Ward, 1937. The title is less exciting than unprepared Irish readers might imagine.

18. The English literary dimension of Easter 1916 deserves a full study, perhaps to originate in a critical biography of MacDonagh. In *The London Review of Books* (16 December 2010), Dickens's use of the resurrection motif is noted by Michael Wood in connection with Joyce's *Finnegans Wake*. Professor Wood (author of *Yeats and Violence*, 2010) and I share the distinction of being rubbished by Peter Brooke (author of *Ulster Presbyterianism*, 1987) in the online *Dublin Review of Books*.

19. Arthur James Balfour (1848–1930) was Chief Secretary 1887–91 when he earned the sobriquet 'Bloody Balfour'; he became Prime Minister in 1902. His article on Bergson in the October 1911 issue of *The Hibbert Journal* initiated a sustained British interest in the French philosopher. The following April, *The Irish Church Quarterly* (an Anglican publication) commended Oliver Lodge in *The Hibbert* on 'Balfour and Bergson', also noting some discussion of Balfour's original article, with discussion also of Civilisation and Decadence. In July 1913, it commended Gerald Balfour's article in *The Hibbert* on 'Telepathy and

Metaphysics'. G.A. Chamberlain contributed an article to the *ICQ* on 'Demonic Possession' (April 1913, pp 143–53) in which Balfour and Bergson are noted, together with a more general reference to the French interest in hysteria. Nowhere is Yeats mentioned in these Irish Anglican chronicles, though his friend John Henry Bernard (1860– 1927) is. See also D.R.C. Hudson, *The Ireland that We Made: Arthur and Gerald Balfour's Contribution to the Origins of Modern Ireland*, Akron: University of Akron Press, 2003.

20. See Catherine B. Shannon, *Arthur J. Balfour and Ireland 1874–1922*, Washington: Catholic University Press of America, 1988, p. 182.

21. A starting point in the voluminous critical literature might be Kenneth Asher, 'T.S. Eliot and Ideology', *ELH*, vol. 55 no. 4 (Winter 1988), pp 895– 915. For specifically Irish debts to Eliot one might consider Daniel Corkery as critic and Eugene Watters (Eoghan Ó Tuairisc) as poet.

22. Quoted by way of translation in Jérôme aan de Wiel, *The Irish Factor 1889–1919: Ireland's Strategic and Diplomatic Importance for Foreign Powers*, Dublin: Irish Academic Press, 2011, p. 229.

23. James Joyce, *A Portrait of the Artist as a Young Man*, London: Penguin, 1963, pp 202–3, 180.

24. Contrast Emer Nolan, *James Joyce and Nationalism* (London: Routledge, 1995) and Trevor L. Williams, *Reading Joyce Politically* (Gainesville: University Press of Florida, 1997).

25. I should point to the extensive assembly of materials in Joseph Connell, *Dublin in Rebellion: a Directory 1913–1923* (Dublin: Lilliput, 2006), which makes scant use of the periodicals examined here, focuses entirely on the apparently victimless 'rebel cause', and laps the events of Easter Week into a synthetic periodisation, opening with the Lockout and including the late months of the Civil War. More positively, it is a very helpful guide to the topography of the rebellion.

26. Quoted in Bernard Bailyn, *The Ideological Origins of the American Revolution*, Cambridge, Mass: Belnap Press, 1967, p. vi.

27. See Henry Parkinson (ed.), *'The Workers' Charter': a Translation of the Famous Encyclical of Pope Leo XIII on the Condition of the Working Classes*, Oxford: Catholic Social Guild, 1929, p. 7.

## Chapter 1

1. See Alan O'Day and John Stevenson (eds), *Irish Historical Documents Since 1800*, Dublin: Gill & Macmillan, 1992, p. 149.

2. Initially, 'Ulster Unionists viewed this rebellion quite complacently, even gleefully …' See Patrick Buckland, *Ulster Unionism and the Origins of Northern Ireland 1886–1922*, Dublin: Gill & Macmillan, 1973, p. 105.

3.  Honor Ó Brolcháin, the Plunkett family historian, says the compilers went to Plunkett's bedside. I have heard it claimed that no surviving copy of the Proclamation bears his signature, but cannot verify the claim.

4.  In connection with the inner council of IRB activists responsible for the Proclamation, it is worth noting that no legal or constitutional expert was involved or available. (Pearse had qualified as a barrister, but took it as a personal merit to have failed in that profession.) In class terms, they had no access to the sort of expertise that might have rendered these phrases less awkward; this too may have been regarded as a 'merit', though it also reflects the hasty formulation of a text intended to get Ireland to the post-war conference table.

5.  Liam de Paor, *On the Easter Proclamation and Other Declarations*, Dublin: Four Courts Press, 1997, p. 77, referring to the Proclamation's fifth paragraph.

6.  But see Paige Reynolds, 'Staging Suffrage: the Events of 1913 Dublin Suffrage Week' in Louise Ryan and Margaret Ward (eds), *Irish Women and the Vote: Becoming Citizens*, Dublin: Irish Academic Press, 2007, pp 60–74.

7.  De Paor, op. cit., p. 46.

8.  'Ireland; the Shirt of Nessus', in Conor Cruise-O'Brien, *Passion and Cunning and Other Essays*, London: Weidenfeld & Nicolson, 1988, p. 220. Though the play of 1902 should not be confused with his earlier 'The Countess Cathleen' (where the sacrifice is supposedly of an immortal soul and the context famine, not insurrection), one can see that the later work functions at one level as an agit-prop version of the earlier which had traceable French origins; on this last point, see Mc Cormack, *Blood Kindred: W.B. Yeats, the Life, the Death, the Politics*, London: Pimlico, 2005, pp 334–5.

9.  Marianne Elliott, *Robert Emmet: the Making of a Legend*, London: Profile Books, 2003, pp 65, 87.

10. *DIB*, vol. 3, p. 217. The source is Grattan's *Life* of John Philpot Curran.

11. See Jesse Goldhammer, *The Headless Republic: Sacrificial Violence in Modern French Thought*, Ithaca: Cornell University Press, 2005, pp 5–7. See also Susan Dunne, *The Deaths of Louis XVI*, Princeton: Princeton University Press, 1994.

12. 'having resolutely waited for the right moment to reveal itself, she now seizes that moment …'

13. Henri Hubert and Marcel Mauss, *Sacrifice: its Nature and Function* (trans. W.D. Halls), London: Cohen and West, 1964, p. 63. See also J.G. Frazer, *The Golden Bough* (1911) vol. 1. Both Pearse and Burgess were the sons of protestant fathers.

14. This was not a unique personal obsession, though Pearse was conscious of an alleged failure to perpetuate racial insurrection in Ireland. Standish O'Grady dwelt on the same theme, though in relation to his own class rather than the Irish nation as any kind of unified entity. In France, anti-Dreyfus rhetoric alleged effeminacy among supporters of the Jewish captain co-relatable with their 'foreign' origins or affiliations; see Christopher E. Forth, *The Dreyfus Affair and the Crisis of French Manhood*, Baltimore: Johns Hopkins University Press, 2004.

15. J.J. Horgan, *From Parnell to Pearse*, Dublin: UCD Press, 2002, pp 285, 291, etc.

16. Patrick H. Pearse, *Complete Work: Political Writings and Speeches*, Dublin: Phoenix, 1924, p. 223. Pearse uses 'last' here in the idiomatic sense of 'latest' though there is a frisson of 'final' also.

17. Ibid., p. 65.

18. Pearse was not the first to use the term in an Irish political context; George Sigerson (1836–1925) responded to the government's execution of the three 'Manchester Martyrs' in 1867 with 'The Holocaust', a newspaper article which gained considerable notoriety; see Ken MacGilloway, 'George Sigerson' [n. p.]: *Stair Uladh*, 2011, pp 21–2, 69, and (for the text) pp 148–9.

19. Ibid., p. 87.

20. De Paor, op. cit., p. 56.

## Chapter 2

1. *Transactions of the Ossianic Society for the Year 1853*, vol. 1, p. 5.

2. See Dominic Daly, *The Young Douglas Hyde: the Dawn of the Irish Revolution and Renaissance 1874–1893*, Dublin: Irish University Press, 1974, pp 21–2.

3. Douglas Hyde, *A Literary History of Ireland* (2nd edition), London: Benn, 1967, p. 116.

4. See entries in Douglas Bennett (ed.), *Encyclopaedia of Dublin*, Dublin: Gill & Macmillan, 1991.

5. W.B. Yeats, *The Poems* (ed. Daniel Albright), London: Dent, 1990, p. 29; see also editorial notes on pp 397–413.

6. Ibid., p. 411.

7. R.V. Comerford, *The Fenians in Context*, Dublin: Wolfhound, 1998, p. 183.

8. For a recent perspective, see Pierre Arnaud, 'Dividing and Uniting; Sports Societies and Nationalism, 1870–1914', in Robert Tombs (ed.), *Nationhood and Nationalism in France: from Boulangism to the Great War 1889–1918*, London: HarperCollins, 1991, pp 182–94. Football is used as the symbol

of unthreatened civilian life in Sean O'Casey's play about the Great War, *The Silver Tassie* (1928).

9. Joseph Valente, 'The Manliness of Parnell', *Éire/Ireland*, vol. 41 (2000).

10. J.P.T. Bury, *France 1814–1940* (5th ed.), London: Routledge, 1985, p. 193.

11. See Herman Lebowicz, *True France, the Wars Over Cultural Identity 1900-1945*, Ithaca: Cornell University Press, 1992, p. 20 (citing Marin's widow as his authority).

12. See Bruce Morris, '"Neptune and Surging Waves"; Paul Borget and W.B. Yeats', *Yeats: an Annual of Critical and Textual Studies*, vol. 13 (1995), pp 225–36. Barrès has virtually disappeared from French bookshops, new and antiquarian, despite having been the idol of a generation; among his advocates in critical times was Ramon Fernandez; see his monograph of 1943, published in Paris by Editions de Livre Moderne. For a generous selection in English translation, see J.S. McClelland (ed.), *The French Right from de Maistre to Maurras*, London: Cape, 1970, pp 143–211. For an excellent summary of Barrès' political and literary positions, see Chapter 11 (pp 226–43) of Eugen Weber, *My France: Politics, Culture, Myth*, Cambridge, Mass.: Belnap Press, 1991.

13. Paul Bourget, *Some Portraits of Women*, London: Downey, 1898, pp 77–140.

14. Ibid., p. 130, original emphasis. For Yeats's treatment of a related folk motif, see 'Ghosts' in his *Fairy and Folk Tales*, London: Walter Scott, 1888, pp 128–9. The example of sprinkled chicken blood in Yeats's little text differs markedly from the occasion of Bourget: according to Yeats, 'The weak souls of very young are in especial danger. When a very young child dies, the western peasantry sprinkle the threshold with the blood of a chicken, that the spirits may be drawn away to the blood.'

15. Pat, 'Democracy in the Free State', *The English Review*, vol. 44 (1927), pp 669–70.

16. Connolly's vocabulary takes on a decidedly religious coloration after the O'Donovan Rossa funeral in the summer of 1915 when Pearse delivered his much lauded ovation. In an article called 'Ireland's Travail and Ireland's Resurrection' (*The Worker's Republic*, 7 August 1915), Connolly declared, 'Never did Ireland see a more soul-stirring of the Gael'; the term 'soul' is repeated throughout his contribution to the *Rossa Souvenir* (July 1915), 'Why the Citizen Army Honours Rossa'. See Liam de Paor, *On the Easter Proclamation and Other Declarations*, Dublin: Four Courts Press, 1997, pp 41, 72.

17. See Ivan Strenski, *Contesting Sacrifice: Religion, Nationalism and Social Thought in France*, Chicago: University of Chicago Press, 2001.

18. W.B. Yeats, 'Man and the Echo', in *The Poems*, p. 392.

19. Friedrich Nietzsche, 'The Case of Wagner'; I have used the translation provided by Walter Kaufmann, but extended it beyond the word 'atoms' for the specific political dimension of the original; see Kaufmann, *Nietzsche, Philosopher, Psychologist, Antichrist*, New York: Meridian Books, 1956, p. 61.

20. The essays began publication in November 1881 (*Nouvelle revue*), and appeared in volume form in 1883. Authors treated were Baudelaire, Ernest Renan, Hippolyte Taine, and Stendal. Subsequent editions were expanded in two volumes. For the Nietzsche/Bourget axis, see Werner Hamacher, *Premises: Essays on Philosophy and Literature from Kant to Celan* (trans. Peter Fenves), Stanford: Stanford University Press, 1996, pp 164–6. Kaufmann refers to *Essais I* (1883), p. 25.

21. György Lukács, *Soul and Form* (trans. Anna Bostock), London: Merlin Press, 1974, p. 113.

22. Cf Yeats's 'The Song of the Happy Shepherd' (1885: *Poems*, pp 33–5) and Eliot's 'Love Song of J. Alfred Prufrock' (1915: *Collected Poems 1909–1962*, London: Faber, 1963, pp 13–17).

23. See also V.M. Crawford, 'Paul Bourget, his Work and Place in French Literature', *Studies* vol. 24 (1935), p. 433.

24. See Proinsias Ó Drisceoil, 'Rebellion in the Artwork: Ó Tuairisc, *Dé Luain*, and the Craig Connection' in Agnes Bernelle (ed.), *Decantations: a Tribute to Maurice Craig*, Dublin: Lilliput Press, 1992, pp 139–47.

25. See the first chapter of *The House of the Seven Gables* (1851), Nathaniel Hawthorne, *The Complete Novels and Selected Tales*, New York: Modern Library, 1937.

26. During the Third Republic, rival symbols of ancient France entered into competition: the more familiar is the Bourbon dynasty's *fleur de lys*. The cockerel flew lower, its associations rural, regional, and non-aristocratic; it is now part of France's sporting iconography. Outside the Nanterre headquarters of the revived Front Nationale, a towering fibreglass cockerel stands guard over a rockery, complementing the figure of Saint Joan who graced the party's earlier years.

27. See C.E. Bechhofer, 'Letters from Ireland IV', *The New Age*, vol. 19, no. 26 (26 October 1916), p. 610; and 'James Connolly', loc. cit., vol. 20, no. 10 (4 January 1917), p. 239. Bechhofer was often condescending or supercilious in writing about Dublin but he took the trouble to incorporate most of the Proclamation into his articles, and to note the economic factors in Ireland injurious to the rebels' intentions. He also visited Belfast and other parts of Ireland.

28. Augusta Gregory, *Seventy Years 1852–1922* (ed. Colin Smythe), Gerrards Cross: Smythe, 1973, p. 308.

29. See notes to *The Collected Letters of W.B. Yeats: Volume II 1896–1900* (ed. Warwick Gould, John Kelly and Deirdre Toomey), Oxford: Clarendon Press, 1997, esp. pp 47–9.

30. Florimond de Basterot, *De Quebec à Lima: journal d'un voyage dans les deux Ameriques en 1858 et en 1859*, Paris: Hachette, 1860. See pp 34, 222, 291, etc.

31. De Basterot, who was a licensed *advocat* in France, had submitted a short thesis on Roman law; he published a second and longer travel journal, *Le Liban, la Galilé, et Rome*, in 1869. His father, Barthélemy (died 1887), was probably the first of the family to acquire property in Ireland. In his early years he published material on the geology of France, and corresponded with the Geological Society in London.

32. For Hone's influence as an intermediary between these continental strains of thought and W.B. Yeats (whose biography he wrote twice), see Mc Cormack, *We Irish in Europe: Yeats, Berkeley and J.M. Hone*, Dublin: UCD Press, 2010.

33. Cf. Mary Ebrill (born c.1867, she became a fluent speaker of Gaelic), 'A Tale of a Mirror', *Irish Monthly*, vol. 32, no. 367 (January 1904), p. 46; 'Rather Let Him Labour', ibid., vol. 38, no. 439 (January 1910), pp 21–2; 'Told in the Valley', ibid., vol. 38, no. 442 (April 1910), pp 210–11; 'Once Upon a Time', ibid., vol. 38, no. 443 (May 1910), pp 283–5; 'Her Garden', ibid., vol. 38, no. 445 (July 1910), pp 382–5; 'The Prayer of Saint Walpurga', ibid., vol. 38, no. 447 (September 1910), pp 520–22.

34. See Thomas Dillon, 'The Origins and Early History of the National University Part II', *University Review*, vol. 1, no. 6 (Autumn 1955), p. 18.

35. *Cork Examiner*, 21 February 1866.

36. She principally wrote short stories, e.g. 'The Unfinished Symphony' and 'The Bit o' Blue' (both 1906); 'Little Mary Cassidy' and 'Rosemary for Remembrance' (both 1907). 'The Egg Trust' appeared in *On Tiptoe: a Collection of Stories and Sketches by Irishwomen* (Dublin: M.H. Gill, 1917).

37. The recent academic literature on Joseph de Maistre is vast, with the Canadian Richard A. Lebrun a major activist. It is instructive to note who anthologised de Maistre, and thus returned him to readerly circulation, at sensitive moments; one fascist trader in these goods was E.M. Cioran in 1957.

38. *An Cailín ón Sibéir* (trans. Father Tomás Mac Eoin), Baile Átha Cliath: Oifig an tSoláthair, 1958. An Irish interest in the de Maistres was assumed in some quarters; in 1952, Burns, Oates and Washbourne forwarded a copy of Béla Menczer's anthology *Catholic Political Thought 1789–1848* to Bord Fáilte Éireann (the Irish Tourist Board) who duly sent it out to

a reviewer. Menczer's introduction to the de Maistre extracts makes much of the Savoyard's debt to Edmund Burke.

39. The translator was Aeneas McDonnell Dawson (1810–1894) who emigrated to Canada; the de Maistrean works were *The Pope* (translated 1850) and *St Petersburg Evenings* (1851).

40. 'The Coming Revolution' in Patrick H. Pearse, *Complete Works: Political Writings and Speeches*, Dublin: Phoenix, 1924, p. 99.

41. For the Kilmainham rebuke, see *The Irish Times*, 21 December 1901, p. 18; 'A great Christian thinker, Count Joseph de Maistre has an argument to the effect that War is a Divine law; he urges that it is so in the mysterious glory which encrowns it; in the protection of great captains …' After some more of this, the primate (William Alexander) prays for peace. Re L'Action francais, see *Cercle Joseph de Maistre*, Paris, 1907.

42. See Thomas Kinsella, *The Messenger*, Dublin: Peppercanister Press, 1978, p. 13. The Oblate Fathers' parent body was the French Assumptionist group, virulently anti-Semitic at the end of the nineteenth century and after; see Ruth Harris, *The Man on Devil's Island: Alfred Dreyfus and the Affair that Divided France*, London: Allen Lane, 2010, pp 218–29. On an ideological continuity from Joseph de Maistre to the Assumptionists, see Strenski, *Contesting Sacrifice*, p. 45.

43. For evidence of the order's place in a conventional forum of Catholic opinion in Ireland on the eve of Pearse's Rising, see R.F. O'Connor, 'The Oblates of Mary Immaculate', *The Irish Monthly*, vol. 44, no. 512 (February 1916), pp 102–7.

44. See Mrs M. Pearde Beaufort, 'Paul Bourget and Ireland', *The Irish Monthly*, vol. 43, no. 509 (November 1915), p. 696.

45. A case is sometimes made that the Military Council (and especially Clarke and MacDermott) anticipated Leninist tactics rather than repeating past models of Fenian organisation. There is certainly no evidence of a Bolshevik influence in the IRB, and the Proclamation is utterly devoid of socialist objectives, let alone communist ones. MacDermott nearly escaped execution, until he was identified among the prisoners by an astute G-man. (His physical disability as a polio victim made it unlikely that he could have remained incognito.) However, even if continuity had been maintained through the survival of a veteran IRB hard man, the likelihood of an Irish soviet-style republic was very slim indeed. Lawrence White, in *DIB*, ably summarises MacDermott's position: 'Ideologically a pure physical-force separatist, single-mindedly devoted to expelling British government from Ireland, he was hostile toward trade-unionism and socialist internationalism as impeding the development of native entrepreneurial industry and diluting national

feeling.' As to metaphysics, Requiem Mass was usual, and Catholicism remained inseparable from republican/nationalist ideology. I am grateful to Michael Laffan for his additional comments on MacDermott's role.

46. Bernard E. Doering, *Jacques Maritain and the French Catholic Intellectuals*, Notre Dame: University of Notre Dame Press, 1983, pp 1, 5. Doering describes Barrès as a Catholic novelist, and this is correct in the political sense, though the confessional aspect was diluted by both scientist and occult interests.

## Chapter 3

1. Some French, however, kept tabs on the secretive movement; see Jean-Marie Lemoine, *L'Irlande qu'on ne voit pas: les Fenians et le Fenianisme aux Etats-Unis*, Paris: Giard et Briève, 1893.

2. See for example the IRB article in Sean Connolly (ed.), *The Oxford Companion to Irish History*, Oxford: Oxford University Press, 1998.

3. For discussion of Joyce's allusion to *The Resurrection of Hungary*, see R.M. Adams, *Surface and Symbol: the Consistency of James Joyce's Ulysses*, New York: Oxford University Press, 1962, pp 99–104. Part of Adams's objective was to point out the anti-Semitism of Sinn Féin's founder.

4. Marnie Hay, *Bulmer Hobson and the Nationalist Movement in Twentieth-Century Ireland*, Manchester: Manchester University Press, 2009, pp 187–96.

5. For the fullest account of Lillie Reynolds (1877–1938), see Donal Nevin's edition of James Connolly, *Between Comrades, Letters and Correspondence 1889–1916*, Dublin: Gill & Macmillan, 2007, p. 647. Her father died when Lillie was young; her mother (Margaret, née Newman) moved the family to Rathmines, in the south Dublin suburbs. Jim Larkin's wife, Elizabeth Brown, was also a protestant, the daughter of a Baptist lay-preacher.

6. Ruth Dudley Edwards, *Patrick Pearse: the Triumph of Failure*, London: Gollancz, 1977, p. 2.

7. Mary Emily Pearse was baptised on 24 January 1865, and James Vincent Pearse on 19 December 1866 in St Peter's (Church of Ireland), Aungier Street, Dublin.

8. Ruth Dudley Edwards, op. cit., pp 2–3. Fr Devine, born James Devine in County Sligo and an Irish speaker, was a member of the Passionist congregation (an Italian eighteenth-century foundation) at Mount Argus in south Dublin. He spent the years 1872–5 travelling in America, north and south; on his return to Ireland, he was posted to Belfast. James Pearse, Fr Devine and other historical figures are characters in Eugene McCabe's one-act play, 'Gale Day' (1979).

9.   See the very useful family tree in Joost Augusteijn, *Patrick Pearse: the Making of a Revolutionary*, Basingstoke: Palgrave Macmillan, 2010, p. 347.

10.  James Stephens, *The Insurrection in Dublin*, Gerrards Cross: Smythe, 1978, pp 17–18.

11.  This is not the place or moment to analyse Great Brunswick Street in detail but, from 1862, one might note Bernard Mulrennin (at No. 23) miniature painter in ordinary to the Lord Lieutenant; Benjamin du Gue (No. 25) professor of French; Messrs Abbey and Harrison (No 27; where James Pearse later set up his business) architectural sculptors and church decorators; the Christian Brethren Chapel (between Nos 28 and 29); Crean W. Giblan (No. 29) cement and stucco plasterer, fountain vase and statue maker; Emily and Florence de Pontonier (No. 40) professors of harp, pianoforte, Italian and French; J.J. Gaskin (No. 40) professor of Wilheim's system of vocal music; and, further east, B.R.K. Shanahan [styled Count de Kavanagh] (No. 147) M.D. and accoucheur. In connection with James Pearse's first marriage, note for investigation James Fox (No. 148) guard at Kingstown Railway Station. By the end of the century, much had changed, not least through the economic difficulties of the 1890s. Demographically, the Catholic residents enjoyed greater numbers but also greater diversity of economic fortune. James Pearse's absorption into the Catholic Church, and his winning an important commission to erect pulpit and altar rails in the Star of the Sea church at Sandymount, might be taken as symbolic of these changes.

12.  James McCaffrey, 'The Catholic Church in 1916', *The Irish Ecclesiastical Record*, vol. 9 (January 1917), p. 13.

13.  P. Coffey, 'The Conscription Crisis in Ireland', *The Irish Ecclesiastical Record*, vol. 11 (June 1918), p. 485.

14.  For his contributions and pseudonyms, see the article on Corcoran in DIB by Patrick Maume.

15.  See the excellent summary account in Tom Clyde, *Irish Literary Magazines: an Outline History with Descriptive Bibliography*, Dublin: Irish Academic Press, 2003, pp 160–61.

16.  *The Catholic Bulletin*, vol. 6. nos 5–6, pp 266–8.

17.  By Thomas H. Burbage, ibid., pp 309–14; continued in vol. 6, no. 7, pp 354–60.

18.  William A. Scott, 'The Reconstruction of O'Connell Street, Dublin', *Studies*, vol. 5, no. 18, unpaged.

19.  Ibid., 'Poets of the Insurrection i — Thomas MacDonagh', pp 179–87 signed X Z.

20. For an account of Joyce's conversation with Fr Darlington, see Stanislaus Joyce, *My Brother's Keeper*, Cambridge, Mass: DaCapo Books, 2003, pp 187–9.

21. In April 1918, as the Great War bled to death, an Irish reviewer of Maurice Barrès' *Diverses Familles spirituelles de la France* defined Claudel as 'the uncompromising Catholic', Bourget as 'the pragmatist Catholic', Péguy as 'the nationalist Catholic', Francis James [sic] as 'the wistful Catholic', Huysmans as 'the aesthetic Catholic', and Barrès himself as 'that eminent pagan Roman Catholic'. The reviewer (and Hone is not a suspect) concludes that the *Entente* can be no better served than by mutual appreciation of British and French literature. The appeal of an emphatically Catholic group of writers was not lost on Ireland. See Anon., 'The Spiritual Families of France', *The Irish Times*, 20 April 1918, p. 5.

22. See Joseph O. Baylen, 'An Unpublished Note on General Georges Boulanger in Britain, June 1889', *French Historical Studies*, vol. 4, no. 3 (spring 1966), pp 344–7. Baylen incorporates a passage from Mrs Crawford's private journal which indicates that she had met Boulanger on some previous occasion who 'remembered me quite well.'

23. *The Irish Times*, 9 June 1892, p. 5.

24. I have argued that details of *The Brook Kerith* may obliquely reflect Moore's response to the Easter Rising, absorbed probably when he was correcting the proofs; see *We Irish in Europe: Yeats, Berkeley and Joseph Hone*, Dublin: UCD Press, 2010, pp 138–42.

25. In the course of her charitable work, she was persistently assailed by an Irish labourer in London whose children she tried to rescue from neglect; see *The Irish Times*, 14 March 1894, p. 6.

26. See J.M. Hone, *The Life of George Moore*, London: Gollancz, 1936, pp 354–7; Karen Offen, 'Sur l'origine des mots "féminisme" et "féministe"', *Revue d'histoire modern et contemporaine*, vol. 34, no. 3 (July–September 1987), pp 492–6.

27. *The Catholic Bulletin*, vol. 6, no. 9 (September 1916), p. 519.

28. Ibid., p. 522.

29. Ibid., vol. 6, no. 10 (October 1916), p. 580.

30. Ibid., vol. 6, no. 12 (December 1916), p. 629. Keogh was a pupil in Saint Enda's, and thus unlikely to have been as old as the *Bulletin* stated; see Joost Augusteijn, *Patrick Pearse: the Making of a Revolutionary*, Basingstoke: Palgrave Macmillan, 2010, pp 310–11.

31. *The Catholic Bulletin*, vol. 7, no. 1 (January 1917), p. 53.

32. Ibid., p. 57.

33. Ibid., p. 53.

34.  Ibid., p. 60. MacNeill was, of course, the Volunteers' commander whom Pearse and the *Bulletin*'s martyrs had deceived and betrayed, while he had tried to prevent the Rising.

35.  Ibid., pp 130, 127, 128.

36.  At least three early works of fiction by Bourget were published in English translation by the Waterford-born and London-based Edmund Downey. These were *A Tragic Idyll* (1896), *Some Portraits of Women* (1898), and *Domestic Dramas* (1901).

37.  Ibid., vol. 7, no. 9, p. 587.

38.  O'Kelly is the subject of a lengthy but partial study by Brian P. Murphy, *The Catholic Bulletin and Republican Ireland, with Special Reference to J.J. O'Kelly ('Sceilg')*, Belfast: Athol Books, 2005.

39.  *The Catholic Bulletin*, vol. 6, no. 8, p. 457. Thomas Kent was executed for the killing; one of his brothers later served as a deputy in Dáil Éireann.

40.  Ibid., p. 459.

41.  Ibid., p. 464.

42.  'Pat', 'Democracy in the Free State', *The English Review*, vol. 44 (1927), pp 673.

43.  *The Capuchin Annual*, No. 5 (1934), p. 185.

44.  *The Capuchin Annual*, No. 1 (1930), p. 40.

45.  Séamas Ó Buachalla, 'Pearse's Emmet' in Anne Dolan (et al, eds), *Reinterpreting Emmet*, Dublin: UCD Press, 2007, p. 217. C. 1911–12 much popular French journalism explored the phenomenon of crowd behaviour, following on Gustave Le Bon's highly successful *Psychologue des foules* (1895), including reconstructions of crowd behaviour in the distant and not so distant past; see Robert A. Nye, *The Origins of Crowd Psychology*, London: Sage, 1975, pp 173–5. Le Bon's one notable precursor on this topic was Hippolyte Taine in *Origines de la France contemporaine*, of which Pearse had studied the sections treating the *ancien regime*. Pearse's image of Emmet is in some respects a distorted reflection of French revolutionary violence, with the Irish rebel a disguised aristo.

46.  An exception might seem to be Yeats's 'Bachelor's Walk (in Memory)' painted, however, in 1922. A note appended to it in the popular 'Masters' series of the 1960s exemplifies the difficulty in maintaining any kind of chronological accuracy: 'This is a direct, classically simple "documentary" painting in which Yeats shows his moving but entirely unsentimental feeling for the Irish dead of the "Troubles" — the grim period between 1916 and 1923 when Irishmen and Englishmen killed each other with an unusually grandiose folly, even for warfare.'

The site, of course, is that of the 1914 shooting by British troops to which Pearse responded with 'unusually grandiose folly'.

47. On Yeats's remote dealings with Maloney, see W. J. Mc Cormack, *Roger Casement in Death*, Dublin: UCD Press, 2002, pp 64–6.

48. Yeats, *The Poems*, p. 355. See also p. 162 below.

**Chapter 4**

1. Jérôme aan de Wiel, *The Irish Factor 1899–1919: Ireland's Strategic and Diplomatic Importance for Foreign Powers*, Dublin: Irish Academic Press, 2011, p. xviii. See also Mark Tierney, 'A Survey of the Reports of the French Consuls in Ireland 1814-1929' in Liam Swords (ed.), *The Irish-French Connection 1578–1978*, Paris: Irish College, 1978, pp 130–41.

2. Thomas Kettle, *The Open Secret of Ireland* (ed. Senia Pašeta), Dublin: UCD Press, 2007, p. 32.

3. The famous speech from the dock was, of course, to a considerable extent constructed or re-arranged in the 1890s, almost a century after its author's execution, the context being centenary commemorations of the 1798 rebellion. Thus Pearse's Emmet is, in a synthetic textual sense, genuinely his contemporary, proving yet another instance of a discounted time-interval; see W.J. Mc Cormack (et al.), 'Political Power: Cromwell to O'Connell', *Field Day Anthology*, Derry: Field Day, 1991, vol. 1, pp 855–960.

4. A gruesome vignette from the Emmet rebellion, detailed in C.R. Maturin's gothic novel, *Melmoth the Wanderer* (1822) re-emerged in the edition of 1892. Most apt for the *fin-de-siècle* was the auto-crucifixion of a witness to Lord Kilwarden's murder by Emmet's irregulars, nailed to the wall by what he saw. This Sebastianisation of the victim/witness impressed Oscar Wilde who, in French exile, called himself Sebastian Melmoth. As Christ is to Sebastian, so Emmet is to Pearse, or so the homo-erotic cult might conclude.

5. 'Royal Hibernian Academy: "Ecce Homo"' in James Joyce, *The Critical Writings* (ed. Ellsworth Mason and Richard Ellmann), Ithaca: Cornell University Press, 1989, p. 36. For discussion of misapplication of the term 'passion' (as in an article called 'The Passion of Padraic Pearse') see Mc Cormack, *'We Irish' in Europe: Yeasts, Berkeley and Joseph Hone*, Dublin: UCD Press, 2010, p. 91, etc.

6. For matriculation in 1898, Pearse would have read some or all of the following — Emile Souvestre, 'Un philosophe sous les toits' (1855); Jean François Casimir Delavigne, 'Les Enfants d'Edouard' (1833); Corneille, 'Polyeucte' (1643); Sandeau, 'Mlle de la Seiglière' (1848), La Fontaine, 'Select Fables', Erckmann-Chatrian, 'L'invasion' (1862). Apart

from the obligatory classic drama, this was essentially a nineteenth-century list; indeed the two co-authors who wrote as Erckmann-Chatrian both lived into the 1890s. For the annual university examinations, he studied more classic texts (by Boileau, Buffon, Corneille, Fenélon, Molière, Racine, Voltaire), but also a range of near-contemporary prose works. Among the latter was Augustin Thierry's 'Récits des temps Merovingiens' (1-3). Hippolyte Taine was represented by *L'Ancien regime* (1876) Parts ii–iv. The full title of Taine's work was *Les Origines de la France contemporaine: l'ancien regime* and, as such, it contributed to the *soi-disant* Marxist Georges Sorel's disenchantment with the Revolution of 1789; see below pp 102–108. Apart from the dramatists, also La Fontaine, Taine, Thierry, etc, minor authors prevailed; there was no Flaubert, Baudelaire or Hugo on the syllabus. Nevertheless, a contemporary sense of French thought was accessible. A full assessment of Pearse and MacDonagh's indebtedness to their university education awaits its moment. The summer 1899 examination (first year, pass level, Section b) in French included four questions, two of which required students to translate seven passages of various lengths: of which no fewer than six related specifically to the military career of General Lazare Hoche or his attempt to land French forces in Bantry Bay. No concern with contemporary French style can explain this proportion.

7.   G.K. Chesterton, 'The Donkey', in *The Wild Knight and Other Poems*, London: Grant Richards, 1900. Cf. 'The fools, the fools, the fools, they have left us our Fenian dead ...' Patrick H. Pearse, *Complete Works: Political Writings and Speeches*, Dublin: Phoenix, 1924, p. 137.

8.   Cf MacDara's last words in 'The Singer' — 'One man can free a people as one Man redeemed the world. I will take no pike, I will go into the battle with bare hands. I will stand up before the Gall as Christ hung naked before men on the tree!' Patrick H. Pearse, *Collected Works: Plays, Stories, Poems*, Dublin: Phoenix, 1924, p. 44. See W.I. Thompson, *The Imagination of an Insurrection*, 2nd ed., West Stockbridge: Lindisfarne Press, 1982, p. 98 on the passage quoted above.

9.   W.I. Thompson, op. cit., pp 49–52, etc.

10.  For a judicious summary see Tom Clyde, *Irish Literary Magazines: an Outline History and Descriptive Bibliography*, Dublin: Irish Academic Press, 2003, pp 161–3. A comprehensive analysis of the advertising pages would be valuable. Take the 8pp of advertisements in the first issue (March 1911): these included one full page for *The English Review*, another for Macmillans, a third for the Pelman School of Memory; half-pages for Murray's tobacco, Edwards' Desiccated Soup, *The Open Window* (magazine), Pohlmann's Pianos, *The Book Monthly*, and

*An Macnaomh* (ed. Pearse). Retail business (including book publishing) predominated, with little or no ecclesiastical patronage of the kind found in the comparable sections of *The Irish Monthly, The Catholic Bulletin, The Capuchin Annual,* etc. Of course, *The Irish Review* had no institutional link to any religious body, and to the best of my knowledge no ordained person figured as a contributor. A thorough analysis of these mundane details might illuminate the notion that the *Review* was more interested in French Catholicism than Irish.

11.   See his *Pan-Germanic Doctrine* (1904) and *England and Germany* (1907).

12.   *The Irish Times,* 10 May 1913, p. 7.

13.   For Harrison (1873–1928), see Martha S. Vogeler, *Austin Harrison and the English Review,* Columbia: University of Missouri Press, 2008.

14.   Sam Hynes, *The Edwardian Turn of Mind,* Princeton: Princeton University Press, 1968, p. 307.

15.   Virginia Woolf, 'Mr Bennett and Mrs Brown' (1923), *Collected Essays,* vol. 3, London: 1966, p. 319.

16.   See Christophe Charle, *Naissance des 'intellectuels', 1880–1900,* Paris: Editions de Minuit, 1990.

17.   *The Irish Review,* vol. 1, no. 6 (August 1911), p. 275.

18.   National Library of Ireland Ms 10,999.

19.   Calvin Bedient, *The Yeats Brothers and Modernism's Love of Motion,* Notre Dame: University of Notre Dame Press, 2009, pp 30, 57–8, etc.

20.   *The Irish Review,* vol. 1, no. 7 (September 1911), pp 331–2.

21.   Loc. cit., vol. 1, no. 8 (October 1911), pp 380–81.

22.   Loc. cit., p. 382.

23.   Joost Augusteijn, *Patrick Pearse: the Making of a Revolutionary,* Basingstoke: Palgrave Macmillan, 2010, pp 91, 103.

24.   *The Irish Review,* vol. 2, no. 13 (March 1912), p. 2.

25.   Bodkin (1887–1961), who became director of the National Gallery of Ireland in 1927, published the bilingual anthology *May it Please Your Lordships: Reproductions of Modern French Poems,* Dublin: Maunsel, 1917.

26.   *The Irish Review,* vol. 2, no. 21 (December 1912), p. 552.

27.   Loc. cit., vol. 3, no. 31 (September 1913), pp 338, 336.

28.   See Joseph Barbier's critical and annotated edition, published in Nancy by Berger-Levrault (1962).

29.   See J.S. Mc Clelland (ed.), *The French Right from de Maistre to Maurras,* London: Cape, 1970, pp 143–4.

30.   See Ronald Schuchard, 'T.S. Eliot as an Extension Lecturer 1916–1919', *Review of English Studies* n s, vol. 25, no. 98 (1974), esp. p. 166. Schuchard elsewhere lists the primary books used by Eliot in this venture:

J-J Rousseau: *The Social Contract: Confessions: De l'origine de l'inegalite*; Jules Lemaitre: *Jean-Jacques Rousseau*; Maurice Barrès: Novels: *Le Jardin de Berenice: Colette Baudoche: La Colline inspirée*; Political writings: *Scenes et doctrines du nationalisme: La Patrie française: Pages choisies*; Charles Maurras: *L'Avenir del'intelligence: La Politique religieuse*; Pierre Lasserre: *Le Romantisme français*; Charles Péguy: *Oeuvres choisies, 1900– 10*; *Le Mystere de la charité de Jeanne d'Arc*; *Notre Patrie*; Georges Sorel: *Reflections on Violence*; Paul Claudel: *Art poetique: The Tidings Brought to Mary: The East I Know*; Henri Bergson: *Introduction to Metaphysics*; Maurice Maeterlinck: *Wisdom and Destiny: The Life of the Bee*; Paul Sabatier: *Modernism: Disestablishment in France: France Today: Its Religious Orientation*; Alfred Loisy: *The Gospel and the Church: War and Religion*. See Schuchard, 'Eliot and Hulme in 1916' PMLA, vol. 88, no. 5 (Oct. 1973), p. 1093. The overlap between Eliot's list of required reading in 1916 and the French authors impinging on Irish literary debate, either through *The Irish Review* and lesser periodicals or through Joseph Hone or through Iseult Gonne's tutoring of Yeats is striking. Loisy's *The Gospel and the Church* (England translation, 1908) was prefaced with a memoir by the Dublin-born Jesuit-Modernist George Tyrell. Rousseau heads the list as the enemy to be vanquished.

Malye (died 1973) published in several issues of *Le Pays Lorrain* c. 1922–3, and may have shared a Lorraine background with Barrès; later he became secretary of the Association Guillaume Budé, a learned society devoted to classical studies and the history of humanism. For some minute details of his career as a French diplomat in Washington, dealing with Irish matters, see Jérome aan de Viel, *The Irish Factor 1899– 1919: Ireland's Strategic and Diplomatic Importance for Foreign Powers*, Dublin: Irish Academic Press, 2011, pp 373–5, 386–77. (This book appeared too late to be adequately treated in these pages.) In 1964 Malye co-edited with James Carney no. VII of *Irish Essays and Studies* (Uppsala).

31.	For an account of the Celtic movement's relationship with major French cultural innovations, see Chapter 4 ('The Body of the Nation: Cubism's Celtic Nationalism') in Mark Antcliff, *Inventing Bergson: Cultural Politics and the Parisian Avant Garde*, Princeton: Princeton University Press, 1993, pp 106–34. Barrès' appeal to Celtic nationalism was not limited to Ireland; as a young soldier in the trenches, Saunders Lewis (1893-1985; founder of the Welsh Nationalist Party) read from Barrès' works; he later admired Charles Maurras. See *Oxford Dictionary of National Biography* — 'he had been profoundly affected by his experiences in France during the war and by the Irish rising of 1916. At university he met Margaret Gilcriest (1891–1984), the daughter of Irish Wesleyan parents who had moved from Wicklow to Liverpool. She read geography and became a teacher, but she also espoused the cause of Irish nationalism, later turning her back on her parents' religion by becoming a Roman Catholic. Both she and Lewis steeped themselves in the works of the Irish literary renaissance and learned the Irish and Welsh languages.'

32. Madelaine Teynier, 'La Mouvement Feminine Francaise', *The Irish Review*, vol. 3, no. 28 (June 1913), pp 191–4.

33. James Bertram, 'Liberty under Capitalism', *The Irish Review*, vol. 3, no. 32 (October 1913), p. 395; Connolly's 'Labour in Dublin' is at pp 385–91.

34. See Leslie Derfler, *Paul Lafargue and the Flowering of French Socialism*, Cambridge, Mass: Harvard University Press, 1998, p. 59.

35. Moritz Bonn, *Wandering Scholar*, London: Cohen and West, 1949, p. 89. Very charitably, he made no reference to the Irish republican alliance with his persecutors in Germany.

36. Edward Martyn, 'Wagner's Parsifal; or, The Cult of Liturgical Aestheticism', *The Irish Review*, vol. 3, no. 34 (December 1913), pp 535–40.

37. W.I. Thompson, op. cit., p. 121.

38. Plunkett's 'White Dove of the Wild Dark Eyes' appeared in *The Irish Review*, vol. 1, no. 4 (June 1911), p. 178. His resistant beloved was Columba (i.e. 'dove' in Latin) O'Carroll.

39. The speech, or passages from it, was preserved by Yeats, *Autobiographies*, London: Macmillan, 1955, p. 424. Joost Augusteijn inexplicably attributes this passage to Fr Eugene O'Growney (see his *Patrick Pearse*, p. 278).

40. Thomas William Hazen Rolleston, *Parsifal, or the Legend of the Holy Grail retold from Ancient Sources with Acknowledgement to the Parsifal of Richard Wagner*, London: Harrap, 1912. For a more detailed account of Rolleston's versions of the Wagnerian tales, see C.H. Rolleston, *Portrait of an Irishman: a Biographical Sketch of T.W. Rolleston*, London: Methuen, 1939, pp 150–56. Rolleston's pamphlets deserve close attention, notably *Ireland and Poland: a Comparison* (1917), *Ireland's Vanishing Opportunity* (1919), and a number of translations from German.

41. Padraic H. Pearse, *Collected Works: Plays, Poems, Stories*, Dublin: Phoenix, 1924, p. 14.

42. Ibid., p. 33. For a longer consideration of Pearse, Péguy and Nietzsche, see *'We Irish' in Europe: Yeats, Berkeley and Joseph Hone*, Dublin: UCD Press, 2010, pp 128–38.

43. Pearse, loc. cit., pp 25 and 24.

44. Ibid., p. xvii.

45. Ibid., p. 31.

46. For a fuller discussion of O'Grady's radical toryism and his pamphlets of the 1880s, see W.J. Mc Cormack, *Ascendancy and Tradition in Anglo-Irish Literary History from 1789 to 1939*, Oxford: Clarendon Press, 1985, pp 228-238.

47. Theodor Adorno, *In Search of Wagner*, London: New Left Books, 1981, p. 79.

48. On Boutroux see Alan D. Schrift, *Twentieth-Century French Philosophy*, Oxford: Blackwell, 2006, pp 6–7, 104–5.

49. Jean Malye, 'Le Home Rule et la France', *The Irish Review*, vol. 4, no. 41 (July–August 1914), p. 273.

50. Bourgeois returned to Ireland during the Troubles and, if memory serves, was arrested in the company of the very young Seán MacBride (who was compromising who?). After the Treaty he corresponded with George Gavan Duffy. In 1925, the first volume of his *Catalogue méthodique des fonds britannique et nord-américains ... La Crise internationale* appeared (Paris: Costes), the final volume in 1931.

51. NLI Ms 22, 934, Thomas MacDonagh to Dominick Hackett, 19 May 1915. Houston may have joined the Georgius Rex corps: at c. sixty, he was ineligible for the Army.

52. Quoted in T.W. Rolleston, *L'Irlande telle qu'elle est, par deux irlandais*, Geneva: Delachaux et Niestlé, 1917, p. 42. For a detailed and balanced account, see Ian McKeane, 'Journées Sanglantes / Days of Blood; the French Press and the Easter Rising' in Ruan O'Donnell (ed.), *The Impact of the 1916 Rising Among the Nations*, Dublin: Irish Academic Press, 2008, pp 119–40.

53. Stuart-Stephens, 'The Secret History of the [sic] Sinn Féin', *The English Review* (May 1916), pp 487–96; 'How I Foretold the Sinn Féin Rebellion', loc. cit. (June 1916), pp 548–61; 'Secret Constitution of the [sic] Shinn [sic] Fane [sic]', loc. cit. Martha S. Vogeler treats the variants of Stuart-Stephens's name as pseudonyms, the unidentified author being responsible for 25 articles published in the EE during the war; see Vogeler, *Austin Harrison and the English Review*, Columbia: University of Missouri Press, 2007, pp 215–16. After Harrison sold *The English Review*, its political orientation swung sharply to the Right. Regular contributors included Montgomery Belgion, Christopher Dawson, Wyndham Lewis, and the Irish baronet Sir Charles Petrie who wrote a Foreign Affairs column. T.S. Eliot made occasional appearances, usually as a reviewer. Against this bias, one finds H.W. Nevinson, Casement's supporter and a valiant anti-colonialist. Retired army officers commanded numerous pages. Among these we might count Arthur Lynch, once an Irish volunteer in the Boer cause and, by 1930, a

successful London doctor. (Vogeler describes him as 'a former intelligence agent'.) He railed (1932, 1933) against Einstein and Freud. The Irish presence was slight, though Petrie favourably reviewed Lennox Robinson's biography of Bryan Cooper, and Francis Stuart contributed a short story ('The Isles of the Blest', December 1934). The attitude towards continental fascism was not entirely complaisant, yet Odon Por's 'Agriculture under Fascism [in Italy]' steered a 'middle' approving course. Hostile, or embarrassed, English responses to Easter 1916, such as those appearing in *The English Review* or *The New Age*, are not treated in Ruan O'Donnell (ed.), *The Impact of the 1916 Rising Among the Nations* (Dublin: Irish Academic Press, 2008). The series of letters appearing in *The New Age* were written from Dublin by Carl Eric Bechhofer (1894–1949) whose subsequent publications indicate a wide familiarity with French, German and Russian literature.

54. Dawson (1889–1970) began to publish c. 1920 in *The Sociological Review*, and subsequently contributed two articles on the cyclical theory of civilisations approved by both Oswald Spengler and W.B. Yeats. He published frequently in *The Dublin Review*, not an Irish-based journal, though the influence of Shane Leslie and others kept the door open. In 1931 he made his first appearance in *Studies* and, in the same year, wrote an introduction to the little volume which constituted the first of Carl Schmitt's works to be translated into English. Part of this introduction also appeared in *The English Review*. One of his few direct comments on Ireland, 'Rome, Ireland and the European Tradition', was published in *G.K.'s Weekly*, vol. 20 (1934). Apart from *The Sociological Review*, all of these publications appeared under explicitly Catholic imprints.

## Chapter 5

1. For Bonn's own account, see *Wandering Scholar*, London: Cohen & West, 1949, especially the fifth chapter, 'The Land of Heart's Desire' (pp 82–101).

2. One of these, Heinrich Zimmer, had died years before the Easter Rising; the other, Kuno Meyer, had been confused with a non-relative of the same surname; see Ian McKeane, 'Journées Sanglantes / Days of Blood; the French Press and the Easter Rising' in Ruan O'Donnell (ed.), *The Impact of the 1916 Rising Among the Nations*, Dublin: Irish Academic Press, 2008, p. 134.

3. Moran, of course, achieved more than an introductory analysis of Pearse in Freudian terms; he also involved Charles Péguy and Georges Sorel in arguments placing Pearse within a European context. Before him, only Conor Cruise O'Brien had dealt with both Pearse and Péguy — though

never in the same article or book; see his *Maria Cross* (1954) for essays on Claudel, Péguy, Bloy amongst others.

4.　*The Irish Times*, 14 October 1910, p. 6.

5.　*The Irish Times*, 1 May 1912, p. 8.

6.　*The Irish Times*, 13 September 1913, p. 6.

7.　See Patrick Sheehan, *A Spoilt Priest & Other Stories*, Dublin: Clonmore and Reynolds, 1954, pp 32–54. First published 1905; by 1919, the collection had been translated into Dutch and German.

8.　This certainly was not the first notice of Sorel to appear in Ireland. In a review of T.J. Gerrard's *Bergson, an Exposition and Criticism from the Point of View of St Thomas Aquinas*, *The Irish Monthly* noted that the author had 'several interesting pages on the connection between the Syndicalism of Sorel and the Evolutionism of Bergson.' See *The Irish Monthly*, vol. 42, no. 487, pp 53–4. According to Jeremy Jennings, Hulme's translation was first published in America (he gives a date of November 1914); thus it is possible (though, I think, unlikely) that Hone had read the *Reflections* in English well in advance of March 1916. In practice, he would have used the original French text.

9.　For the only extensive account of Hone, see W.J. Mc Cormack, *'We Irish' in Europe: Yeats, Berkeley, and Joseph Hone*, Dublin: University College Dublin Press, 2010. A preliminary checklist of his publications, not including the review of Sorel now proposed as his work, appears on pp 185–9.

10.　Seillière is largely forgotten, even in France. However, a 2001 thesis accepted at the University of Paris x (Nanterre), by Laetitia de Cazenove, presents him as a theoretician of imperialism and also, with careful punctuation, as 'père de fascism?' The latter title, of course, has been widely distributed to many (including, by the Protocols of Athol, Edmund Burke!).

11.　Hulme remains an under-known figure; but see Ronald Schuchard, 'Eliot and Hulme in 1916: Toward a Revaluation of [T.S.] Eliot's Critical and Spiritual Development', *PMLA*, vol. 88, no. 5 (October 1973), pp 1083–94.

12.　Georges Sorel, *Reflections on Violence* (ed. Jeremy Jennings), Cambridge: Cambridge University Press, 1999, p. xxxvii.

13.　Daniel Halévy, *The Life of Friedrich Nietzsche* (trans. J. M. Hone), London: Fisher Unwin, 1911, p. 18. As an account of the German philosopher, the book was fatally compromised by its reliance on the work of Nietzsche's manipulative sister.

14.　Writing about 1913, Pádraig Yeates notes a number of contrasting instances where the syndicalist vocabulary is cited or implied. A stolid middle-class citizen complains through *The Irish Times* of being caught, in effect, between rising costs and 'the epidemic of labour unrest which has spread over these islands.' In *Sinn Féin*, a more adventurous thinker (Séamus Ó hAodha) pointed out that the employers had been the first party to the conflict which used 'sympathetic' action to reinforce its position (cf the 'sympathetic strike' regarded as a syndicalist tactic). He went on to declare that 'if we were within three hours' sail of France or Belgium or Germany, and the workers in those countries realised that our fear of being regarded as "taking sides" prevented us succouring our hard-hit women and children, do you think they would realise the duty of sending food?' The busy IRB-man Earnán de Blaghd regarded the general strike as a weapon of limited value, but emphasised the power of voluntarism and the ideological impulse to transform potential — an alternative couched in recognisably Sorelian terms. De Blaghd duly progressed as a skinflint minister for finance in the 1920s into full-blooded support for fascism. See Yeates, *Lockout Dublin 1913*, Dublin: Gill & Macmillan, 2000, pp 168, 357, 358.

15. This theme has been linked by an American critic of Sorel's to the theology of Saint Augustine; see Richard Humphrey, *Georges Sorel, Prophet without Honor: a Study in Anti-Intellectualism*, Cambridge, Mass: Harvard University Press, 1951, pp 168–70.

16. Sorel, *Reflections on Violence*, esp. pp 230–34.

17. Sorel, op. cit., p. 67. For an account of journalistic circles in which Bonnier and Sorel moved in 1893 (just two years after Parnell's death) see Leslie Derfler, *Paul Lafargue and the Flowering of French Socialism 1882–1911*, Cambridge, Mass: Harvard University Press, 1998, pp 169–81.

18. See McKeane, op. cit., p. 132.

19. Two co-presidents were elected at the Congress, and the person alluded to here was Fritz Kater (1861–1945). Ironically, the dominant French syndicalist organisation boycotted the London congress.

20. Sorel's most concentrated discussion of myth is to be found in the Letter to Daniel Halévy which served as Introduction to the book-version of *Reflections*; see Sorel, op. cit., pp 3–36.

21. The meaning of this proverbial phrase is not thoughtlessly to 'fool about', but consciously to act the part of a jester, stage-fool, etc.

22. The letter-writer's view is entirely at odds with Sorel's own insistence; see Sorel, op. cit., pp 21, 29.

23. Again the letter-writer is at odds with Sorel's own published views, but the latent point may refer to the extent workers ignored or remained ignorant of these publications while acting in accordance.

24. *Irish Independent*, 29 September 1913, p. 4.

25. Michael J. Phelan, 'A Gaelicised or a Socialised Ireland — Which?', *Catholic Bulletin and Book Review*, vol. 3. no. 11 (November 1913), pp 769–74.

26. See John J. Silke, 'Irish Scholarship and the Renaissance 1580–1673' in *Studies in the Renaissance*, vol. 20 (1973), pp 201–2, citing Renan's *Histoire littéraire de la France* (1869).

27. *Irish Independent*, 27 January 1914, p. 5.

28. *Irish Independent*, 12 August 1912, p. 8 — 'anti-State, anti-militant, anti-patriotic'. The middle term should be taken to means 'anti-military'.


## Chapter 6

1.  For vivid details of Barrès' attention to the working class in 1898, see Chapter Three of Pierre Birnbaum, *The Anti-Semitic Moment* (Chicago: University of Chicago Press, 2011), especially pp 126–32. The immediate excitement in France was Emile Zola's conviction, in relation to his Dreyfusard protests; for Maud Gonne and her circle, the moment was devoted to the United Irishmen centenary, celebrated in nationalist rather than Jacobin terms. There was a degree of anti-English overlap in these heated sentiments. There is no extensive biography of Millevoye, but his long association with Boulangism can be traced in detail in Bertrand Joly, *Deroulède: L'inventeur du nationalisme*, [n.p.] Perrin, 1998.

2.  M. Pearde Beaufort, 'A French Nationalist', *The Irish Monthly*, vol. 44, no. 514 (April 1916), pp 258–66; see pp 259 and 266–7.

3.  Hone not only introduced Montégut's *Mitchel*, he also translated and published it (via Maunsel). While his 1918 selection of writings by James Fintan Lalor (1807–1849) could hardly be thought evidence of a rightward political shift, Lalor was an interest Hone did not maintain, whereas Mitchel he successfully insinuated into Yeats's pantheon of anti-democratic heroes.

4.  Perhaps the great thinker was Joyce, who certainly had some of Bergson's work on his bookshelves; see John McCourt (ed.), *Roll Away the Reel World: James Joyce and Cinema*, Cork: Cork University Press, 2010, pp 123–4.

5.  Liam de Paor, *On the Easter Proclamation and Other Declarations*, Dublin: Four Courts Press, 1997, p. 28.

6.  Thomas Clarke and Pearse made public interventions sympathetic to the workers, the former to condemn police violence, and the latter mockingly to compare the employers to 'poor Marie Antoinette'; see Yeates, op. cit., pp 219–20.

7.　The sardonic coinage 'Cuchullainoid' was J.M. Synge's, alluding to Standish O'Grady's fiction and (possibly) Yeatsian drama.

8.　Ramsay MacDonald, *Syndicalism, a Critical Examination*, London: Constable, 1912, p. v.

9.　Arthur D. Lewis, *Syndicalism and the General Strike: an Explanation*, London: Fisher Unwin, 1912, p. 57.

10.　Walter McDonald, *Some Ethical Questions of Peace and War*... (1919) is an exception to several rules. Most of the material was written before 1916, and all of it is light on specifics; see pp 116–21, 'Trade Unionism, Syndicalism, Socialism', where Fr McDonald regards or presents syndicalism as driven by evolution not revolution.

11.　Quoted in Sean Farrell Moran, *Patrick Pearse and the Politics of Redemption: the Mind of the Easter Rising 1916*, Washington DC: Catholic University of America Press, 1994, p. 180.

12.　Moran, op. cit., p. 180, referring to passages in the *Reflections*.

13.　P.H. Pearse, 'Some Aspects of Irish Literature', lecture to the National Literary Society, 9 December 1912.

14.　NLI Ms 22, 934, Thomas MacDonagh to Dominick Hackett, 19 May 1915.

15.　See Schuchard, 'Eliot and Hulme in 1916', p. 1089.

16.　See Louis Roche's, *Anthology of French Poetry: Filíocht Mheán-Teistiméireachta* (Dublin: Brown and Nolan [c.1952]).

17.　*The Irish Times*, 12 September 1915, p. 5.

18.　After the Franco-Prussian War, veneration of Martin of Tours as soldier-saint gained great popularity; for Foch in this context, see Brian Brennan, 'The Revival of the Cult of Martin of Tours in the Third Republic', *Church History*, vol. 66, no. 3 (September 1997), p. 500.

19.　Plunkett, a much younger man than Yeats, read French poetry through a selection rooted in the nineteenth-century, *Anthologie des Poètes Francais Contemporains* (1866–1906), 3 vols, ed. G. Walch.

20.　Strenski, p. 2.

21.　Ronald Schuchard, 'Eliot and Hulme in 1916', PMLA, vol. 88, no. 5 (October 1973), pp 1088–9.

22.　A brief passage by Montégut appears on the title-page of Arland Ussher's *The Face and Mind of Ireland* (London: Gollancz, 1949) — 'This race is at the same time inferior and superior to the rest of humanity. One may say of the Irish that they find themselves in a false position here below. Placed between memory and hope, the race will never conquer what it desires, and it will never discover what it regrets.' I owe this detail to Liam de Paor.

23.　*The Irish Times*, 26 March 1916, p. 3.

24. *The Irish Times*, 26 April 1916, p. 6. Barrès' source was a Dutch (hence neutral) traveller's report of visiting Cologne and Berlin.

25. Moritz Bonn, *Modern Ireland and Her Agrarian Problem*, Dublin: Hodges Figgis, 1906, p. 78.

26. Moritz Bonn, *Irland und die irische Frage*, Munich, Leipzig: Duncker & Humblot, 1918, p. 255; see also pp 238, 250. The foreword is dated 28 December 1917.

27. A.J. Balfour to John Henry Bernard, 10 May 1916; quoted in Catherine B. Shannon, *Arthur J. Balfour and Ireland 1874–1922*, Washington: Catholic University of American Press, 1988, p. 213.

28. Georges Sorel, *Reflections on Violence* (ed. Jeremy Jennings), Cambridge: Cambridge University Press, 1999, p. 24.

29. Ibid., p. 49.

**Chapter 7**

1. See Patrick Bridgwater, *Nietzsche in Anglosaxony: a Study of Nietzsche's Impact on English and American Literature*, Leicester: Leicester University Press, 1972.

2. Carl Schmitt, *Theodor Däubers 'Nordlicht': Drei Studien über die Elemente, den Geist under die Aktualität des Werkes* (republished Cologne, 1982).

3. Richard Ellmann, *James Joyce*, New York: Oxford University Press, 1959, p. 128. When Stanislaus Joyce enquired what his brother would have done in the event of the challenge materialising, the latter mentioned the first train out of Paris; see Stanislaus Joyce, *My Brother's Keeper: James Joyce's Early Years*, [n.p.]: Da Capo Press, 2003, p. 200.

4. For a brief local contribution to what will be Schmitt's grand continental theme, see William O'Brien, MP, *The Downfall of Parliamentarianism: a Retrospect for the Accounting Day*, Dublin, London: Maunsel, 1918. O'Brien (1852–1928), whose Jewish wife was a Francophone Russian, ended his political days in Fianna Fáil.

5. Carl Schmitt, *The Crisis of Parliamentary Democracy* (trans. Ellen Kennedy), Cambridge, Mass: MIT Press, 1994, p. 75. The essay available in French includes the same passage with, however, the use of Gaelic *Padraic* for Patrick.

6. Carl Schmitt, *Roman Catholicism and Political Form* (trans. G.L. Ulmen), Westport, Conn.: Greenwood, 1996, p. 7. In 1931 the London firm of Catholic publishers, Sheed & Ward, issued a short book by Schmitt under the title *The Necessity of Politics*. The title-page verso declares this to be a translation of *Römischer Katholizmus und Politische Form*. While this earlier publication has a certain period quality, and

the translation differs in style, I have opted to cite the somewhat more accessible recent version.

7. See Michael Marder, 'Carl Schmitt's "Cosmopolitan Restaurant": Culture, Multiculturism, and Complexio Oppositorum', *Telos*, no. 142 (Spring 2008), pp 29–47.

8. Schmitt, *Roman Catholicism*, p. 5.

9. Pádraig Yeates, *Lockout Dublin 1913*, Dublin: Gill & Macmillan, 2000, pp 296, 574. Many priests were antagonistic towards the trade unions in 1913, and towards charitable efforts to feed, clothe and house the children of workers. In that context, Fr Aloysius was generally an exception. In 1916, however, he and his order, together with other clergy, were engaged in widespread ministration to rebels and civilians alike. Schmitt's parable nimbly merges these two occasions and confuses the proportions.

10. Carl Schmitt, *Political Theology: Four Essays on the Concept of Sovereignty* (trans. George Schwab), Chicago: University of Chicago Press, 2005, p. 5.

11. Ibid., p. 6.

12. *Die Verfassung des Irischen Freistaats* was published in Tubingen in 1928; the English edition, with a preface by Hugh Kennedy, Irish chief justice, was issued by Allen & Unwin. I am grateful to Tom Garvin for drawing this material to my attention. See also Michael Rynne, *Die Völkerrechtliche Stellung Irlands*, Munich: Dunchker und Humblot, 1930.

13. 'Pat', 'Democracy in the Free State', *The English Review*, vol. 44 (1927), p. 671.

14. See 'The Wild Goose' in George Moore, *The Untilled Field*. As with much of Moore's fiction, the text was several times revised, and the phrase quoted by Schmitt does not appear in editions from 1926 onwards. For the original, see *The Untilled Field*, London: Fisher Unwin, 1903, pp 301–93, esp. p. 378.

15. Bonn, *Wandering Scholar*, p. 330.

16. See biographical notes in Joachim Fischer and John Dillon (eds), *The Correspondence of Myles Dillon 1922–1925*, Dublin: Four Courts Press, 1999, pp 279–89.

17. Reinhard Mehring, *Carl Schmitt: Aufstieg unter Fall: Eine Biographie*, Munich: Beck, 2009, p. 131, etc.

18. A copy of this little work, perhaps the only one in the British Isles, is preserved in the Warburg Institute, London. Touchingly, Schmitt listed it in the bibliography attached to the 1926 edition of his critique of parliamentary democracy.

19. See Fernand Rossignol, *La Pensée de G. Sorel*, Paris: Bordas, 1948, pp 4–50.

20.  See Yves Charles Zarka (ed.), *Carl Schmitt, ou le mythe du politique*, Paris: PUF, 2009. This collection of essays concludes with Denis Trierweiler's translation of the brief 1923 essay on the political theory of myth, already referred to; note (p. 197) the spelling of Pearse's Christian name as Padraic, strongly indicating an Irish and Gaelic-conscious source.

21.  On Taine's long career, see Theodore Zeldin, *France 1848–1945: vol. 2, Intellect, Taste and Anxiety*, Oxford: Clarendon Press, 1977, pp 604–8.

22.  Schmitt, *The Crisis*, p. 75.

23.  Schmitt, *The Crisis*, p. 110, n.24. That's three mysts in one footnote.

## Chapter 8

1.  Sham, opportunism or something else, Schmitt's anti-Semitism went so far as veritably to identify the Jews with the Devil himself, by calling for a 'holy exorcism'; see Christian Joerges and Navraj Singh Ghaleigh (eds), *Darker Legacies of Law in Europe: the Shadow of National Socialism and Fascism over Europe and its Legal Tradition*, Oxford: Hart, 2003, p. 203. In mid-war Joshua Trachtenberg recalled a related North African folk-tale or belief, that certain mediaeval Jews were the product of intercourse between widows and the graves of their murdered husbands, the only true begetter being the Devil; his source was Leo Frobenius whose anthropological work greatly impressed Ezra Pound and, briefly, W.B. Yeats. See Trachtenberg, *The Devil and the Jews*, New Haven: Yale University Press, 1943, pp 225–6, n.19.

2.  Franzen, p. 282. The academic exchange programme in Dublin was organised by Helmut Clissmann, an Abwehr agent and member of the Nazi party.

3.  See *The Irish Times*, 21 February 1938, p. 9.

4.  Sigmund Freud, *Totem and Taboo and Other Works*, London: Vintage etc., 2001, p. 46. (His source was Frazer's *Golden Bough*.)

5.  Ibid., p. 47. One might add that this recourse had the advantage of ensuring a condition of exogamy at the top of the social group.

6.  Ibid., pp 4–5.

7.  See Artur Nussbaum, 'Debts Under Inflation', *The University of Pennsylvania Law Review*, vol. 86, no. 6 (April 1938), pp 571–601 for a pointed allusion to Franzen (p. 593, n.140). Schmitt is treated at length in Marc Linder, *The Supreme Labor Court in Nazi Germany* (1987).

8.  For some late comments on Victor Bruns' and Schmitt's role in the Habilitation of 1938, and on the Irish constitution, see Franzen, *Im Wandel des Zeitgeistes, 1931–1991: Euphorien, Angste, Herausforderunge*, Munich: Universitas, 1992, pp 77–81. In an autobiographical summary (p. 331), Franzen records that, between 1943 and 1945, he was attached to the Indian

Legion of Subhas Chandra Bose. For Bruns on neutrals in time of war see *Der Britische Wirkschaftskriege und das geltende Seekriegsrecht* (Berlin: Max-Planck-Gesellschaft zur Förderung der Wissenschaften Institut fûr ausländlisches öffentliches Recht und Völkerrecht, 1940). See also Anthony Carty and Richard M. Smith, *Sir Gerald Fitzmaurice and the World Crisis: a Legal Adviser in the Foreign Office, 1932–1945*, The Hague, London: Kluwer Law International, 2000, pp 587–93 on Bruns.

9. See Chapter Seven of Bernard G. Krimm, *W.B. Yeats and the Emergence of the Irish Free State 1918–1939*, Troy (NY): Whitston, 1981, pp 201–45 and notes.

10. Franzen, 'Ireland und Grossbritannien', pp 289, 290n, 293, 301, 351.

11. These were Wilhelm Dibelius (born 1876, an Anglophile with religious interests, not a legal authority); Hans Kersen (1881–1973, a major intellectual figure but by Franzen reduced to his surname), Kohn (pointedly characterised as a Jew, with the qualifier 'deutschen' bracketed), Müller-Ross (for a magazine article), Spindler (for his nautical account of Casement's last days at sea). There is no reference to Moritz Bonn, nor to the more decidedly left-wing accounts of Connolly.

12. Franzen, loc. cit., pp 341–2.

13. Franzen, loc. cit., p. 288n.

14. See Michael Rynne, *Die Volkerrechtliche Stellung Irlands*, Munich: Duncker & Humblot, 1930. It dealt with Ireland in relation to the League of Nations. Papers of Rynne's are preserved in the library, National University of Ireland, Galway.

15. *The Irish Times*, 12 December 1931, p. 4.

16. Franzen, loc. cit., p. 351.

17. Hans Franzen, *Aus Meinem Leben und Mein Zeit*, Wiesbaden [c. 1981], p. 61.

18. Franzen, p. 62.

19. Seamus Deane, 'Walter Benjamin; the Construction of Hell', *Field Day Review* (ed. Seamus Deane and Breandán Mac Suibhne), no. 3 (2007), pp 2–27. Luke Gibbons at a seminar in the Royal Irish Academy invoked Schmitt's theory of the exception in connection with a supposed traumatic origin of modern Irish literary sensibility in the trial and execution of Fr Nicholas Sheehy (1728–1766). A later obeisance to Schmitt by someone working with the Notre Dame cadre can be found in Seán D. Moore, *Swift, the Book and the Irish Financial Revolution: Satire and Sovereignty in Colonial Ireland*, Baltimore: Johns Hopkins University Press, 2010, p. 37.

20. See John Hellmann, *The Knight-Monks of Vichy France: Uriage 1940–1945*, Liverpool: Liverpool University Press, 1997, pp 153–5.

21. Hellmann, op. cit., p. 179.
22. The final chapter of D'Astorg's *Aspects de la literature européenne depuis 1945* (Paris: de Seuil, 1952) was devoted to Stuart's post-war novels; see *A Festschrift for Francis Stuart on His Seventieth Birthday* (ed. W.J. Mc Cormack), Dublin: Dolmen Press, 1972, pp 28–39 for Richard York's translation.
23. Quoted in Mc Cormack, *From Burke to Beckett: Ascendancy, Tradition and Betrayal in Literary History*, Cork: Cork University Press, 1994, p. 295.
24. See Luca Crispi and Sam Slote (eds), *How Joyce Wrote* Finnegans Wake: *a Chapter by-Chapter Genetic Guide*, Madison: University of Wisconsin Press, 2007.
25. James Joyce, *Finnegans Wake*, London: Faber, 1975 (1939), p. 8.
26. Roland McHugh, *Annotations to* Finnegans Wake, Baltimore: Johns Hopkins University Press, 2006 (3rd ed.), spots Byng, Boyne, Byng, Cambronne, Crimea, Grouchy, Stonewall Jackson, Magenta Napoleon, Waterloo, to mention just a few.
27. See Sigmund Freud, *Jokes and their Relation to the Unconscious*, London: Vintage, etc, 2001, pp 71, 239, quoting Jakob von Falke, *Lebenserinnerungen*, Leipzig: Meyer, 1897, p. 271. Von Falke (1825–1897) records several other expressions heard in Ireland which he found amusing, e.g. 'I am not so young as I used to be some twenty years ago.'
28. The couple married on 2 April 1859 in St Thomas's parish church (Church of Ireland), Dublin. The bride's father was Humphrey Stevenson, of 3 Upper Sackville Street.
29. Seamus Heaney, 'Whatever You Say Say Nothing', in *North*, London: Faber, 1975, p. 54.

**Chapter 9**

1. Liam de Paor, *On the Easter Proclamation and Other Declarations*, Dublin: Four Courts Press, 1997, p. 72.
2. W.B. Yeats, *The Collected Works: Volume II, the Plays* (ed. David R. Clarke and Rosalind E. Clark), London: Palgrave, 2001, p. 542.
3. Donald T. Torchiana, *W.B. Yeats & Georgian Ireland*, Evanston: North Western University Press, 1966, pp 340–65.
4. Quoted in David O'Donoghue, *The Devil's Deal: the IRA, Nazi Germany and the Double Life of Jim O'Donovan*, Dublin: New Island, 2010, p. 96.
5. In March 2011 the National Archives at Kew released a January 1939 report from a British official in Dublin, throwing light on Eamon de Valera's attitude to the IRA's bombing campaign in England. Its seems that the Taoiseach, citing the dangers for his internal security of too robust a crack-down on the bombers, requested any information British

Intelligence could supply which would might help to portray IRA chief-of-staff Sean Russell as a Soviet agent. Russell had (according to Irish sources) travelled to Moscow in 1925, though none of this altered the extensive later record of his Nazi contacts in Ireland, the United States and (in 1940) Germany. Russell, incidentally, had travelled to Moscow with Gerry Boland who was later Minister for Justice in de Valera's war-time cabinet. Though the chief of staff was a pious Catholic (and a daily communicant), de Valera evidently preferred to brand him with atheistic communism (abhorred in Ireland) rather than with fascism. See *The Irish Times*, 29 March 2011, pp 1, 3.

6. Eric Hobsbaum, *On History*, London: Weidenfeld, 1997, p. 248. Lenin did regard Easter 1916 with some approval, and Brendan Behan was fond of quoting him. In summer 1917 some Bolsheviks had advised against precipitous action.

7. Liam de Paor spoke frequently about the unhelpful influence of 'The Battle of Algiers' on the Irish generation below him, citing a total misapprehension of apparent resemblances. See Mc Cormack (ed.), 'Six Letters (1940–1942) written by George Plant (1904–1942)', *Tipperary Historical Journal* (2008), pp 158–63.

8. T.W. Rolleston, *Ireland's Vanishing Opportunity*, Dublin: Talbot Press, 1919, pp 3–4. See also *The Irish Times*, 11 July 1919, p. 3. Rolleston insists that the Grail story is originally Celtic.

9. See Lucien Goldmann, *The Hidden God: a Study of Tragic Vision in the Pensées of Pascal and the Tragedies of Racine* (trans. Philip Thody), London: Routledge, 1964.

10. See W. Irvine, *The Boulanger Affair Reconsidered*, New York: Oxford UP, 1989, pp 157–8. And note p. 7 on 'determining link'.

11. Burns, p. 52.

12. Maurice Bourgeois, *John Millington Synge and the Irish Theatre*, London: Constable, pp v, 290.

13. See *The Worker's Republic*, 5 February 1916, quoted in Desmond Ryan, *James Connolly*, Dublin: Talbot Press; London: The Labour Publishing Company, 1924, p. 92.

14. Fearghal McGarry, *Frank Ryan*, Dundalk: Historical Association of Ireland, 2002, pp 14–16.

15. *The Irish Times*, 18 February 1924, p. 4; 16 February 1924, p. 9.

16. Anon, 'A Daughter of France', *The Irish Times*, 26 September 1924, p. 2. The book in question was Elizabeth Saint-Marie Perrin, *St Colette and Her Reform: a Page from the History of the Church* (trans. Mrs Conor Maguire), London: Sands, 1923.

17. See Ghesquiere, n.275, etc. Passage translated by Jean-Paul Pittion.

18.  POST SCRIPTUM. On Saturday 2 April 2011, republican dissidents murdered a police constable in Omagh, by placing a bomb under his car. In noting that he was a Catholic, one should not only point to the terrorism of a campaign to drive Catholics out of, or away from, the ranks of Northern Ireland's new police service, and thus re-create the sectarian monopoly of Stormont days. One should also specify and name the underlying sacrificial 'politics' in which terrorists choose targets from a small group with which they share powerful 'identity' (in religious background).

19.  For the text, see Yeats, *The Plays* (ed. Clark and Clark), pp 307–16.

20.  Moritz Bonn, *Die englische Kolonisation in Irland*, Stuttgart, Berlin: Cotta'sche, 1906, 2 vols.

21.  There are distinct verbal echoes of 'The Dreaming' in 'Purgatory', specifically referring to ancestry and the dead's perpetual memory; cf use of the term 'grandam/grand-dam'.

22.  W.B. Yeats, *The Poems* (ed. Daniel Albright), London: Dent, 1990, p. 384.

23.  Yeats's use of proper nouns and the names of historic personages calls for discrimination in the critical reader; referring specifically to 'Parnell's Funeral' (a poem dating from 1932/3), I have suggested use of the term *persona* to distinguish the Yeatsian construct from the historical person. Yeats was fond of a story which related how, when accused of abetting assassination, Parnell had maintained absolute *sang froid* in the House of Commons, though 'when he came among his followers his hands were full of blood, because he had torn them with his nails.' In one perspective, the detail suggests a species of self-crucifixion (involving a play on 'nails'); in another, it hints at an admission of abetting violent crime because Parnell ends up with (quite literally) blood on his hands. 'Parnell's Funeral' meditates on the consequences of Easter 1916 by comparing De Valera, Cosgrave, and O'Duffy unfavourably with The Chief. Only Kevin O'Higgins is commended (partly because he was dead and had been assassinated). See W.J. Mc Cormack, *Dissolute Characters*, Manchester: Manchester University Press, 1993, pp 194–7.

24.  Yeats, *The Poems*, p. 355. The editor, Daniel Albright, sees the poem as a 'populist sequel to "Easter 1916" — less a keening over futile courage than an incitement to war'. Written in January 1937, the poem was published in 1938. He reads the 'bland commonplace question' which serves as a chorus as indicating a coming storm, but adds that the original refrain had been 'Praise the Proud' (pp 789–90).

25.  The stanza concludes with the line 'Had travelled half the night', which links the second-last line into a self-contained non-rhyming couplet.

But, as quoted above, the lines present a visual image of a solitary who has deliberately kept others from joining him.

26. Ezra Pound, *The Cantos*, New York: New Directions, 1993, p. 62 (Canto XIV, which refers to the 'murderers of Pearse and MacDonagh', adding the intriguing detail, 'Captain H, the chief torturer').

27. James Longenbach, *Stone Cottage: Pound, Yeats and Modernism*, New York: Oxford University Press, 1988, pp 251–69.

28. See John Unterecker (ed.), *Yeats and Patrick McCartan: a Fenian Friendship*, Dublin: Dolmen Press, 1967.

29. Quoted in J.J. Horgan, *Parnell to Pearse*, Dublin: UCD Press, 2009, p. 244. Horgan suggested that the blood sacrifice motif was introduced into Irish nationalist rhetoric by Casement, and found Pearse's view of Emmet 'bordering on the blasphemous'. Yeats's efforts to set up his own grandfather as a friend of Emmet's have never found any independent verification.

30. Information supplied by his grand-niece, Honor Ó Brolcháin.

31. Yeats to Henry James August [1915], from Coole Park. Access No. 2749.

32. Yeats, *Later Essays*, p. 61. In relation to the last clause, 'angelic spirits seem to awaken them', it might be asked — seem *to whom*?

33. 'Passing the gap' initiates the action of Synge's 'The Well of the Saints' (1905), a very different drama.

34. In 1937, a diligent scholar (Pól Breathnach) published (in English) an article entitled 'Gaelic Genealogies of the Plunkets [sic]'. This made no reference to J.M. Plunkett's direct family line, nor did it argue that the Plunketts were in any sense Gaelic; there were, however, genealogies in the Gaelic language mainly accessible through annalistic sources — see *Irish Book Lover*, vol. 25, no. 1 (January–February 1937), pp 50–57.

## Chapter 10

1. See the illustrated catalogue 'Ireland 1916–1922' issued by Carraig Books Ltd in April 2011.

2. Unfortunately, librarians disposed of the supplements as surplus to need, thus spoiling the effect for latter-day readers. There is a lesson here for university managers who think that digitisation of a text in any one version dissolves the need for preservation of others.

3. See *The Catholic Bulletin*, vol. 26, no. 10 (October 1936), pp 783–7.

4. Donal O'Donovan, *Little Old Man Cut Short*, Bray: Kestrel, 1998, p. 61.

5. Owen Sheehy Skeffington (1909–1970) was the only son of Frank Skeffington (1878–1916), a pacifist executed by a supposedly deranged British officer during Easter Week. His mother, Hanna Sheehy (1877–1946), became an intransigent republican. Owen Sheehy Skeffington

studied French at Trinity College, joined the French Communist Party (and the Irish Labour Party), and lectured at TCD until his death.

6.  David O'Donoghue, *The Devil's Deal: the IRA, Nazi Germany and the Double Life of Jim O'Donovan*, Dublin: New Island, 2010, pp 77–82. Poets whose work appeared in *Ireland To-day* included Brian Coffey, Denis Devlin, Ewart Milne, Niall Montgomery and Arland Ussher.

7.  Lucy wrote an autobiography, *There's a Devil in the Drum*, published by Faber in 1938. Terry Cave's Introduction to a 1993 reprint from The Naval & Military Press provides some details of J.F. Lucy's odd career.

8.  See J.B. Desmond [a pseudonym], 'The Republic in 1916–1923', *Ireland To-day*, vol. 2, no. 1 (January 1937), pp 28–34, and John Dowling, 'The Abbey Attacked I', loc. cit., pp 35–43.

9.  See Seán D. Moore, *Swift, the Book and the Irish Financial Revolution: Satire and Sovereignty in Colonial Ireland*, Baltimore: Johns Hopkins University Press, 2010, p. 37. The second source is Bruno Bosteels, 'The Obscure Subject: Sovereignty and Geopolitics in Carl Schmitt's *The Nomos of the Earth*', *South Atlantic Quarterly*, vol. 104, no. 2 (spring 2005), pp 295–305. Schmitt published *Der Nomos der Erde im Völkerrecht des Jus Publicum Europeaum* in 1950 as a contribution to his own de-Nazification; a translation by G.L. Ulmen appeared in 2003.

10.  John Dowling, 'The Abbey Attacked I', *Ireland To-day*, vol. 2, no. 1 (January 1937), pp 39–40. Dowling is named in passing by Ernie O'Malley in a letter of this period, though the editors are unable to add any biographical detail: Ernie O'Malley, *Selected Letters* (ed. Conor O'Malley and Nicky Allen), Dublin: Lilliput Press, 2011, p. 135.

11.  An invoice, dated 14 April 1940, indicates that more than £90 was still owed to the magazine's printers, two years after *Ireland To-day* ceased publication; the docket is additionally inscribed '12 letters missing', probably an archival note. See NLI Ms 21, 155(3).

12.  Sean O'Callaghan, *The Jackboot in Ireland*, London: Allan Wingate, 1958, pp 12–13.

13.  See O'Donoghue, *The Devil's Deal*, p. 168. For the date of Clissmann's Nazi party membership (1 May 1934) see ibid., p. 296 n.5. Hoven was attached to the German Legation in Dublin, and contributed to the foundation of the Brandenburg regiment, an SAS-type unit in which Clissmann served after the outbreak of war.

14.  O'Donoghue, *The Devil's Deal*, pp 250–51.

15.  O'Donoghue, *The Devil's Deal*, p. 116; those participating included Jim O'Donovan, Oskar Pfaus and Sean Russell.

16.  See NLI Ms 21, 155 (3).

17.  O'Donoghue, *The Devil's Deal*, p. 191.

18. NLI Ms 21,155 (5).
19. 'The Church is a juridical person, though not in the same sense as a joint-stock company. The latter, a typical fruit of an age of production, is a system of accountancy, whilst the Church is a concrete personal representation of concrete personality. That she embodies in a supreme degree the spirit of the law and faithfully carries on the traditions of Roman jurisprudence has been conceded hitherto by all who have known her ... She represents the *civitas humana* and constitutes throughout the ages the historic bond with Christ's Incarnation and the Sacrifice of the Cross. She personally represents Christ Himself, the God Who in historic reality became Man. It is in her representative character that she rises superior to an age of economic thought.' Schmitt, *The Necessity of Politics*, London: Sheed and Ward, 1931, p. 56. Part of the book, a translation of *Römischer Katholizismus und Politische Form* (1923), had previously appeared in *The English Review*.
20. Ibid., pp 33, 36.
21. NLI Ms 21, 155 (4) pp 1–2.
22. Ibid., p. 4.
23. Liam de Paor, op. cit., p. 77.
24. James Joyce, *Ulysses*, London: Bodley Head, 1960, p. 24.
25. There is perhaps an echo of American terminology in the numbering of presidents; early in 1919, the president of Dáil Éireann was Cathal Brugha (aka Charles William St John Burgess), soon replaced by Eamon de Valera on his escape from Lincoln Gaol.
26. The text was devised by William O'Brien and Thomas Johnson (both of the Irish Labour Party), then trimmed by Seán T. O'Kelly of Sinn Féin, and incorporated to the proceedings of the first Dáil on 21 January 1919:

We declare in the words of the Irish Republican Proclamation the right of the people of Ireland to the ownership of Ireland, and to the unfettered control of Irish destinies to be indefeasible, and in the language of our first President, Pádraíg Mac Phiarais, we declare that the Nation's sovereignty extends not only to all men and women of the Nation, but to all its material possessions, the Nation's soil and all its resources, all the wealth and all the wealth-producing processes within the Nation, and with him we reaffirm that all right to private property must be subordinated to the public right and welfare.

We declare that we desire our country to be ruled in accordance with the principles of Liberty, Equality, and Justice for all, which alone can secure permanence of Government in the willing adhesion of the people.

We affirm the duty of every man and woman to give allegiance and service to the Commonwealth, and declare it is the duty of the Nation to assure that every citizen shall have opportunity to spend his or her strength and faculties in the service of the people. In return for willing service, we, in the name of the Republic, declare the right of every citizen to an adequate share of the produce of the Nation's labour.

It shall be the first duty of the Government of the Republic to make provision for the physical, mental and spiritual well-being of the children, to secure that no child shall suffer hunger or cold from lack of food, clothing, or shelter, but that all shall be provided with the means and facilities requisite for their proper education and training as Citizens of a Free and Gaelic Ireland.

The Irish Republic fully realises the necessity of abolishing the present odious, degrading and foreign Poor Law System, substituting therefor a sympathetic native scheme for the care of the Nation's aged and infirm, who shall not be regarded as a burden, but rather entitled to the Nation's gratitude and consideration. Likewise it shall be the duty of the Republic to take such measures as will safeguard the health of the people and ensure the physical as well as the moral well-being of the Nation.

It shall be our duty to promote the development of the Nation's resources, to increase the productivity of its soil, to exploit its mineral deposits, peat bogs, and fisheries, its waterways and harbours, in the interests and for the benefit of the Irish people.

It shall be the duty of the Republic to adopt all measures necessary for the recreation and invigoration of our Industries, and to ensure their being developed on the most beneficial and progressive co-operative and industrial lines. With the adoption of an extensive Irish Consular Service, trade with foreign Nations shall be revived on terms of mutual advantage and goodwill, and while undertaking the organisation of the Nation's trade, import and export, it shall be the duty of the Republic to prevent the shipment from Ireland of food and other necessaries until the wants of the Irish people are fully satisfied and the future provided for.

It shall also devolve upon the National Government to seek co-operation of the Governments of other countries in determining a standard of Social and Industrial Legislation with a view to a general and lasting improvement in the conditions under which the working classes live and labour.

27. Michel de Montaigne, *The Complete Essays* (trans. M. A. Screech), London: Penguin, 1993, p. 122 (Book I, Chapter 23).

# Select Bibliography and Further Reading

## 1. Ireland, General

Bedient, Calvin, *The Yeats Brothers and Modernism's Love of Motion*, Notre Dame: University of Notre Dame Press, 2009.

Bonn, Moritz, *Die englische Kolonization in Irland*, Stuttgart, Berlin: Cotta'sche, 1906, 2 vols.

Bonn, Moritz, *Modern Ireland and Her Agrarian Problem* (trans with preface by T.W. Rolleston), Dublin: Hodges Figgis, 1906.

Bourgeois, Maurice, *John Millington Synge and the Irish Theatre*, London: Constable, 1913.

Buckland, Patrick, *Ulster Unionism and the Origins of Northern Ireland 1886–1922*, Dublin: Gill & Macmillan 1973.

Clyde, Tom, *Irish Literary Magazines: an Outline History and Descriptive Bibliography*, Dublin: Irish Academic Press, 2003.

Comerford, R.V., *The Fenians in Context: Irish Politics and Society 1848–82*, Dublin: Wolfhound, 1998.

Costello, Peter, *James Joyce: the Years of Growth 1882–1915, a Biography*, London: Kyle Cathie, 1992.

Cruise-O'Brien, Conor, *Passion and Cunning and Other Essays*, London: Weidenfeld & Nicolson, 1988.

Cruise O'Brien, Conor, 'The Roots of My Preoccupations', *The Atlantic Monthly*, vol. 274, no. 1 (July 1994), pp 73–81.

Cruise O'Brien, Conor (ed.), *The Shaping of Modern Ireland*, London: Routledge, 1960.

Daly, Dominic, *The Young Douglas Hyde: the Dawn of the Revolution and Renaissance 1874–1893*, Dublin: Irish University Press, 1974.

De Paor, Liam, *Divided Ulster*, Harmondsworth: Penguin, 1970.

De Paor, Liam, *Landscapes with Figures: People, Culture and Art in Ireland and the Modern World*, Dublin: Four Courts, 1998.

De Paor, Liam, *The Peoples of Ireland from Prehistory to Modern Times*, London: Hutchinson, 1986.

De Paor, Liam, *Unfinished Business*, London: Radius, 1990.

Donoghue, Denis, *Irish Essays*, Cambridge: Cambridge University Press, 2011.

Donoghue, Denis, *Yeats*, London: Fontana Modern Masters, 1971.

Dubois, Paul, *Contemporary Ireland*, Dublin: Maunsel, 1908.

Elliott, Marianne, *Robert Emmet: the Making of a Legend*, London: Profile Books, 2003.

Ellmann, Richard, *James Joyce*, New York: Oxford University Press, 1959.

Foster, R.F., *W.B. Yeats, a Life: II the Arch-Poet*, Oxford: Oxford University Press, 2003.

Franzen, Hans, 'Irland und Grossbrittanien seit 1919; ein Beitrag zum Verfrassungsleben', *Jahrbuch des Offentlichen Rechts* vol. 25 (1938), pp 280–375.

Geoghegan, Patrick, *Robert Emmet, a Life* (2nd ed.), Dublin: Gill & Macmillan, 2004.

Ghesquière, Amélie, *La Construction de la politique étrangère de l'Irlande: analyse francaise d'une specifité irlandaise? (1921–1949)*, Lille: University of Lille, 2004 (thesis).

Hartley, Stephen, *The Irish Question as a Problem in British Foreign Policy, 1914–1918*, Basingstoke: Macmillan, 1986.

Hay, Marnie, *Bulmer Hobson and the Nationalist Movement in Twentieth-Century Ireland*, Manchester: Manchester University Press, 2009.

Horgan, J.J., *Parnell to Pearse: Some Recollections and Reflections* (2nd ed. with a biographical introduction by John Horgan), Dublin: UCD Press, 2009.

Hudson, David R.C., *The Ireland that We Made: Arthur and Gerald Balfour's Contribution to the Origins of Modern Ireland*, Akron: University of Akron Press, 2003.

Joyce, James, *The Critical Writings* (ed. Ellsworth Mason and Richard Ellmann), Ithaca: Cornell University Press, 1989.

Joyce, James, *Dubliners* (ed. Robert Scholes, illus. Louis Le Brocquy), Dublin: Lilliput Press, 1992.

Joyce, Stanislaus, *My Brother's Keeper: James Joyce's Early Years* (ed. Richard Ellmann, with an intro. by T.S. Eliot), Cambridge, Mass: Da Capo Books, 2003 (First pub. 1958).

Krimm, Bernard G., *W.B. Yeats and the Emergence of the Irish Free State 1918–1939: Living in the Explosion*, Troy (NY): Whitston, 1981.

MacEvilly, Michael, *A Splendid Resistance: the Life of* IRA *Chief of Staff Dr Andy Cooney*. Dublin: Éamonn de Burca, 2011.

McGarry, Fearghal, *Frank Ryan*, Dundalk: Historical Association of Ireland, 2002.

Malins, Edward, *Yeats and the Easter Rising*, Dublin: Dolmen, 1965.

Malye, Jean, *La Littérature Irlandaise contemporaine*, Paris: Sansot, [c. 1912].

Marsden, John, *Redemption in Irish History*, Dublin: Dominican Publications, 2005.

Maume, Patrick, *'Life that is Exile': Daniel Corkery and the Search for Irish Ireland*, Belfast: Institute of Irish Studies, 1993.

Maume, Patrick, *The Long Gestation: Irish Nationalist Life 1891–1918*, Dublin: Gill & Macmillan, 1999.

Meredith, James Creed, *The Rainbow in the Valley*, Dublin: Brown and Nolan, 1939.

Mitchell, Arthur, *Labour in Irish Politics 1890–1930: the Irish Labour Movement in an Age of Revolution*, Shannon: Irish University Press, 1974.

Moore, George, *Hail and Farewell* (ed. Richard Cave), Gerrards Cross: Smythe, 1976.

Moore, George, *The Untilled Field*, London: Fisher Unwin, 1903.

Moore, Seán D., *Swift, the Book, and the Irish Financial Revolution: Satire and Sovereignty in Colonial Ireland*, Baltimore: Johns Hopkins University Press, 2010.

Morrissey, Thomas J., *William O'Brien 1881–1968: Socialist, Republican, Dáil Deputy, Editor and Trade Union Leader*, Dublin: Four Courts, 2007.

Murphy, Cliona, 'The Religious Context of the Women's Suffrage Campaign in Ireland' *Women's History Review*, vol. 6, no. 4 (1997), pp 549–65.

Newsinger, John, *Rebel City: Larkin, Connolly and the Dublin Labour Movement*, London: Merlin Press, 2004.

O'Connor, Emmet, *Syndicalism in Ireland 1917–1923*, Cork: Cork University Press, 1988.

O'Donnell, Peadar, *Monkeys in the Superstructure*, Galway: Salmon, 1986.

O'Donoghue, David, *The Devil's Deal: the* IRA, *Nazi Germany and the Double Life of Jim O'Donovan*, Dublin: New Island, 2010.

O'Donoghue, David, 'New Evidence on IRA/Nazi Links', *History Ireland*, vol. 19, no. 2 (March/April 2011), pp 36–9.

O'Donovan, Donal, *Little Old Man Cut Short*, Bray: Kestrel, 1998.

O'Leary, Philip, *The Prose Literature of the Gaelic Revival 1881–1921: Ideology and Innovation*, Pennsylvania: Pennsylvania State University, 1994.

O'Rahilly, Aloysius, *Studies, an Irish Quarterly Review: General Index of Volumes 1–50, 1910–1961*, Ros Cré: An Fáisceán Liath, 1966.

Rolleston, C.H., *Portrait of an Irishman: a Biographical Sketch of T.W. Rolleston*, London: Methuen, 1939.

Rolleston, T.W., *L'Irlande telle qu'elle est, par deux Irlandais*, Geneva: Delachaux et Niestlé, 1917.

Rolleston, T.W., *Ireland's Vanishing Opportunity*, Dublin: Talbot Press, 1919.

Ryan, Desmond, *Unique Dictator: a Study of Eamon de Valera*, London: Barker, 1936 (German translation by Senta Bernecker, Berlin: Frundsberg, 1938).

Shannon, Catherine B., *Arthur J. Balfour and Ireland 1874–1922*, Washington: Catholic University Press of America, 1988.

Shaw, G.B., *Collected Letters 1911–1925* (ed. Dan H. Lawrence), London: Max Reinhardt, 1985.

Sheehan, Patrick, *The Spoilt Priest & Other Stories*, Dublin: Clonmore and Reynolds, 1954 (First pub. 1905).

Silke, John J., 'Irish Scholarship and the Renaissance, 1580–1673', *Studies in the Renaissance*, vol. 20 (1973), pp 169–206.

Swords, Liam (ed.), *The Irish-French Connection 1578–1978*, Paris: Irish College, 1978.

Tierney, Mark, 'A Survey of the Reports of the French Consuls in Ireland 1814–1929' in Swords, op. cit. above, pp 130–41.

Unterecker, John (ed.), *Yeats and Patrick McCartan, a Fenian Friendship*, Dublin: Dolmen Press, 1967.

Valente, Joseph, *The Myth of Manliness in Irish National Culture 1880–1922*, Urbana: University of Illinois Press, 2011.

Wiel, Jérôme aan de, *The Irish Factor 1899–1919: Ireland's Strategic and Diplomatic Importance for Foreign Powers*, Dublin: Irish Academic Press, 2011.

Williams, Trevor (ed.), *Reading Joyce Politically*, Gainesville: University of Florida Press, 1997.

Yeates, Pádraig, *Lockout Dublin 1913*, Dublin: Gill & Macmillan, 2000.

Yeats, W.B., *Collected Works: Volume II, the Plays* (ed. David R. Clark and Rosalind E. Clark), London: Palgrave, 2001.

Yeats, W.B., *The Poems* (ed. Daniel Albright), London: Dent, 1990.

Yeats, W.B., *Writings on Irish Folklore, Legend and Myth* (ed. Robert Welch), London: Penguin, 1993.

Yeats, W.B., and George Yeats, *The Letters* (ed. Ann Saddlemeyer), Oxford: Oxford University Press, 2011.

## 2. Easter 1916

Anon., 'Did Telefís Éireann Overlook the Catholic Inspiration of the 1916 Heroes?', *The Catholic Standard*, 29 April 1966.

Augusteijn, Joost, *Patrick Pearse: the Making of a Revolutionary*, Basingstoke: Palgrave Macmillan, 2010.

Bateson, Ray, *They Died by Pearse's Side*, Dublin: Irish Graves Publications, 2010.

Bechhofer, C.E., 'Letters from Ireland' *The New Age* vol. 19, no. 23 (5 October 1916) p. 540; vol. 19, no. 24 (12 October 1916) p. 562; vol. 19, no. 25 (19 October 1916) pp 588–9; vol. 19, no. 26 (26 October 1916) p. 610; vol. 20, no. 1 (2 November 1916) p. 14; vol. 20, no. 2 (9 November 1916) p. 35; vol. 20, no. 3 (16 November 1916) pp 62–3; vol. 20, no. 4 (23 November 1916) p. 85; vol. 20, no. 5 (30 November 1916) pp 107–8; vol. 20, no. 6 (7 December 1916) pp 134–5; vol. 20, no. 7 (14 December 1916) pp 159–60; vol. 20, no. 8 (21 December 1916) pp 180–81; vol. 20, no. 9 (28 December 1916) pp 206–7; vol. 20, no. 10 (4 January 1917) pp 228–9; vol. 20, no. 11 (11 January 1917) p. 256; vol. 20, no. 12 (18 January 1917); vol. 20, no. 13 (25 January 1917) pp 303–4. See also by Bechhofer in the same journal, 'A Complaint from Ireland', vol. 20, no. 2 (9 November 1916) p. 45, and 'James Connolly', vol. 20, no. 10 (4 January 1917) p. 239.

Beckett, Samuel, *Murphy*, London: Routledge, 1938.

Bonn, Moritz, *Irland und die irische Frage*, Munich: Duncker & Humblot, 1918.

Caulfield, Max, *The Easter Rebellion*, London: New English Library, 1965.

Coates, Tim (ed.), *The Irish Uprising 1914–21: Papers from the British Parliamentary Archive*, London: HMSO, 2000.

Coffey, Thomas M., *Agony at Easter: the 1916 Irish Uprising*, London: Harrap, 1970.

Connell, Joseph E.A., *Dublin in Rebellion: a Directory 1913–1923*, Dublin: Lilliput, 2006.

Connolly, James, *Between Comrades: Letters and Correspondence 1889–1916* (ed. Donal Nevin), Dublin: Gill & Macmillan, 2007.

Connolly, James, *Collected Works* (ed. Michael O'Riordan), Dublin: New Books, 1988, 2 vols.

Coogan, T.P., *1916: the Easter Rising*, London: Phoenix, 2005 (2nd ed.).

Cruise O'Brien, Conor, 'The Embers of Easter, 1916–1966', *The Irish Times*, 7 April 1966.

Daly, Mary E., and Margaret O'Callaghan, *1916 in 1966: Commemorating the Easter Rising*, Dublin: Royal Irish Academy, 2007.

De Paor, Liam, *On the Easter Proclamation and Other Declarations*, Dublin: Four Courts Press, 1997.

Doherty, Gabriel, and Dermot Keogh (eds), *1916: the Long Revolution*, Cork: Mercier, 2007.

Dudley Edwards, Owen, and Fergus Pyle (eds), *1916: the Easter Rising*. London: MacGibbon and Kee, 1968.

Dudley Edwards, Ruth, *Patrick Pearse: The Triumph of Failure*, London: Gollancz, 1977.

Foy, Michael, and Brian Barton, *The Easter Rising*, Stroud: Sutton, 1999.

Githens-Mazer, Jonathan, *Cultural and Political Nationalism in Ireland: Myths and Memories of the Easter Rising 1916*, London School of Economics, PhD thesis, 2005.

Greaves, Desmond, *The Life and Times of James Connolly*, London: Lawrence & Wishart, 1961.

Ireland, John de Courcy, *The Sea and the Easter Rising 1916*, [Dun Laoghaire:] Maritime Institute of Ireland, 1966.

Jeffrey, Keith (ed.), *The GPO and the Easter Rising*, Dublin: Irish Academic Press, 2006.

Laffan, Michael, *The Resurrection of Ireland: the Sinn Féin Party, 1916–1923*, Cambridge: Cambridge University Press, 1999.

McKeane, Ian, 'Journées Sanglantes / Days of Blood: the French Press and the Easter Rising' in Ruan O'Donnell (ed.), *The Impact of the 1916 Rising Among the Nations*, Dublin: Irish Academic Press, 2008, pp 119–40.

Martin, F.X. (ed.), *Leaders and Men of the Easter Rising, Dublin 1916*, London: Methuen, 1967.

Martin, F.X. (ed.), *1916 and University College Dublin*, Dublin: Brown and Nolan, 1966.

Moran, Seán Farrell, *Patrick Pearse and the Politics of Redemption: the Mind of the Easter Rising 1916*, Washington: Catholic University of America Press, 1994.

Morgan, Austen, *James Connolly: a Political Biography*, Manchester: Manchester University Press, 1988.

Murdoch, Iris, *The Red and the Green*, London: Chatto and Windus, 1965.

Nevin, Donal, *James Connolly: 'a Full Life'*, Dublin: Gill & Macmillan, 2005.

ní Dhonnchadha, Máirín, and Theo Dorgan (eds), *Revising the Rising*, Derry: Field Day, 1991.

Nowlan, Kevin B. (ed.), *The Making of 1916: Studies in the History of the Rising*, Dublin: Stationery Office, 1969.

O'Casey, Sean, *Collected Plays*, Vol. 1 (including 'The Plough and the Stars'), London: Macmillan, 1949.

O Cathasaigh, P. [i.e. Sean O'Casey], *The Story of the Irish Citizen Army*, Dublin, London: Maunsel, 1919.

Ó Conaire, Pádraic, *Seacht mBuaidh an Éirghe-amach*, Baile Átha Cliath, Lonndain: Maunsel, 1918.

Ó Drisceoil, Proinsias, 'Rebellion in the Artwork: Ó Tuairisc, *Dé Luain* and the Craig Connection' in Agnes Bernelle (ed.), *Decantations: a Tribute to Maurice Craig*, Dublin: Lilliput Press, 1992, pp 139–47.

O'Kelly, Seamus, *The Glorious Seven*, Dublin: Irish News Service, 1965.

O'Rahilly, Aodogán, *Winding the Clock: O'Rahilly and the 1916 Rising*, Dublin: Lilliput, 1991.

Pearse, Patrick H., *Collected Works*, Dublin: Phoenix, 1924. 5 vols.

Queneau, Raymond, *On est toujours trop bon avec les femmes*, Paris: Gallimard, 1971.

Reilly, Tom, *Joe Stanley: Printer to the Rising*, Dingle: Brandon, 2005.

Ryan, Desmond, *James Connolly, His Life Work and Writings*, Dublin: Talbot Press; London: Labour Publishing Company, 1924.

Ryan, Desmond, *The Man Called Pearse*, Dublin: Maunsel, 1919.

Ryan, Desmond (ed.), *The 1916 Poets*, Dublin: Figgis, 1963.

Slater, Montagu, *Easter: 1916*, London: Lawrence and Wishart, 1936.

Stephens, James, *The Insurrection in Dublin* (with an introduction and afterword by John A. Murphy), Gerrards Cross: Colin Smythe, 1978 (First published 1916).

Thompson, William Irwin, *The Imagination of an Insurrection: Dublin, Easter 1916*, New York: Oxford University Press, 1967.

Townshend, Charles, *Easter 1916: the Irish Rebellion*, London: Allen Lane, 2005.

Wills, Clair, *Dublin in 1916: the Siege of the GPO*, London: Profile, 2009.


*Periodicals*

> *The Capuchin Annual, The Catholic Bulletin, The English Review, Ireland To-day, The Irish Review, The Irish Ecclesiastical Record, The Irish Monthly, Studies.*


## 3. Europe

Adorno, Theodor, *In Search of Wagner* (trans Rodney Livingstone), London: New Left Books, 1981.

Asher, Kenneth, 'T.S. Eliot and Ideology', *English Literary History*, vol. 55, (winter 1988), pp 895–915.

Balfour, Arthur James, 'M. Bergson', in *The Hibbert Journal* of October 1911.

Baylen, Joseph O., 'An Unpublished Note on General Georges Boulanger in Britain, June 1889', *French Historical Studies*, vol. 4, no. 3 (Spring 1966), pp 344–7.

Beaufort, M. Pearde, 'A French Naturalist' [i.e. Maurice Barrès], *The Irish Monthly*, vol. 44 (April 1916), pp 258–66.

Beaufort, M. Pearde, 'Paul Bourget and Ireland', *The Irish Monthly*, vol. 43 (November 1915), pp 695–703.

Berlin, Isaiah, *The Crooked Timber of Humanity: Chapters in the History of Ideas*, London: John Murray, 1990.

Bergson, Henri, *Creative Evolution* (trans. Arthur Mitchell), London: Macmillan, 1911.

Bergson, Henri, *Matter and Memory* (trans. Nancy Margaret Paul and W. Scott Palmer), London: Allen and Unwin; New York: Macmillan, 1912.

Bergson, Henri, *Time and Free Will: an Essay on the Immediate Data of Consciousness* (trans. F.L. Pogson), London: Swan Sonnenswein, 1910.

Birnbaum, Pierre, *The Anti-Semitic Moment: a Tour of France in 1898* (trans. Jane Marie Todd), Chicago: University of Chicago Press, 2011.

Bonn, Moritz, *The Crisis of European Democracy*, New Haven: Yale University Press, 1925.

Bosteels, Bruno, 'The Obscure Subject: Sovereignty and Geopolitics, in Carl Schmitt's *The Nomos of the Earth*', *South Atlantic Quarterly*, vol. 104, no. 2 (spring 2005).

Bourget, Paul, *Some Portraits of Women* (trans. William Marchant), London: Downey, 1898.

Brennan, Brian, 'The Revival of the Cult of Martin of Tours in the Third Republic', *Church History*, vol. 66, no. 3 (September 1997), pp 489–501.

Bridgwater, Patrick, *Nietzsche in Anglosaxony: a Study of Nietzsche's Impact on English and American Literature*, Leicester: Leicester University Press, 1972.

Burns, Michael, *Rural Society and French Politics: Boulangism and the Dreyfus Affair 1886–1900*, Princeton: Princeton University Press, 1984.

Butler, Hubert, *Escape from the Anthill*, Mullingar: Lilliput, 1985.

Carr, Helen, *The Verse Revolutionaries*, London: Cape, 2009.

Carty, Anthony, and Richard M. Smith, *Sir Gerald Fitzmaurice and the World Crisis: a Legal Adviser in the Foreign Office 1932–1945*, The Hague, London: Kluwer Law International, 2000.

Cazamian, Louis, *The Social Novel in England, 1830–1850: Dickens, Disraeli, Mrs Gaskell, Kingsley* (trans. Martin Fido), London: Routledge, 1973.

Charlet, Nicholas, *Yves Klein, un matérialisme mystique*, [n. p.], 2004.

Conway, Martin, *The Crowd in Peace and War*, London: Longmans, 1915.

Copleston, Frederick, *Friedrich Nietzsche, Philosopher of Culture*, London: Search Press, 1975.

Crawford, Virginia M., 'Feminism in France', *The Fortnightly Review* (April 1897), pp 524–34.

Crawford, Virginia M., 'Maurice Barrès, an Appreciation', *Studies*, vol. 13, no. 49 (March 1924), pp 76–84.

Crawford, Virginia M., 'Paul Bourget and Some Successors', *Studies*, vol. 24 (September 1935), pp 433–41.

Crawford, Virginia M., 'The Rise of Fascism and What it Stands for', *Studies*, vol. 12, no. 48 (December 1923), pp 539–52.

Crawford, Virginia M., *Studies in Foreign Literature*, London: Duckworth, 1899.

Crawford, Virginia M., *Switzerland To-day: a Study in Social Progress*, London, Edinburgh: Sands, 1911.

Cruise O'Brien, Conor [under the name, Donat O'Donnell], *Maria Cross: Imaginative Patterns in a Group of Modern Catholic Writers*, London: Chatto, 1954.

Cruise O'Brien, Conor, 'Foreword' to Susan Dunn, *The Deaths of Louis xvi* (below).

Curran, Vivian Grossewald, 'Formalism and Anti-Formalism in French and German Judicial Methodology' in Christian Joerges and Navraj Singh Ghaleigh (eds), *Darker Legacies of Law in Europe: the Shadow of National Socialism and Fascism over Europe and its Legal Tradition*, Oxford: Hart, 2003, pp 205–28.

Deane, Seamus, 'Water Benjamin: the Construction of Hell', *Field Day Review* (eds Seamus Deane and Breandán Mac Suibhne), no. 3 (2007), pp 2–27.

de Maistre, Joseph, *Considerations on France* (trans. Richard A. Lebrun), Cambridge: Cambridge University Press, 1994.

Derfler, Leslie, *Paul Lafargue and the Flowering of French Socialism, 1882–1911*, Cambridge, Mass.: Harvard University Press, 1998.

Doering, Bernard E., *Jacques Maritain and the French Catholic Intellectuals*, Notre Dame: University of Notre Dame Press, 1983.

Dunn, Susan, *The Deaths of Louis xvi*, Princeton: Princeton University Press, 1994.

Eliot, T.S., *Collected Poems 1909–1962*, London: Faber, 1963.

Eliot, T.S., *The Waste Land: a Facsimile and Transcript of the Original Drafts Including the Annotations of Ezra Pound* (ed. Valerie Eliot), London: Faber, 1971.

Falke, Jakob von, *Lebenserunnerungen*, Leipzig: Meyer, 1897.

Fischer, Joachim, and John Dillon (eds), *The Correspondence of Myles Dillon 1922–1925: Irish-German Relations and Celtic Studies*, Dublin: Four Courts, 1999.

Forth, Christopher E., *The Dreyfus Affair and the Crisis of French Manhood*, Baltimore: Johns Hopkins University Press, 2004.

Forth, Christopher E., *Zarathustra in Paris: the Nietzsche Vogue in France 1891–1918*, De Kolb: North Illinois University Press.

Franzen, Hans, *Aus Meinem Leben und Meiner Zeit*, Wiesbaden [privately printed; n.d. c. 1973].

Franzen, Hans, *Im Wandel des Zeit-Geistes 1931–1991: Euphorien, Ängste, Herausforderungen*, Munich: Universitas Verlag, 1992.

Freud, Sigmund, *The Standard Edition of the Complete Psychological Works* (ed. James Strachey et al.) — vol. 8, *Jokes and their Relation to the*

*Unconscious;* vol. 13, *Totem and Taboo and Other Works;* vol. 23, *Moses and Monotheism, An Outline of Psycho-Analysis and Other Works,* London: Vintage, the Hogarth Press, and the Institute of Psycho-Analysis, 2001.

Gillies, Mary Ann, *Henri Bergson and British Modernism,* Montreal: McGill-Queens University Press, 1996.

Greene, E.J.H., *T.S. Eliot et la France,* Paris: Boivin, 1951.

Habermas, Jurgen, *The New Conservatism: Cultural Criticism and the Historians' Debate* (trans. Shierry Weber Nicholsen), Cambridge: Polity Press, 1989.

Hamacher, Werner, *Premises: Essays on Philosophy and Literature from Kant to Celan* (trans. Peter Fenves), Stanford: Stanford University Press, 1996.

Harris, Ruth, *The Man on Devil's Island: Alfred Dreyfus and the Affair that Divided France,* London: Allan Lane, 2010.

Hobsbaum, Eric, *On History,* London: Weidenfeld and Nicolson, 1997.

Horowitz, Irving Louis, *Radicalism and the Revolt against Reason: the Social Theories of Georges Sorel,* Carbondale: Southern Illinois University Press, 1968.

Hubert, Henri, and Marcel Mauss, *Sacrifice: its Nature and Functions* (trans. W. D. Halls), Chicago: University of Chicago Press, 1981.

Hulme, T.E., *Collected Writings,* Oxford: Oxford University Press,

Hutton, Patrick H., *The Cult of the Revolutionary Tradition: the Blanquists in French Politics 1864–1893,* Berkeley: University of California Press, 1981.

Hynes, Sam, *The Edwardian Turn of Mind,* Princeton: Princeton University Press, 1968.

Irvine, W.D., *The Boulanger Affair Reconsidered: Royalism, Boulangism and the Origins of the Radical Right in France,* New York: Oxford University Press, 1989.

Kahn, Victoria, 'Hamlet or Hecuba: Carl Schmitt's Decision', *Representations,* no. 83 (summer 2003), pp 67–96.

Kaufmann, Walter, *Nietzsche, Philosopher, Psychologist, Antichrist,* New York: Meridian Books, 1956.

Koehn, Barbara, *La Révolution conservatrice et les élites intelllectuelles,* Rennes: Presses Universitaires de Rennes, 2003.

Kuelpe, Otto, *Philosophy of the Present in Germany,* London: Allen & Unwin, 1913.

Kurth, Godefroid, *Saint Clotilda* (trans Virginia M. Crawford with an introduction by Rev. George Tyrrell sj), London: Duckworth, 1898.

Le Bon, Gustave, *The Crowd,* New Brunswick: Transaction Books, 1995.

Lebovics, Herman, *True France: the Wars over Cultural Identity 1900–1945,* Ithaca: Cornell University Press, 1992.

Lewis, Arthur D., *Syndicalism and the General Strike: an Explanation*, London: Fisher Unwin, 1912.

Locas, Claude, 'Christopher Dawson: a Bibliography', *The Harvard Theological Review*, vol. 66, no. 2 (April 1973), pp 177–206.

Longenbach, James, *Stone Cottage: Pound, Yeats and Modernism*, New York: Oxford University Press, 1988.

Loughlin, Claire E., *Foch, the Man*, New York: Revell, 1918.

Lukács, György, *Soul and Form* (trans. Anna Bostock), London: Merlin Press, 1974.

Luxemburg, Rosa, *The Essential Rosa Luxemburg* (ed. Helen Scott), Chicago: Haymarket Books, 2008.

Luxemburg, Rosa, *The Letters* (ed. Georg Adler et al.; trans. George Shriver), London: Verso, 2011.

McClelland, J.S. (ed.), *The French Right from de Maistre to Maurras*, London: Cape, 1970.

McCormick, John P., *Carl Schmitt's Critique of Liberalism: Against Politics as Technology*, Cambridge: Cambridge University Press, 1997.

McCormick, John P., 'Political Theory and Political Theology: the Second Wave of Carl Schmitt in English', *Political Theory*, vol. 26, no. 6 (December 1998), pp 830–54.

MacDonald, Ramsay, *Syndicalism: a Critical Examination*, London: Constable, 1912.

MacLeod, Catherine, 'Charles Péguy, 1873–1914', *The Irish Monthly*, vol. 65, no. 770 (August 1937), pp 529–41.

Marder, Michael, 'Carl Schmitt's "Cosmopolitan Restaurant": Culture, Multiculturalism, and Complexio Oppositorum', *Telos*, no. 142 (spring 2008), pp 29–47.

Mehring, Reinhard, *Carl Schmitt, Aufstieg und Fall*, Munich: Beck, 2009.

Meisel, James H., *The Genesis of Georges Sorel: an Account of his Formative Period Followed by a Study of His Influence*, Ann Arbor: Wahr, 1951.

Mohler, Armin, *Georges Sorel: Erzvater der Konservativen Revolution*, Schnellroda: Editions Antaios, 2004.

Montaigne, Michel de, *The Complete Essays* (trans. M.A. Screech), London: Penguin, 1991.

Morris, Bruce, '"Neptune and Surging Waves": Paul Bourget and W.B. Yeats' in *Yeats: an Annual of Critical and Textual Studies*, vol. 13 (1995), pp 225–36.

Murray, Kathleen, *Taine und die Englische Romantik*, Munich: Duncker & Humblot, 1924.

Nietzsche, Friedrich, *Ecce Homo: How One Becomes What One Is* (trans. R.J. Hollingdale), London: Penguin, 2004.

Nora, Pierre, *Realms of Memory: the Construction of the French Past* (trans. Arthur Goldhammer), New York: Columbia University Press, 1996–1998, 3 vols.

Nye, Robert A., *The Origins of Crowd Psychology: Gustave LBon and the Crisis of Mass Democracy in the Third Republic,* London: Sage, 1975.

Offen, Karen, 'Sur l'origine des mots "feminine" et "féministe"', *Revue d'histoire modern et contemporaine,* vol. 34, no. 3 (July–September 1987), pp 492–6.

O'Hegarty, P.S., [Obituary for Paul Bourget] *Dublin Magazine,* (April–June 1936).

Péguy, Charles, *Portal of the Mystery of Hope* (trans. D. L. Schneidler), London, New York: Continuum, 1996.

Renan, Ernest, *The Poetry of the Celtic Races, and Other Studies,* London: Walter Scott, [1896]. (Includes, 'What is a Nation?')

Roberts, Michael, *T.E. Hulme,* London: Faber, 1938.

Roche, Louis (ed.), *Anthology of French Poetry: Filíocht Mheán-Teistiméireachta,* Dublin: Brown and Nolan [c.1952].

Roth, Jack J., *The Cult of Violence: Sorel and the Sorelians.* Berkeley: University of California Press, 1980.

Rouanet, S.P., 'Irrationalism and Myth in Georges Sorel', *Review of Politics,* vol. 20, no. 1 (January 1964), pp 45–59.

Sand, Shlomo, *The Words and the Land: Israeli Intellectuals and the Nationalism Myth,* Los Angeles: Semiotext(e), 2011.

Schmitt, Carl, *The Crisis of Parliamentary Democracy* (trans. Ellen Kennedy), Cambridge, Mass: MIT Press, 1988.

Schmitt, Carl, *The Necessity of Politics: an Essay on the Representative Idea in the Church and in Europe* (trans. E.M. Codd), London: Sheed & Ward, 1931.

Schmitt, Carl, *Political Theology: Four Chapters on the Concept of Sovereignty* (trans. George Schwab), Chicago: University of Chicago Press, 2005.

Schrift, Alan D., *Twentieth-Century French Philosophy: Key Themes and Thinkers,* Oxford: Blackwell, 2006.

Schuchard, Ronald, 'Eliot and Hulme in 1916: Toward a Revaluation of Eliot's Critical and Spiritual Development', *PMLA,* vol. 88, no. 5 (October 1973), pp 1083–94.

Schuchard, Ronald, 'T.S. Eliot as an Extension Lecturer, 1916–1919', *Review of English Studies,* n. s., vol. 25, no. 98 (May 1974), pp 163–73.

Scott, J. W., *Syndicalism and Philosophical Realism: a Study in the Correlation of Contemporary Social Tendencies,* London: Black, 1919.

Sloterdijk, Peter, *Rage and Time* (trans. Mario Wenning), New York: Columbia University Press, 2010.

Sorel, Georges, *Reflections on Violence* (ed. Jeremy Jennings), Cambridge: Cambridge University Press, 1999.

Strenski, Ivan, *Contesting Sacrifice: Religion, Nationalism, and Social Thought in France*, Chicago: University of Chicago Press, 2002.

Synan, Arthur, 'Catholicity and Conservatism: a Review of Paul Bourget's L'Etape', *New Ireland Review*, vol. 27 (June 1907), pp 227–33.

Taine, Hippolyte, *The Ancien Régime* (trans. John Durand), London: Daldy, 1876.

Trachtenberg, Joshua, *The Devil and the Jews: the Mediaeval Conception of the Jew and its Relation to Modern anti-Semitism*, New Haven: Yale University Press, 1943.

Triomphe, Robert, *Joseph de Maistre: Étude sur la vie et sur la doctrine d'un matérialiste mystique*, Geneva: Droz, 1968.

Vogeler, Martha S., *Austin Harrison and the English Review*, Columbia: University of Missouri Press, 2008.

Ward, Maisie, *Insurrection Versus Resurrection: the Wilfrid Wards and the Transition II*, London: Sheed and Ward, 1937.

Weber, Eugen, *My France: Politics, Culture, Myth*, Cambridge, Mass.: Belnap Press, 1991.

Weber, Eugen, *The Nationalist Revival in France, 1905–1914*, Berkeley and Los Angeles: University of California Press, 1969.

Weber, Eugen, *Peasants into Frenchmen: the Modernisation of Rural France 1880–1914*, Stanford: Stanford University Press, 1976.

Wilson, David R., 'Clemenceau's Contacts with England', *Diplomacy and Statecraft*, vol. 17, no. 4 (December 2006), pp 715–30.

Wilson, Edmund, *To the Finland Station: a Study in the Writing and Acting of History*, London: Secker and Warburg, 1941.

Zarka, Yves Charles, *Carl Schmitt ou le mythe du politique*, Paris: Presses Universitaires de France, 2009.

Zeldin, Theodore, *France 1848–1945*, 2 vols, Oxford: Clarendon Press, 1977.

## 4. Some Related and Recent Work by W. J. Mc Cormack

*Ascendancy and Tradition in Anglo-Irish Literary History from 1789 to 1939*, Oxford: Clarendon Press, 1985.

*Blood Kindred: W.B. Yeats, the Life, the Death, the Politics*, London: Pimlico, 2005.

'Church, State, Childhood and Youth 1865–1885' in David Holderman and Ben Levitas (eds), *Yeats in Context*, Cambridge: Cambridge University Press, 2010, pp 15–24.

*Dissolute Characters: Irish Literary History through Balzac, Sheridan Le Fanu, Yeats and Bowen*, Manchester: Manchester University Press, 1993.

'Edmund Burke's Reflections on the Revolution in France: a Modified Codicological Approach', forthcoming.

'*Edmund Burke, Yeats and Leo Frobenius: the State a Tree?*', in S.P. Donlan (ed.), *Edmund Burke's Irish Identities*, Dublin: Irish Academic Press, 2007, pp 226–62.

*From Burke to Beckett: Ascendancy, Tradition and Betrayal in Literary History*, Cork: Cork University Press, 1994.

'Obituary: Liam de Paor', *The Independent* (London), 26 August 1998.

'Oliver Goldsmith's *Deserted Village* (1770) and Retrospective Localism', in Martin Morris and Fergus O'Ferrall (eds), *Longford: History and Society*, Dublin: Geography Publications, 2010, pp 259–81.

'Robert Emmet and Roger Casement', in Anne Dolan, Patrick M. Geoghegan and Darryl Jones (eds), *Reinterpreting Emmet: Essays on the Life and Legacy of Robert Emmet*, Dublin: UCD Press, 2007, pp 219–26.

*Roger Casement in Death: Or, Haunting the Free State*, Dublin: UCD Press, 2003.

'Sheridan Le Fanu and Greater Chapelizod', in Motoko Fujita (ed.), *In the Shadow of James Joyce: Chapelizod and Environs*, Dublin: Lilliput Press, 2011, pp 77–82.

'Six Letters (1940–1942) written by George Plant (1904–1942)', *Tipperary Historical Journal* (2008), pp 158–63.

'Universal Language (1641) to Universal War (1814): a Reading of Maria Edgeworth's *Patronage*', in Danielle Westerhof (ed.), *The Alchemy of Medicine and Print in the Edward Worth Library, Dublin*, Dublin: Four Courts Press, 2010, pp 89–109.

'*We Irish' in Europe: Yeats, Berkeley and Joseph Hone*, Dublin: UCD Press, 2010.

# Index

Only those notes (pp 187–222) which contain substantial argument or information have been indexed.